# TAX POLITICS IN EASTERN EUROPE

# TAX POLITICS IN EASTERN EUROPE

## Globalization, Regional Integration, and the Democratic Compromise

HILARY APPEL

THE UNIVERSITY OF MICHIGAN PRESS

ANN ARBOR

Published in the United States of America by
The University of Michigan Press
Manufactured in the United States of America
∞ Printed on acid-free paper

2014 2013 2012 2011 4 3 2 1

*A CIP catalog record for this book is available from the British Library.*

Library of Congress Cataloging-in-Publication Data

Appel, Hilary.
Tax politics in Eastern Europe : globalization, regional integration, and the democratic compromise / Hilary Appel.
p. cm.
Includes bibliographical references and index.
ISBN 978-0-472-11776-5 (cloth : alk. paper) —
ISBN 978-0-472-02751-4 (e-book)
1. Taxation—Europe, Eastern. 2. Europe, Eastern—Politics and government. 3. Europe, Eastern—Economic integration. I. Title.

HJ2305.A66 2011
336.200947—dc22 2011003379

# Contents

# Acknowledgments

I am grateful to many individuals and institutions for their support of this project. This book could not have been written without the generous funding of the National Council of Eurasian and East European Research and the Kennan Institute at the Woodrow Wilson International Center for Scholars. I would like to thank these organizations as well as the Keck Center for International and Strategic Studies, the Lowe Institute for Political Economy, and the Dean of Faculty's research fund at Claremont McKenna College for their support of this project. This book has also benefited from the substantial research assistance of my undergraduate students at Claremont McKenna College, including David Ernst, Luke Penn-Hall, Drew Patterson, and most important David Nahmias and Carissa Tudor. I feel very fortunate to have spent the past decade working in this intellectually rich, ambitious community of scholars and students.

In addition, I am extraordinarily grateful to the many political actors, local scholars, and government officials in Washington, DC, Brussels, and throughout Eastern Europe who sat down with me and shared their experiences, insights, and data. My understanding of the politics of taxation benefited tremendously from the generosity and openness of countless policymakers and tax specialists in eight postcommunist countries: Poland, Hungary, Czech Republic, Bulgaria, Slovakia, Serbia, Ukraine, and Russia. Some of these officials were kind enough to meet with me repeatedly to respond to my questions, including Pavel Mertlík, Václav Klaus, Leszek Balcerowicz, and Andrei Illarionov. I would also like to extend special thanks to the students and scholars in the region who provided invaluable support while I conducted research in the field, especially Piotr Skolimowski in Poland, Josef Takacs in Hungary, and Mihail Tzintzarov in Bulgaria. I am also grateful to the entire Lyovin family for their support in Russia.

I would also like to thank numerous friends and scholars who have commented on either parts or all of the manuscript at various phases of the project. My interest in taxation was sparked by the conference organized by Anna Grzymala-Busse and Pauline Jones Luong at Yale University; their comments on earlier versions of my manuscript were extremely valuable. I also benefited tremendously from the comments by seminar participants at the University of Pennsylvania, Georgetown University, Harvard University, University of Michigan, University of California, Berkeley, and the Woodrow Wilson International Center for Scholars during presentations of this research. I am grateful to many individual colleagues for their thoughtful feedback on the manuscript and their generosity in sharing their research contacts (not to mention the years of stimulating discussion and good company at academic conferences and seminars), with special appreciation for the comments and contributions of Juliet Johnson, Peter Rutland, Yoshiko Herrera, Andrew Barnes, Venelin Ganev, Gerald Easter, Slavi Slavov, Roderic Camp, William Ascher, John Gould, and Kevin Deegan-Krausse. I would also like to express my gratitude to Melody Herr at the University of Michigan Press for her immediate interest in this project and then for her superb handling of my manuscript throughout the whole publication process. I also appreciate the hard work and professional excellence of Susan Cronin at the Press.

I am pleased to have permission to reprint material from two articles I have published elsewhere: "International Imperatives and Tax Reform: Lessons from Postcommunist Europe," *Comparative Politics* 39, no. 1 (October 2006): 43–62; and "Is It Putin or Is It Oil? Explaining Russia's Fiscal Recovery," *Post-Soviet Affairs* 24, no. 4: 301–23, copyright Bellwether Publishing, Ltd., 8640 Guilford Road, Suite 200, Columbia, MD 21046. All rights reserved.

In addition, I would like to heartily thank the members of my family for their support. I want to express how fortunate I feel to receive so much moral support and encouragement from my parents, Marjorie and Jeffrey Appel, my sister Deborah, and my Auntie Linda and how lucky I am to have the exuberant affection of my three tireless little boys, Nicholas, Matteo, and Sebastian. I also want to thank my husband, Vincenzo Quadrini, who is unflappable and unwavering in his support for my scholarship and all of my professional undertakings.

Finally, I want to acknowledge my wonderful grandparents, Adele and Edward Bearman. They have served as role models to me in so many ways throughout my life. With love, I dedicate this book to them.

CHAPTER 1

# The Decline of Tax Politics in Eastern Europe

After the collapse of the communist regimes in Eastern Europe and the abandonment of the command economy system, newly elected leaders had to create the basic institutions of a capitalist tax system. Within this process a staggering number of profound policy choices had to be made within a short period of time. Public officials had to decide, for instance, which sectors of the economy should shoulder the greatest burden for revenue generation. They needed to set the distribution of the personal income tax across different income classes. They needed to consider how to tax real property and intellectual property, whether to tax nonprofit organizations differently from profit-seeking ones, and whether to tax small domestic firms differently from large foreign corporations. Officials needed to determine whether to introduce a sales tax or a value-added tax and on which goods to levy excise duties.[1] How should social welfare taxes be organized? Should there be an inheritance tax? Should there be tax allowances for large families? The new and generally inexperienced promarket policymakers in Eastern Europe were not simply tinkering at the margins of the existing tax systems. They were designing the fundamentals of a new fiscal system.

Given that leaders were reconceptualizing the country's basic approach to raising revenue, one would expect the development of the new tax system to have been highly controversial and politicized. After all, these reforms held important distributional consequences for multiple groups in society. Certain aspects of capitalist tax reform did create political friction, yet the evolution of the tax regime overall was less sensitive to domestic political logics than one might expect. When the new democratic leaders introduced dramatic changes to the fiscal system, they seldom faced controversy or popular resistance, even though ordinary citizens with almost no experience paying taxes under communism were now required to pay taxes on the goods they consumed and income they earned, with little input as to how that burden should be distributed across different actors and sources of revenue. Even the positions of political parties across the ideological spectrum were surprisingly similar on numerous areas of taxation.

Similarities in approaches to taxation emerged across countries as well. Many tax programs and fiscal trends have been shared across countries as politically and economically diverse as Bulgaria, Hungary, Slovakia, Lithuania, Romania, the Czech Republic, and Poland. Their common approaches in taxation are all the more surprising when compared to the rather wide variation in other areas of economic policy-making, like exchange rate policy, financial regulation, wage controls, international aid, and privatization (Aslund 2007).

Some interesting puzzles emerge in the study of postcommunist taxation: Why are there such pronounced commonalities in tax trends across a strikingly diverse region? For example, why did the tax systems in postcommunist Europe become decreasingly progressive over time, such that those individuals with a lower ability to pay contributed proportionately more sales and income tax over time? Why did the tax obligations of corporations drop so consistently and dramatically across postcommunist Europe? Why did the governments in countries with economic and political conditions as diverse as Russia, the Czech Republic, Ukraine, Serbia, Slovakia, Macedonia, Romania, Kazakhstan, and many more adopt a flat tax—a single tax rate on all income brackets? Most strikingly, why did citizens and political elites defer so much policy-making authority to external actors, like the Organization for Economic Cooperation and Development (OECD), the International Monetary Fund (IMF), and, most important, the European Union (EU), in developing their tax structures? How powerful was the European Union in taxation, and was there any backlash from East European citizens or policymakers against the EU's dictates in fiscal policy?

Unfortunately there is not one simple answer to these questions. However, turning to international factors sheds much light upon the evolution of key areas of postcommunist taxation and tax politics. For example, in the largest area of revenue, indirect taxes—the taxes levied on consumption, including all forms of sales tax, import and export duties, and excise taxes—the EU absolutely dominated. The preparations for joining the European Union took precedence over many domestic political priorities. As part of the process of preparing for membership, East European leaders adopted in full the consumption tax regime that the West European states had collectively developed. This process of tax harmonization, as it was called, left little room for variation across acceding countries. Their tax laws had to be harmonized with existing EU law, and all areas of indirect taxes had to follow the *acquis communautaire*, the body of EU law whose adoption was required for membership. The taxes on tens of thousands of goods stood within the EU's domain, and aspiring EU members lacked the right to diverge from the EU tax laws and regulations. In practice this meant that the East Europeans imported their consumption tax regime from abroad with virtually no concessions to domestic groups. Since consumption taxes generate the largest portion of tax revenue, the loss of control over taxation was enormous.

In the accession process, tax harmonization extended beyond even formal membership negotiations devoted solely to it. For example, the East European policymakers who designed tax incentives for corporations also worked closely with European Commission authorities to avoid violating EU competition policy. Hence, the EU not only dictated indirect tax policy outright, it also had jurisdiction over some aspects of direct taxation as well. Leaders thus had to pay close attention to the EU's competition policy in designing the taxation of profits. Recognizing these constraints, the leaders worked closely with European Commission officials in drawing up plans to tax large investors. For instance, consider the Czech case in which leaders demonstrated an extraordinary willingness to defer to the European Union in tax policy-making. When the Social Democratic government was reforming CzechInvest, the government body established to develop investment incentives to attract foreign investors, the Ministry of Finance regularly sent partial drafts of the legislation to the European Commission for comment. According to the finance minister at the time, Pavel Mertlík, CzechInvest's strategy was to ask the office of the EU commissioner for competition, Mario Monti, to approve each paragraph of the law as it was under construction. When asked whether the investment law was tentatively approved paragraph by paragraph by the European Commission as it was being drafted and whether that was acceptable to him, the former finance minister elaborated, "Yes, paragraph by paragraph. . . . Definitely you lose some sovereignty. But we want[ed] to be part of some entity [the EU]." The former minister's frank response exemplifies the acquiescence and acceptance with which tax policy-making authority was ceded to Brussels for the sake of EU membership.[2]

In the same vein, it is striking to contrast the interactive policy-making process with Brussels officials with the noninteractive, domestic policy-making process in Prague. The main hurdle in reforming the tax incentive program was not winning the support of Mertlík's fellow Social Democratic Party members or the approval of the opposition parties, or even obtaining the passing vote by the Czech legislature as a whole. Like most laws required for tax harmonization, this law was rubber-stamped by the parliament, with the understanding that a departure from EU law was not an option unless the country was willing to abandon the overarching goal of European Union membership. In short, the crucial hurdle in designing the tax incentive program was obtaining the European Commission's approval and not passing it through the domestic legislative process. Indeed in tax reform regional integration determined the most minute policy choices.

The analysis of various tax areas in this book suggests that in Eastern Europe domestic political conditions—like the extent of partisan turnover or interest group activity—had very little bearing on key areas of taxation. After decades of absorbing Moscow's policy dictates, it is curious to see how soon after the Cold War the East Europeans ceded policy-making control to a powerful external body, the European Union. Why didn't the taxpayers, the voting publics, or interest groups object more strenuously to their government's loss of autonomy, especially in the tax areas where they would most likely absorb the costs? Likewise, why did political elites so freely relinquish their policy-making authority after finally achieving a position to influence policy-making? After all, taxing and spending are central to what governments do. Yet in tax policy-making, the democratic legislative process became hollow due to external priorities.

The dominance of external factors over internal ones is seen especially clearly in the area of indirect taxation and the European Union. However, even in corporate profit taxes, external factors *not stemming from the EU* importantly constrained policy-making. Here the external influences are much more complex since the European Union had competency over some aspects of taxes on corporations but not others. For example, the EU did not dictate the rate on corporate income taxes at all, but a common trend in corporate taxes emerged in postcommunist Europe nonetheless. In particular, East European governments in country after country repeatedly lowered corporate tax rates over two decades of capitalist transformation. Curiously, the decline of corporate taxation is consistent throughout the region, regardless of whether the Right or the Left controlled the government. The consistency of this pattern across Eastern Europe suggests that government leaders, regardless of their primary constituent base, may not have perceived much flexibility in their approach to corporate taxation. Instead, they felt common pressures stemming from global economic integration to keep corporate taxes low. Once again it is striking how little domestic politics mattered within this trend and how consistent this tax approach was across the entire region.

What could account for this trend, given that the tax on corporate profits lies outside the EU's competence? The argument advanced in this book looks to global economic integration. Given the competitive realities of integrated markets and global investment, postcommunist governments needed to create a tax regime that helped attract foreign capital. After the Cold War, the East Europeans seemed to find themselves in the predicament of many small states at the end of the twentieth century. They lacked adequate domestic capital for their economic development and needed to supplement domestic investment with foreign capital. It became common to use the tax regime to attract and sustain foreign and domestic investment. Shifting the tax burden away from corporations and onto consumers and workers was a common approach to meeting budgetary obligations while competing in the global economy for mobile capital. The loss of control over corporate taxation due to the imperatives of globalization is not as direct or literal as the losses due to regional integration, but the effect has been similar: East European governments—either as small states, as transitioning states, or as aspiring members of regional bodies—followed the same downward trend in corporate taxation, regardless of differing domestic political conditions. Indeed, leaders on the right and the left have shifted the tax burden away from corporations over the past two decades.

A surprising development in corporate tax trends in Europe is that the new East European members of the European Union lowered their corporate income tax to such a degree that the older West European members have been trying to keep up with the augmented competitive pressure. Ironically, the East Europeans have become the leaders in this fiscal movement, rather than the followers of the West Europeans. This book examines this development in detail and shows that, despite the efforts of the West Europeans, especially France, Germany, and Sweden, to thwart this trend, the East Europeans' efforts to become attractive environments for foreign investors have intensified the very pressures to which they were reacting. Ultimately the West European governments failed to dissuade the East Europeans from slashing corporate income taxes, and instead joined them in the race to lower tax rates—thereby creating more attractive corporate tax regimes themselves.

The one area where domestic politics has made an important difference in postcommunist taxation is in the development of personal income taxes (PIT).[3] In contrast to other sources of revenue, the approach to taxing personal income in Eastern Europe remained reflective of domestic political conditions. For two decades, political battles raged over tax rates and the special exemptions like deductions for families with children, disabled members, home renovations, and other areas within personal income taxation. Most fundamentally, domestic partisan politics has shaped debates and outcomes over the progressivity of personal income taxes—that is, over the distributive implications of the tax burden across income levels. In particular, domestic politics has factored importantly in the move to adopt a flat tax in many postcommunist countries. The flat tax is an approach that taxes the population at one rate across all income levels and that allows a limited number of exemptions and deductions. As this book illustrates, personal income taxes constitute the most significant remaining terrain where domestic groups and political parties go to battle. However, the increasing popularity of the flat tax in the region could weaken the future role of domestic politics in this otherwise politicized tax area. Due to the simplification of the system, there should be fewer and fewer opportunities in the future for domestic groups to lobby for differentiated rates, exemptions, and deductions within flat-tax countries. Moreover, there is evidence showing that as the number of countries implementing a flat tax increased, the tendency for other countries to also adopt a flat tax—despite very different political conditions—has also increased.

The surprisingly weak role of domestic politics in key tax areas has motivated the writing of this book. As I began to study taxation in postcommunist Europe, I had expected to find that politics drove fiscal policy in pervasive and powerful ways. Instead, I found myself searching for areas where politics still meaningfully determined taxation outcomes. In identifying which tax areas are highly constrained by external factors and which tax areas remain flexible and responsive to domestic conditions, this book seeks to provide a better understanding of the politics of postcommunist taxation and East European political development.

## Why Taxation?

There are many reasons to deepen our understanding of Eastern Europe's fiscal development. The story of Eastern Europe taxation is fascinating in its own right—full of dramatic changes and policy experiments too radical to be supported, let alone attempted, by any mainstream party in the United States or Western Europe. The scope of tax reform after the fall of communism has been immense. Moreover, the design of the tax system reveals much about each country's new role and evolving identity in a highly integrated international economy.

At the same time, postcommunist taxation bears relevance to several broader debates in the political science and political-economy literatures. For example, studying the evolution of fiscal institutions and tax policy-making can shed light upon the nature of East European domestic politics in an era of increasing regional integration. The loss of policy-making authority of East European governments occurred in numerous economic, social, and political areas due to regional integration. The indirect tax negotiations constituted only one of twenty-nine policy areas, or chapters, in the accession negotiations. The vastness of the *acquis communautaire*—the body of law adopted before accession—is legendary. This body of law famously reached 85,000 pages at the time of the first wave of postcommunist accession in 2004 and has been growing since. Social scientists interested in regional integration can learn much by looking at the declining role of politics in taxation in Eastern Europe that emerged out of the profound sacrifices these new governments were willing to make in order to join a regional federative-like body. An analysis of postcommunist taxation contributes thus to a sizable literature on regional integration and EU enlargement that lies at the crossroads of comparative politics and international relations (Jacoby 2006; Vachudova 2005; Cameron 2002; Grzymala-Busse and Innes 2002; Grabbe 2002; Schimmelfennig 2003). Tax harmonization through the accession negotiations illustrates in stark relief the lengths to which East European policymakers went in order to satisfy the criteria for EU membership.

Second, the study of postcommunist taxation bears direct relevance to a core question in the political science literature, namely, to what extent does domestic politics mediate the forces of globalization in economic policy-making? A rather contentious literature has emerged examining the effects of globalization on both welfare spending and revenue generation (Kaufman and Segura-Ubiergo 2001; Mosley 2000; Burgoon 2001; Campbell 1995). Based on the experiences of advanced industrialized countries and, to a lesser extent, developing countries, scholars have analyzed whether governments can still afford past welfare commitments given global economic integration and the competition for investment. Some argue that globalization and the competition for foreign investors have eroded welfare states (Rodrik 1997). Their intellectual opponents counter that firms do not shy away from countries with strong welfare states or corporatist bargaining structures given the other advantages that such environments offer (Garrett and Mitchell 2001). Another strand of research on globalization and fiscal policy examines whether convergence is occurring in corporate tax policy due to globalization. Scholars ask whether various countries' corporate tax policies diverge according to differences in political institutions (Garrett 1998; Garrett and Lange 1996) or national politics (Berger 1996; Kitschelt et al. 1999). Looking at tax policy, Winner

(2005), for example, finds that capital mobility has depressed capital tax rates and increased the effective tax rate on labor income in OECD countries. Similarly, Swank and Steinmo (2002) argue that globalization has led to a decline in statutory corporate income tax rates, but they find no evidence of a decline in effective tax rates in fourteen advanced industrialized economies. Genschel (2002) looks at OECD data and concurs with Garrett (1998) that globalization does not set off a race to the bottom in corporate taxation among countries with large welfare states, and he finds no evidence in the data of a shift from corporate to labor taxes. In Genschel's assessment, globalization does, however, lead to "more austerity, more deficit finance, and a less employment-friendly tax mix," and it diminishes policy autonomy (2002, 246).

The analysis of tax trends in Eastern Europe in this book bears direct relevance to these theoretical debates and provides new empirical information by directing the focus to Eastern Europe. A common feature of the existing literature is its reliance on data from OECD countries, and typically the advanced industrialized countries within this group. The postcommunist countries are not included in this research, not even those that are members of the OECD, largely due to the limitations of the data when these works were published. As a result, the scholarship on the impact of globalization on fiscal policy largely ignores the postcommunist experience.[4] However, studying the East European cases is valuable for understanding the impact of globalization on policy-making in newly democratic and democratizing countries. While numerous scholars conclude that domestic politics and domestic political institutions still mediate the forces of globalization, they are not considering environments, as Campbell notes, in which political institutions are new, politicians are inexperienced, and civil society is weak (2001a). It would be helpful theoretically to consider the constraints of regional and global integration on less-established political systems if we want to understand the *global* effects of globalization, and not just the effects on countries with extensive time-series data. The accumulation of data since the publication of these other studies allows for new statistical analysis of the effect of globalization on domestic politics in key areas of tax policy-making. Indeed, further analysis of the effects of regional and global integration on taxation is necessary to fill both a regional gap and a theoretical lacuna in this scholarship.

Moreover, focusing on fiscal development in Eastern Europe provides important insights into how different countries cope with the loss of policy autonomy under deepening conditions of globalization. Indeed the recent trends in taxation in postcommunist Europe provide a striking example of the declining economic-policy autonomy of states—in this case, newly autonomous states with a great sensitivity to issues of national sovereignty.

Third, the study of taxation is integral to the growing body of analysis on state building after communism. The repercussions of weak state capacity have become increasingly apparent over the past decade, and thus more and more scholars of East European politics are turning their attention to the process of state building. In the initial years of postcommunist transformation, scholars undervalued the need to improve basic infrastructure, to fortify the social safety nets to cushion those most hurt by the capitalist reforms, to enforce property rights and adjudicate disputes, and to provide security against a rising tide of crime and social instability (Holmes 1997). The transitions literature in the 1990s, especially in political economy, was more concerned with how to diminish the behemoth, bloated states inherited from communism than with how to make them stronger and more effective—at collecting taxes, providing security, building infrastructure, ensuring stability, and so on. In other words, many early studies of postcommunist transition overlooked the necessity of building up the institutional and organizational capacity of postcommunist states. However, with the passage of time, even the most convinced antistatists began to recognize that fortifying public institutions and strengthening state capacity were the essential but underappreciated building blocks for countries undergoing economic and political liberalization (Fukuyama 2004).

A new generation of scholars has called for more theoretical and empirical work on state-building processes that takes into account the distinct features of postcommunism (Grzymala-Busse and Jones Luong 2002; Way 2002; Easter 2008; Gehlbach 2008). According to Grzymala-Busse and Jones Luong (2002), much of the older theoretical work on state building that was drawn from the West European experience has limited relevance to postcommunist Europe for three reasons. First, postcommunist state building was taking place over the span of decades or years, and not over centuries. Second, state builders were using formal *and* informal structures and practices to establish authority. The existing literature examined only formal structures since, with the passage of time, little information about the informal practices relevant to West European state building survived. Third, postcommunist state building was influenced "by unique international pressures, such as the pull of the European Union and the demands of globalization" (Grzymala-Busse and Jones Luong 2002, 531). In short, because political scientists developed their past theories on state building by examining the West European experience that started centuries ago, the analysis began with recognized centers of authority that extracted revenue to fund armies and defend territories. By contrast, in the postcommunist state-building process, Grzymala-Busse and Jones Luong argue, "the emphasis is no longer on the ability to defend one's borders, which demands both military and extractive institutions, but on the ability to compete economically, which often mandates certain representative as well as market institutions" (536).

Modern East European states still must defend against external threats and provide basic public goods for their own citizens, all the while creating a competitive economy for outside investors. This is central to garnering the resources necessary to achieving domestic objectives and remaining in power. The state's very approach to resource extraction is a balancing act between domestic responsibilities and external constraints. In order to understand postcommunist state building, scholars must develop a deeper knowledge of how states created tax systems that were legitimate to the citizenry and acceptable to investors who could transfer their resources elsewhere. This is no simple task. East European state building and revenue generation are riddled with contradictions and paradoxes: On the one hand, the state must be able to raise some revenue from mobile corporations without diminishing the corporate tax base overall. On the other, for the state to extract revenue and provide public goods, the state—or the institutions of the central government—must attain the legitimacy and authority to extract wealth from businesses and individuals, thereby convincing productive actors to relinquish part of their income. Indeed, studying taxation in Eastern Europe after communism is important since taxation is central not only to the development of state capacity but also to the awakening of the postcommunist citizenry—the *demos* in a democracy. The state's ability to raise revenue is influenced by the citizen's recognition of the state's claims to authority and its ability to provide public goods. Hence, the ability to extract revenue is both an outcome and a prerequisite of state capacity. The central government's right to tax rests upon its recognized authority, especially vis-à-vis other sources of authority in society, like regional governments, local mafias, and even local employers. When extraction must occur under democratic conditions, the legitimacy of the political leadership is directly at issue. And when democratic processes are compromised for the sake of regional integration, democratic development is directly affected.

The still rather small body of literature in political science on postcommunist taxation emphasizes the problems of state capacity in revenue extraction (Gehlbach 2008; Easter 2009; Berenson 2006). This book instead emphasizes how states cope with competing domestic and international constraints in revenue generation. Thus, I examine state capacity in this book primarily as it relates to fiscal development within the current international context. The main emphasis here is that state capacity is not only a function of domestic institutions and conditions, state capacity is also a function of prevailing international conditions. It is important to understand how state officials can maintain enough public support to achieve their goals and fulfill their responsibilities while relinquishing to international bodies their control of many political and economic tools that could be employed to build and maintain that public support.

## Eastern Europe as a Region

This book examines salient trends in the politics of taxation for postcommunist Europe. It draws primarily from those former communist countries that joined the European Union in 2004 and 2007. Initially the chapters present data from as many countries as available in order to provide the basis for regional generalizations. The analysis of these regional trends is then followed by a more in-depth discussion of several individual country cases to illustrate, and hopefully provide greater insight into, the broader trend.

Certainly, the variable specific to postcommunist Europe that most critically drives the low politicization of taxation is EU accession. As noted, the European Union and the prospect of membership loomed very large over the development of the tax systems in postcommunist Europe. European tax exemplars proved important for those countries expecting, or at least imagining, a future within the European Union. Although diverse external pressures and constraints matter crucially for fiscal development in many regions of the world, the external influence of the EU on tax reform, especially when compounded with broader global influences, is outstanding if not unique. Simply put, non-EU-aspiring countries were not importing an indirect tax regime wholesale. EU factors altered the political and economic landscape and amplify the conclusions we can draw about tax policy-making and national autonomy in an era of globalization.

At times the analysis draws from other non-EU postcommunist countries when helpful—in particular because certain dimensions of fiscal development can be found throughout the postcommunist world. Indeed, the citizenry has had little experience in directly paying taxes or mobilizing politically throughout the postcommunist region. Interest groups remain feeble in much of the former Soviet bloc. Furthermore, East European governments are not the only ones using favorable corporate tax regimes to compete for investment; so are governments in the Caucasus, Central Asia, and developing countries throughout the world. Likewise, there are many states whose political institutions are relatively new, evolving, and often unstable. Such conditions characterize large sections of the postcommunist world: former Soviet satellite states and former Soviet republics alike. By the same token, certain tax trends, like the adoption of the flat tax, have spread throughout the postcommunist region; and the flat tax momentum in Eastern Europe was accelerated by the adoption of the flat tax in the postcommunist region as a whole. In this sense, certain tax trends in Eastern Europe are not only found in, but also reinforced by, trends in the former Soviet bloc more broadly.

Moreover, East European countries like Serbia, Macedonia, Georgia, or Ukraine have important external influences that deserve careful consideration—whether stemming from the IMF, from Russia as a regional power, or from multinational corporations, even if not from the EU. At points in this book, such developments are raised in tandem. However, this book focuses primarily on postcommunist Europe, drawing repeatedly from the examples of the Czech Republic, Hungary, Poland, Slovakia, Bulgaria, and Estonia in the first five chapters. In the final two chapters, this book compares the findings on tax politics in postcommunist Europe to tax politics in Russia and Western Europe in order to reflect more broadly on the role of politics in taxation and in order to understand whether the decline of politics in tax policy-making is unique to postcommunist Europe or shares certain characteristics with other countries or regions.

Despite sharing certain challenges and embarking upon similar fiscal experiments like the flat tax, many scholars have noted *fundamental* differences in the tax systems of East European states and most former Soviet states. As many have noted, the tax systems in East European countries began more quickly to draw upon a broad mix of revenue sources than the tax systems in the former Soviet Union (save the Baltics), where tax systems continued to rely more extensively on taxing traditional revenue sources—namely, the large, monopolistic enterprises in certain industries that existed in a prior form under communism (Gehlbach 2008, 6; Tanzi and Tsibouris 2000, 17; Mitra and Stern 2002). These differences in the revenue mix are plotted in figures 1, 2, and 3, using World Bank data from Mitra and Stern 2002.

Gehlbach (2008) explains the divergence between Eastern Europe and the former Soviet space as follows. In the former Soviet Union (minus the Baltics), the tax bureaucracies were less effective at collecting taxes from smaller enter-

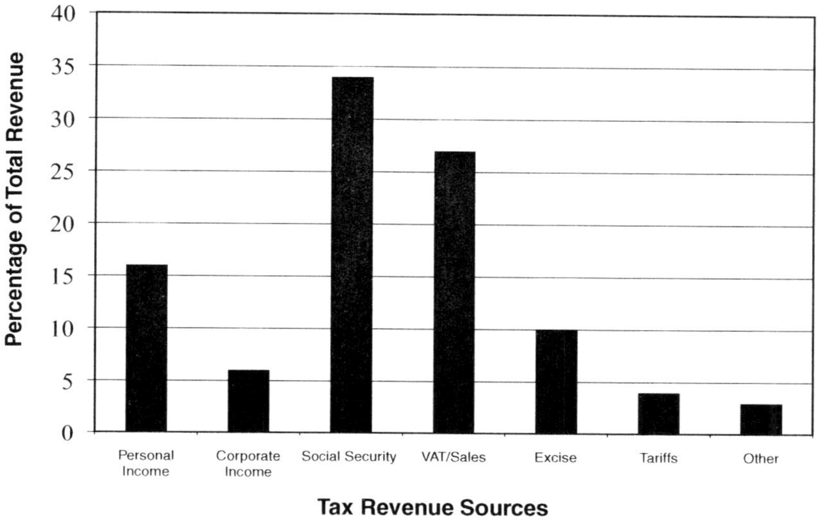


Fig. 1. Structure of tax revenues in East Central Europe, 1999–2000

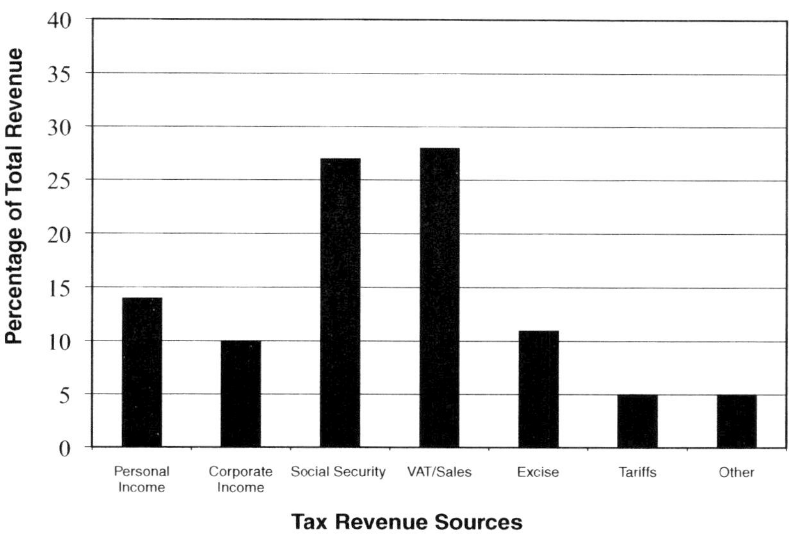


Fig. 2. Structure of tax revenues in former Soviet states, 1999–2000

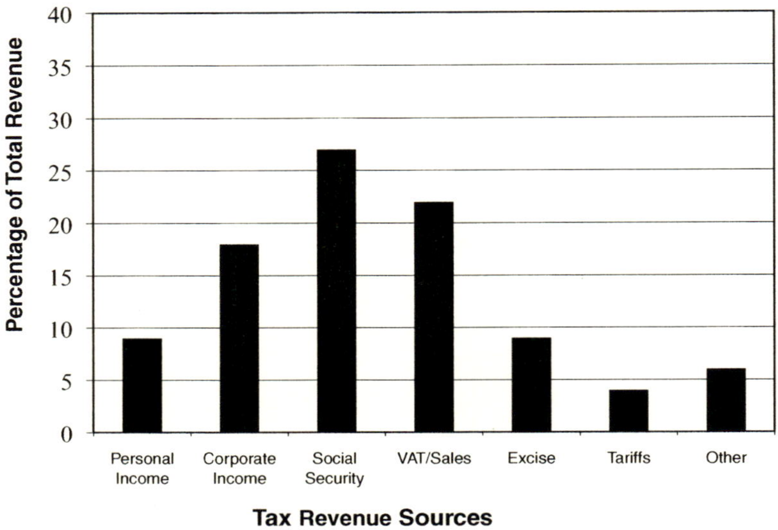


Fig. 3. Structure of tax revenues in Russia, 1999–2000

prises and from particular industries. And, as a result, governments created tax systems that relied extensively upon large industrial producers and chose to support those large enterprises that could less effectively hide profits and evade taxes (Gehlbach 2008, 19). This led to certain biases in the industrial structure of most former Soviet states since scarce public resources were allocated not according to the relative growth of potential of industries or types of enterprises but according to an industry's "taxability." East European governments created a more favorable environment for small and medium enterprises (SMEs), and the taxes from personal income and SMEs became important revenue sources (Gehlbach 2008; Mitra and Stern 2002). The process of European integration pulled East European governments away from previous patterns of revenue extraction, whereas former Soviet states more often became trapped in old fiscal patterns. The different trajectories of postcommunist Europe and the former Soviet Union, especially Russia, are importantly impacted by EU membership.

## Plan of the Book

The next chapter, chapter 2, begins by identifying the main challenges of creating capitalist tax systems after communism. The first part of the chapter explores the initial conditions under which the new tax systems had to be created. It examines the difficulties leaders faced in generating enough revenue given the extraordinary contraction of postcommunist economies in the early 1990s and the loss of traditional revenue sources following the collapse of foreign trade and the privatization of state-owned enterprises. The chapter then examines the barriers to tax collection stemming from the informal economy and the undermonetization of exchange. The second half of the chapter discusses the new institutions and the normative shifts that were required to create a reliable system of revenue generation that would mesh with existing attitudes about inequality and wealth distribution, and that would ultimately raise revenue effectively under challenging political and economic conditions. Three levels of transformation are discussed: the creation of the new tax structure, the development and training of tax bureaucracies, and the development of a taxpaying habit among citizens.

Chapter 3 examines the impact of European integration on taxation, focusing explicitly on the evolution of consumption taxes. This chapter draws from the first- and second-round applicants in order to illustrate the profound implications of EU accession on the taxation authority of East European governments. The chapter reviews the EU's Chapter Ten negotiations, which governed indirect taxation, and the process of tax harmonization. During the accession negotiations, leaders agreed to a tax regime that affected the tax rates on tens of thousands of goods with virtually no exceptions made for domestic political or economic circumstances. Indeed, no government successfully negotiated any permanent exemptions, managing at most to obtain a brief transitional period for implementing minimum tax rates on a handful of goods. After highlighting the scope of tax harmonization and the paucity of tax policy exemptions, the chapter argues that European accession greatly curtailed the autonomy of East European states in setting their own tax policy and limited the ability of government officials—willingly or unwillingly—to respond to those domestic interest groups standing to lose from tax harmonization.

Chapter 4 examines in depth corporate tax trends in Eastern Europe. As in consumption taxation, corporate taxation is shaped in part by EU rules governing fair competition. East European governments are not only highly constrained by formal agreements with the European Union, they are also limited by informal pressures stemming from global economic integration. This chapter studies the development of corporate income tax policy and the investment incentive programs in the region. I argue that despite varied political environments, East European countries have reduced corporate tax rates consistently and repeatedly in the postcommunist period. In order to demonstrate the persistent decline of corporate tax rates irrespective of domestic politics, the chapter first presents the regional trends in corporate income tax rates. It then turns to the income tax policies of Poland, Hungary, the Czech Republic, and Slovakia in order to illustrate the near irrelevance of traditional left-right divisions in shaping leaders' choices over shifting the tax burden away from the business sector and onto workers and consumers.

Chapter 5 examines personal income taxes in Eastern Europe. While large portions of tax policy are driven by external constraints, personal income taxes remain sensitive to domestic political conditions. Chapter 5 contends that partisan politics still determines the degree of progressivity of income taxes. More than any other factor, partisan politics has either facilitated or blocked the adoption of a flat tax in numerous countries. After discussing the spread of the flat tax on a broad regional level, the chapter draws from the experiences of Estonia, Slovakia, and, more briefly, Ukraine and Bulgaria in order to provide greater detail on the role that traditional domestic political variables play in determining fiscal outcomes, emphasizing the role of right-wing political actors and parties in the move away from more progressive tax systems. By looking at the conditions precipitating the adoption of a flat income tax program, I conclude that political leaders maintain much more policy-making authority despite their commitments to regional and global economic integration. The analysis of flat taxes also demonstrates how new economic ideas or paradigms spread among like-minded politicians in the region. The primary intent of this chapter is to shed light upon a tax policy area where policymakers still respond to domestic political pressures.

The broader implication of the declining role of domestic politics in taxation relates to the economic sovereignty of postcommunist Europe in an era of increasing regional and global integration. Chapter 6 contextualizes the findings of the previous chapters by examining why there is much greater policy-making autonomy in Russian taxation. Russia diverges from the postcommunist countries to the west in important ways that speak directly to a core debate motivating this study. While the previous chapters suggest that states are highly constrained—and in the East European cases, extraordinarily constrained—in taxation given the imperatives of regional and global integration, there are countries that, despite their great dependence on the international economy, maintain policy-making autonomy. The Russian case helps to reveal which economic characteristics give policymakers more room to maneuver in setting tax policy according to either domestic political considerations or other political priorities. In particular, the changing role of domestic politics in Russian tax policy and the leadership's relatively greater policy-making autonomy suggest that the structure of the economy, the size of the internal market, or the international terms of trade can give countries greater policy flexibility. The Russian case, in which energy taxes have been crucial, makes the essential point that globalization may profoundly undermine the influence of domestic politics in economic policy-making in some countries but less so in others. By identifying certain factors that contribute to the autonomy of policymakers in taxation, the Russian case also tempers grander generalizations that one might draw from this region in particular on the penetrating effects of international economic integration on domestic policy-making.

The final chapter presents statistical analysis to examine further the role of domestic politics on tax policy-making with special consideration of how politics as a variable differs among East and West European states. It investigates the association between tax policies and an ideology index of the elected representatives in the countries. The relationship of tax policies with other variables, such as international economic integration, is also investigated. The regression analysis of this chapter complements the more in-depth analysis of tax policy-making conducted in earlier chapters of the book. The conclusion then returns to taxation in Eastern Europe and reviews and further reflects upon the conditions within these countries that have depressed the level of politicization of tax policy-making.

The diminished role for domestic politics in tax policy is disconcerting—whether resulting from the global competition for investment, from leaders who pay more attention to tax trends in neighboring countries than to tax pressures from below, or from the requirements stemming from regional accession. The harmonization of consumption taxes required the comprehensive adoption of legislation that did not emerge from the domestic political process but from legislative developments within the European Union. Given that the new tax codes evolved outside the domestic political sphere and given that EU law takes precedence over all national laws after accession, the impact on democratic development is important. Does the limited role of domestic actors, political parties, or legislators in tax policy-making after the communist period erode the quality of democratic governance? As important as the EU was for promoting democratic practices, its export of tax codes to Eastern Europe with limited to no input from the mass publics or local leaders paradoxically weakened democratic development. Indeed, when governments are compelled to set policy in response to the directives of a non–popularly elected body like the European Commission rather than according to the preferences of domestic constituents, it results in the hollowing out of public participation and democracy.

Ironically, the development of the tax system itself was traditionally associated with the rise of representative government in Western Europe. Many political economists have argued that representative government in several European states has its roots in the sovereign or the state's "revenue imperative" (Levi 1988; Brewer 1989; North and Weingast 1989; Tilly 1992; Bates 2001; Mahon 2005). The ruler entered into a contractual relationship with taxpayers (creating the "fiscal contract") in order to collect revenues more effectively. The debate continues over the relationship between taxation and democratization outside of Western Europe (Waterbury 1997; Cheibub 1998; Boix 2001; Ross 2004; Bräutigam 2008). However, one point is certain: the bargaining between state actors and domestic groups, which creates the "fiscal contract" and which can lead to more consensual tax relations, was circumvented in Eastern Europe. Instead, the evolution of postcommunist taxation exemplifies the weakness of traditional domestic political actors in shaping economic policymaking in emerging democracies within a globalized economy.

CHAPTER 2

# Creating a Capitalist Tax Structure after Communism

Even in the best of times, extracting resources from a population has eluded leaders who aspire to increase revenue. In the Soviet era, leaders in communist regimes managed to extract revenue by closely controlling all formal economic activity. Collecting taxes was an administrative task within the overarching structure of (near total) state control of the economy. Garnering taxes amounted thus to little more than withdrawing revenue from various enterprise accounts to which the state had full access. That said, communist states still failed to control absolutely all economic activity, as pockets of informal private economic activity occurred beyond the state's reach.

The private activity that had been previously illegal and thus hidden became legal and necessarily encouraged within the new postcommunist capitalist regimes. Nevertheless, the new bureaucracies could not easily tax it. Encouraging and tapping new private economic activity became the new challenge for the emerging capitalist states. After communism, bureaucratic capacity was weak in many sectors, but it was especially weak in the tax bureaucracy given the almost-automated, administrative nature of taxation under the past planned economy. Achieving the authority and capacity to tax economic activity quickly daunted the newly elected postcommunist leaders. Tax laws had to be fundamentally redesigned. The new tax laws would need to reallocate responsibility for tax revenue within the population, establish a new approach to taxing consumption, and identify and evaluate the usefulness of entirely new tax forms that would have made little sense under a communist system, like property taxes or inheritance taxes. Elected officials lacked experience in distributing the revenue burden effectively across different economic actors and activities; bureaucrats lacked the resources and practical experience of collecting taxes; and taxpayers had little if any experience in recognizing and meeting their fiscal obligations to the state. This lack of experience all around rendered the modern state's revenue imperative extraordinarily difficult to meet after the collapse of communism.

This chapter provides a broad overview of the initial challenges to creating new tax systems in Eastern Europe, focusing on the early transitional recessions, the loss of traditional revenue sources, and the undermonetization of the economy in the early and mid-1990s. This discussion seeks to elucidate the overwhelming task of designing tax structures that would reliably generate revenue, mesh with existing attitudes about inequality and wealth distribution, and ultimately raise revenue sufficiently and efficiently under challenging political and economic constraints. This chapter then examines three necessary aspects of the fiscal transformation. First, the postcommunist governments had to develop a tax system that functioned within a private property, private business environment. Second, these governments had to expand, retrain, and empower the tax bureaucracies to collect the new taxes. Third, the populations had to learn to adapt to and abide by the new capitalist tax regime. After exploring these three areas, the chapter closes with some discussion of the distributional implications of the evolving tax regimes in postcommunist economies.

## Fiscal Reform under Recessionary Conditions

When the East Europeans began to redesign a tax system more appropriate for a private capitalist economy, economic conditions were dire. Fiscal reformers faced four inhospitable and mutually incompatible conditions under which they had to reorient the tax system: falling economic output, rising unemployment, growing demand for social protection, and the political vulnerability of new politicians.

In virtually all East European countries, a severe contraction in production and trade followed the collapse of communism. The contraction of the postcommunist economies immediately limited the pool of resources from which revenue could be drawn. While some economic decline was expected with the collapse of Soviet-era trading relations and the closure of inefficient state enterprises, the degree of contraction in the early years of transition was severe. For instance, during the first three years of transition, Hungary's GDP declined by 17.6 percent, Poland's GDP by 15.6 percent, and Czechoslovakia's GDP by 15.4 percent. Economies to the east were hit even harder. The GDP contracted 26.4 percent in Ukraine, 25.6 percent in Bulgaria, and 25.0 percent in Romania.[1] In the case of Russia, this contraction was even higher and lasted much longer, approaching 40 percent by 1998 (Appel 2008). These early transitional recessions confounded fiscal reform because as the tax base shrunk, the generation of revenue became particularly difficult while the need for social protections ballooned. The postcommunist governments faced growing numbers of citizens who, for the first time in their lives, found themselves without jobs or income.

Unemployment numbers grew steadily in much of the region, as table 1 reports. Hungary, Poland, Romania, and Bulgaria experienced some of the most significant early increases in unemployment. In 1990 unemployment levels were negligible; but by 1992, unemployment levels reached 12.3 percent in Hungary, 13.6 percent in Poland, 8.2 percent in Romania, and 15.3 percent in Bulgaria. In 1993 unemployment rose further by a couple percentage points in Poland (16.4 percent), in Romania (10.4 percent), and in Bulgaria (16.4 percent). The number of newly unemployed workers during the early transition recessions created a burden on the public sector as it tried to provide social safety nets for those without work. It should be noted, however, that the unemployment figures for some countries were much lower, such as Czechoslovakia, Russia, and Ukraine, as reported in table 1. Czechoslovakia, and later the Czech Republic, did not follow the same employment pattern as most of its neighbors; a higher percentage of workers remained employed. Low unemployment was a source of pride for Václav Klaus's government, and it helped to sustain his long tenure in office. However, Premier Klaus's detractors interpreted the low Czech unemployment as a sign of stalled reform and of the distorted financial-industrial ownership structure (Gitter and Scheuer 1998; Mertlík 1997).

In Ukraine and Russia the low number of people who were formally unemployed in the early 1990s may have also reflected a lack of restructuring, however in these former Soviet republics workers were only nominally employed. After the dissolution of the Soviet Union, many employed people had no reliable income due to the widespread problem of wage arrears. That is, even if public sector workers and workers in large enterprises formally maintained their employed status, they often failed to receive their wages for extended periods of time (Alfandari and Schaffer 1996; Commander, Dolinskaya, and Mumssen 2000). Household survey data captures the magnitude of this problem in Russia and Ukraine. In Russia, over 40 percent of workers surveyed reported wage arrears in 1994 (Lehmann, Wadsworth, and Acquisti 1999, 602). By 1996, the percentage of workers suffering wage arrears reached closer to 60 percent (602).[2] The proportion of workers who experienced wage arrears in Ukraine was similarly high, with over 60 percent of workers surveyed in 1996 reporting wage arrears (Boyarchuk, Maliar, and Maliar 2005, 541). Even worse, not only did workers suffer through long periods without receiving their salaries, once they finally did receive them, inflation had significantly eroded the value of their compensation. Thus the relatively low unemployment figures in table 1 hide the depressed condition of workers in the 1990s and the pressures on the state to protect basic social welfare in both Ukraine and Russia. In short, the low unemployment levels in these post-Soviet countries did not mean that social safety nets were less needed and that the fiscal pressures were not great. On the contrary, demands for social protections were high, and the state budgets could not easily cope with the growing demand for help from struggling citizens.

At a time when the tax base was shrinking and spending demands growing, newly elected leaders faced great political uncertainty. Would these leaders survive the economic crisis, and could democratization continue under such challenging conditions? Some feared that the instability and pain associated with capitalist transformation and the limited ability of postcommunist governments to support a struggling population would lead to a backlash against postcommunist politicians pursuing political and economic liberalization. Large numbers of unemployed people could spur a voter backlash that would drive out the reform-oriented democrats responsible for institutionalizing a capitalist system. The former communists would then return to power (Dahrendorf 1990; Przeworski 1991). Western academics pondered whether simultaneous political and economic liberalization was truly possible or whether these countries would ultimately return to some version of communism or authoritarianism. While a certain amount of nostalgia for the communist past did emerge during the painful process of capitalist transition in Eastern Europe, the left-wing parties and successor parties to the national communist parties did not press for a reversion to a command economy or

**TABLE 1. Unemployment Figures in Eastern Europe**

| Country | 1990 | 1991 | 1992 | 1993 | 1994 | 1995 | 1996 | 1997 | 1998 |
|---|---|---|---|---|---|---|---|---|---|
| Hungary | 1.7 | 8.5 | 12.3 | 12.1 | 10.4 | 12.0 | 10.7 | 10.4 | 9.6 |
| Poland | 6.5 | 11.8 | 13.6 | 16.4 | 16.0 | 14.9 | 13.2 | 10.3 | 10.4 |
| Czech Republic | 0.7 | 4.1 | 2.6 | 3.5 | 3.2 | 2.9 | 3.5 | 5.2 | 7.5 |
| Romania | 1.3 | 3.0 | 8.2 | 10.4 | 10.9 | 9.5 | 6.6 | 8.8 | 10.3 |
| Ukraine | — | — | — | 0.4 | 0.4 | 0.6 | 1.5 | 2.7 | 4.3 |
| Bulgaria | 1.7 | 11.1 | 15.3 | 16.4 | 12.8 | 11.1 | 12.5 | 13.7 | 12.2 |
| Russia | — | 0.1 | 0.8 | 5.7 | 7.5 | 8.9 | 9.9 | 11.3 | 13.3 |

*Source:* Figures for Romania from 1990 to 1998 are from the Statistical Appendix of the United Nation's Economic Commission on Europe, *Economic Survey of Europe*, Tables A.10 and B.7, http://www.unece.org/ead/pub/052/052statapp.pdf (accessed November 4, 2008). For all other countries, International Labor Office Bureau of Statistics database Unemployment, http://www.ilo.org/global/What_we_do/Statistics/lang--en/index.htm (accessed May 22, 2009).

embrace authoritarianism in most of Eastern Europe. Many scholars have analyzed the possible reasons for the better-than-expected democratic outcomes under these severe recessionary conditions, highlighting nonfiscal variables like aspects of the first postcommunist elections, a country's geographical position, the incentives of EU and NATO membership, and even the precommunist educational system, in order to explain many countries' ultimate success in abandoning communism (Darden and Grzymala-Busse 2006; Fish 1998; Kitschelt 2003; Kopstein and Reilly 2000; Vachudova 2005).

Few scholars explore the relationship between fiscal spending and democratic transformation. One notable exception, Mitchell Orenstein, finds that democratic consolidation correlates with the maintenance of high welfare spending in postcommunist countries. However, Orenstein's analysis examines how democracy helped sustain higher social spending rather than the reverse (2008). Occasionally observers have posited a causal relationship between the maintenance of social protections and democratization, suggesting that social spending seemed to have played some role in defending the simultaneous political and economic transformations (Kramer 1997; EBRD Transition Report 2000). However, even if some scholars suggest that social spending dampened the public backlash and partially insulated the populace from the economic downturn (Kramer 1997), little systematic attention has gone to examining how welfare spending contributed to the "communist exit" (Darden and Gryzmala-Busse 2006).

There is some anecdotal evidence that high social spending, especially in the area of unemployment benefits, was in fact aimed at dampening political instability and easing the social dislocation during the early period of democratic transition. Several governments initially offered especially high unemployment assistance that would not be affordable in the medium term (Gardawski 2002). For example, in Poland the newly elected government provided generous unemployment benefits to insulate the mass publics from the pain of capitalist reform. In December 1989 the newly elected parliamentarians adopted a program that indefinitely offered to an unemployed worker payments ranging from 40 to 70 percent of the worker's most recent pay. Those who had never been employed (or had recently graduated but had not found work yet) received payments ranging from 100 to 200 percent of the minimum wage indefinitely (Gardawski 2002). Given the high cost of the program, successive governments scaled back the scope of unemployment benefits in multiple waves starting in 1990. That said, the unemployment benefits remained quite generous until 1996. Hungary also offered generous benefits for unemployed workers in the early years of reform. In 1989 Hungary developed an unemployment compensation system that expanded in 1991 to an insurance-type unemployment benefit system. Initially the period of compensation could be as long as 540 days with a payment level reaching a maximum of twice the minimum wage (depending on previous earnings). However, the burden that this program placed on the national budget led to cuts in the level and length of compensation already by 1993 (Wolff 2001, 5–6; Micklewright and Nagy 1994).

In the Czech Republic and the Slovak Republic unemployment insurance initially allowed a maximum of twelve months of benefits equal to at least 70 percent of the minimum living standard; but in 1992, the maximum duration of benefits was cut in half (Vodopivec, Wörgötter, and Raju 2005, 623–24). In Romania, unemployment benefits were protected in the 1991 constitution in article 43. The first legislation guaranteeing unemployment insurance granted Romanians who had worked at least half of the previous year up to twelve months of benefits equal to about half of the net average basic salary (Cerami 2006, 140). By 1996, the maximum duration of benefits was reduced to nine months (Vodopivec, Wörgötter, and Raju 2005, 624).[3]

The relevant point for the purposes of this study is that when the new capitalist fiscal systems were under development, the political need for high welfare spending accompanied the contraction of the tax base. The earliest benefits were quite generous and helped to preserve (or even advance) democratic transformation. But these benefits were scaled back shortly, as the early economic recessions made them unsustainable. Economic contraction put the new fiscal reformers in the challenging position of needing to increase welfare expenditures—due to rapidly increasing unemployment—while their available resources were in decline. Many individual politicians and political parties could not survive the contraction of benefits, yet the *system* of democracy did survive, and capitalism over time became further institutionalized. Paradoxically, the early recessions put the postcommunist leaders in the position of needing to increase the welfare state despite the ultimate goal of shrinking the public sector in the long term—a central aspect of shifting from a communist to a capitalist economy.

## New Revenue Sources

Given the persistently high social-spending needs, shrinking economies, and the uncertain and unstable political environments, how could leaders in the region extract enough revenue in the early postcommunist period? In the past the state would finance expenditures primarily by transferring revenue from state firms to the federal budget, or, as John Campbell writes, "from one of the state's pockets to another" (1995, 763). With a large portion of these enterprises undergoing privatization, the state had to collect more revenue from private sector production and from private individuals.

The privatization programs themselves did little to alleviate budgetary shortfalls. Unlike the privatization programs in advanced industrialized countries, which included much less property but were designed explicitly to generate budgetary revenue, privatization programs in Eastern European generated little cash. Postcommunist privatization relied extensively upon the (nearly) free distribution of property through a voucher system enabling the transfer of property to citizens, factory workers, and managers. Because domestic ownership was a priority, nearly every country implemented a version of voucher privatization, with the notable exception of Hungary. The voucher method of privatization was a quick way to transfer large portions of the economy to private citizens and businesses. It privileged regime change over revenue generation.

As a result of the voucher approach, privatization generated little revenue for cash-starved budgets. In most countries the receipts from privatization (i.e., the privatization of the property *not* freely distributed) served at best as a limited measure, with such gains quickly spent. For example, despite transferring more than 80 percent of GDP to the private sector, privatization receipts in the Czech Republic averaged only 0.9 percent of GDP from 1991 to 1997 (Davis et al. 2000, table 1, 5). In Russia, privatization receipts averaged 0.3 percent of GDP from 1991 to 1998; in Estonia, they averaged 2.9 percent of GDP from 1992 to 1998 (Davis et al. 2000, table 1, 5). In Bulgaria, privatization receipts averaged 1.3 percent from 1993 to 1997 (World Bank).[4] Even in Hungary, which is the one country in the region that did not rely on the free distribution of state property, the privatization receipts only raised an average of 4 percent of GDP from 1991 to 1998 (Davis et al. 2000, table 1, 5).

More commonly, privatization saddled the state with debts from unprofitable firms and weak financial institutions. It is necessary to recall that a privatizing state was more successful in transferring or selling off profitable enterprises than it was in shedding loss-making firms. In fact, in order to rid itself of the responsibility for less profitable enterprises through privatization, the state frequently had to assume enormous debts or had to keep the unwanted residual shares of enterprises under the care of finance ministries, national property funds, or other state institutions (Schwartz 1997). Further compounding fiscal imbalances, many governments found it politically and economically prudent to assume the losses of failing banks undergoing privatization. According to World Bank calculations, the cost for governments to absorb bad debt during banking privatization was quite high in many states: Between 1991 and 1998, the government in Bulgaria spent 26.5 percent of GDP, in the Czech Republic 20.6 percent of GDP, in Hungary 12.9 percent of GDP, and in Poland 8.2 percent of GDP. The cost to the government was lower in the Baltic countries due to a decision to liquidate rather than privatize troubled banks. The government in Estonia spent 1.4 percent of GDP, in Latvia 2.6 percent of GDP, and in Lithuania 1.7 percent of GDP during the same period (Tang, Zoli, and Klytchnikova 2000, table 9, 22–23). In short, even if privatization did rid the state sector of unprofitable enterprises, which lightened the fiscal burden over time, it nevertheless left the state with large debts in the process, especially due to the privatization of the financial sector. Most important, the traditional sources of revenue for state budgets, the large state-owned enterprises, were no longer easy sources of income, as profits could no longer be simply appropriated by state organs. Convincing private actors to contribute to state coffers was a new task for tax officials.

## Raising Revenue in Partially Monetized Economies and Informal Economies

Another challenge to the development of new fiscal systems related to the high level of informal and nonmonetized economic activity. Simply put, tax officials faced the challenge of taxing economic activity that was beyond their direct knowledge or reliable measurement. Informal economic activity and secondary employment existed at modest levels during the communist period but grew to much larger levels in the postcommunist period as citizens sought ways to cope with wage arrears, forced unpaid leave, and the risk of impoverishment (Klugman and Kolev 2001). Hidden employment in the informal sector was a crucial survival mechanism that contributed to social stability in turbulent times. Yet informal employment also became a significant portion of economic activity that remained beyond the reach of the state. Alexandre Kolev explains the vicious circle that emerges.

> The growing informal sector jeopardizes the ability of the state to regulate the economy by reducing its revenues. The state's difficulty in collecting taxes in turn decreases the extent of social welfare in the regular economy and hinders

the capacity of the government to pay wages and pensions on time, which could provide additional incentives for firms and individuals to join the informal sector. (1998, 3)

As Kolev points out, the growth of the informal economy and the state's inability to collect taxes were problems that mutually reinforced each other. As the state was unable to achieve its revenue imperative, it became further unable to pay salaries to public workers or provide social protections to those without employment. And, as public workers went unpaid and the unemployed went without adequate social safety nets, both groups gravitated more and more toward informal economic activity to survive.

Estimates of informal economic activity vary significantly for each country, given the inherent difficulty of measuring hidden activity. At times different methodologies generate significantly different estimates (Feige and Urban 2008). The various estimates for the size of the unofficial economy in the 1990s are in most cases rather large, as table 2 shows. One curious observation in the data is that the trajectories range so significantly among similar type of economies. In some countries the unofficial economy increased during the institutionalization of capitalism (like Bulgaria, Latvia, Russia, and Ukraine) between 1991 and 1995. In other countries, however, the unofficial economy shrank over the same period (like Poland, Slovakia, and Estonia) or remained about the same (like the Czech Republic, Hungary, and Lithuania). That said, the informal economies—which as a share of GDP in 1995 reached as high as 35.3 percent in

**TABLE 2. Share of the Unofficial Economy as Percentage of GDP in Early Transition**

| Country | 1991 | 1993 | 1995 |
|---|---|---|---|
| Bulgaria | 23.9 | 29.9 | 36.2 |
| Czech Republic | 12.9 | 16.9 | 11.3 |
| Hungary | 32.9 | 28.5 | 29.0 |
| Poland | 23.5 | 18.5 | 12.6 |
| Romania | 15.7 | 16.4 | 19.1 |
| Slovakia | 15.1 | 16.2 | 5.8 |
| Estonia | 26.2 | 24.1 | 11.8 |
| Latvia | 19.0 | 31.0 | 35.3 |
| Lithuania | 21.8 | 31.7 | 21.6 |
| Russia | 23.5 | 36.7 | 41.6 |
| Ukraine | 25.6 | 38.0 | 48.9 |

*Source:* Johnson and Kaufmann 2001, 215.

Latvia, 36.2 percent in Bulgaria, 41.6 percent in Russia, and 48.9 percent in Ukraine—significantly hampered the ability of the state coffers to meet the population's needs and expectations (Johnson and Kaufman 2001, 215).

Further obscuring economic activity and complicating revenue generation was the preponderance of nonmonetized forms of exchange within the regular economy. In the former planned economy, money did not demarcate value or play a significant role as a means of facilitating exchange. Across the communist world, shortages and the hoarding of goods were common manifestations of the undermonetized economy. Indeed, under communism, personal access and special connections determined one's access to goods as much as, if not more than, money. Given this communist legacy, money had to regain meaning as the marker of value, and thereby drive the allocation of goods (Ganev 2007). Several scholars like Janos Kornai (1990), David Woodruff (1999), and Venelin Ganev (2007) examine the problem of the demonetized economy for the development of the tax state. They argue that until firms conducted business with money and paid taxes with money, and until they reduced or eliminated their reliance on barter, promissory notes, and payment in kind, the state could not effectively raise the revenue it needed for the budget.

Nonmonetized exchange occurred in virtually all transition countries in the 1990s with a few exceptions. The Russian case offered especially dramatic examples of the havoc wrought by demonetized exchange on fiscal development, with over 71 percent of firms surveyed reporting the use of nonmonetized exchange (see table 3). The stories of Russian workers receiving their wages in goods rather than rubles are legendary, like the stories of the workers at a large paper factory in Novosibirsk receiving their wages in toilet paper or the fishermen of the Preobrazhensk Trawler Fleet in Primorskii Krai receiving their wages in vodka (*Vedomosti*, November 26, 1997; World Bank 1998, 6–7). While this topic is pursued further in chapter 6, it is useful to note briefly here the impact on revenue generation and the consolidation of state authority.

Gaddy and Ickes (2002) write how tax offsets and swaps of promissory notes among enterprises, local governments, and the federal government diminished the power of political leaders to meet their responsibilities or even to set budgetary allocations for much of the 1990s. In-kind tax payments meant the state often lacked the cash to pay child benefits, pensions, health care, military personnel, and government workers; and such groups suffered tremendously within Russia's "virtual economy" (Gaddy and Ickes 2002). Because the Russian state had no choice but to accept tax offsets, debt swaps, and in-kind payments, central and local governments lost control over determining the state's spending priorities and taxpayers' fiscal obligations. For example, spending priorities were determined by the availability of in-kind payments that enterprises (indebted usually to local and regional governments) could provide. Gaddy and Ickes (2002) give the example of a tax-delinquent firm that would "pay its taxes" by constructing a subway station. The local government would accept this payment in kind because the enterprise had no cash to pay taxes and the publicly minded project was better than nothing at all. However, this meant that the spending priorities of the local government (and by extension the federal government, which would have received a portion of the tax as part of the tax-sharing arrangement) were moot. Officials could not allocate the money to a project that they deemed of greater importance than subway construction—or whatever the project on offer. That is, if leaders determined that public resources should go toward increasing pensions or teachers' pay (instead of construction projects), they could not make these allocations. This removed the state's traditional authority over the budget. It also allowed the firm to set its own level of taxation since, according to Gaddy and Ickes, in-kind payments were grossly overvalued, thereby reducing the enterprise's de facto obligation (2002). Even when firms paid taxes with truly useless goods, desperate regional governments would typically accept these forms of payment in the hopes of exchanging them for something of greater value. This practice was highly inefficient, and it delayed the consolidation of state authority and tax collection. It also allowed firms to continue producing products that no one would want to buy (Carlin et al. 2000).

Scholarly analysis of barter and other forms of nonmonetary exchange elucidates the intransigence of various domestic economic actors in the shift to a capitalist tax system (Woodruff 1999; Gaddy and Ickes 2002). Indeed nonmonetary exchange and tax offsets persisted for many years in postcommunist countries since powerful economic actors—regional governments and the large Soviet-era firms that produced at a loss—colluded to resist change (Ganev 2007; Gaddy and Ickes 2002, 177–79). Because so many well-connected economic actors benefited from the unconsolidated monetary order, the government found it difficult to fully monetize the economy.

Moreover, the social and political costs of monetizing the economy were especially high since monetization required terminating de facto tax subsidies to many large industrial enterprises that provided social services, safety nets, and the only formal sector jobs available to a local workforce. As a leading IMF tax economist explains, the tax arrears were a political problem as much as, if not more than, an institutional problem. The problem was not simply that countries like Russia lacked the institutions to collect taxes. Rather, leaders understood the consequences of truly forcing enterprises to pay their taxes in cash. Forcing enterprises to make good on their tax obligations would bankrupt cash-strapped firms and lead to higher unemployment and the collapse of many supporting social institutions.[5]

While demonetization reached much higher levels in the post-Soviet Republics, it existed in nonnegligible levels in Central and Eastern Europe late into the 1990s. Evidence of the persistence of barter in Eastern Europe is found in the World Bank-EBRD World Business Environment Survey. This survey conducted in 1999 asked firms to report the percentage of nonmonetary transactions they engaged in (question 67). The survey results show that some level of barter or nonmonetary exchange occurred in 43.4 percent of firms surveyed in Slovakia, 51.8 percent of firms in Estonia, 35.2 percent of firms in Bulgaria, and 34.2 percent of firms in Poland. Likewise, the survey reports that some level of barter or nonmonetary exchange occurred in 27.2 percent of firms surveyed in Romania and 25.2 percent of firms surveyed in the Czech Republic. Only in Hungary was the number of firms reporting barter and nonmonetary transactions quite low (10.2 percent of firms). Table 3 reports with more detail the extent to which firms engaged in nonmonetized exchange late into the 1990s.

## Creating Tax Bureaucracies

Raising enough revenue when the economy was not fully monetized was all the more challenging given the condition of the postcommunist tax bureaucracies. The creation of the tax state required myriad new institutions and pro-

**TABLE 3. Percentage of Firms in Sample Reporting Level of Barter and Nonmonetary Transaction**

| Country | None | 1–9 | 10–25 | 26–50 | 51–75 | 76–100 | Firms Surveyed |
|---|---|---|---|---|---|---|---|
| Bulgaria | 64.8 | 24.8 | 7.2 | 1.6 | 1.6 | 0 | 125 |
| Czech Republic | 74.8 | 17.0 | 5.2 | 3.0 | 0 | 0 | 135 |
| Estonia | 49.2 | 42.2 | 6.1 | 2.3 | 0 | 0 | 132 |
| Hungary | 89.8 | 8.6 | 1.6 | 0 | 0 | 0 | 128 |
| Poland | 65.8 | 21.6 | 8.1 | 3.6 | 0.9 | 0 | 222 |
| Romania | 72.8 | 10.4 | 8.8 | 4.0 | 0.8 | 3.2 | 125 |
| Russia | 28.4 | 19.1 | 16.8 | 15.3 | 12.6 | 7.8 | 524 |
| Slovakia | 56.6 | 13.2 | 7.8 | 3.9 | 3.9 | 14.7 | 129 |
| Ukraine | 28.6 | 21.4 | 16.1 | 11.6 | 11.2 | 11.2 | 224 |

*Source:* European Bank for Reconstruction and Development Enterprise Survey 1999.

cedures: the transformation and expansion of the existing tax bureaucracy and the creation of national treasury systems, budget offices, and accounting and reporting systems, as well as the establishment of new agencies for macroeconomic and statistical analysis (Bonker 2007, 50).

To create new institutions, the postcommunist governments relied substantially upon the fiscal specialists trained under the previous system. However, existing tax specialists were too few in number, and their previous experience often did not prepare them well for their new responsibilities. Given the behemoth socialist-era bureaucracies, why were there too few tax officials? As noted in brief, the past communist economic systems did not require large bureaucracies to collect taxes because the state relied primarily on a small number of large state-owned companies for taxation. In the past, the monobank determined how to settle enterprise payments and then processed enterprise payments by directly withdrawing from their single monobank account. Hence, an elementary tax bureaucracy could meet the revenue collection needs of the communist state (Tanzi and Tsibouris 2000, 13–14). After communism, however, the number and the types of potential revenue sources changed. The first areas of the formal economy to grow in size and profitability, like services and small enterprises, were more challenging to tax than the large state monopolies of the previous regime (Tanzi 2001, 54–55; Gehlbach 2008). The number of taxpayers increased substantially, and the shift from large formal activity to small informal activity complicated tax collection efforts (Ebrill and Havrylyshyn 1999; Martinez-Vazquez and McNab 2000; Joshi and Ayee 2008).

Furthermore, in the early years of reform, little emphasis was placed on reforming, expanding, and training existing bureaucracies, and civil service reform was delayed in many countries.[6] National budgets allocated inadequate resources to modernize tax collection, including insufficient funds to pay for computer equipment and for computer training for tax collection officials. The new political officials who inherited undertrained and underresourced bureaucracies were overwhelmed by the task of generating revenue. The elected officials were seldom prepared to design and run a tax system oriented toward a market economy. Stoyan Aleksandrov, the Bulgarian finance minister from 1992 to 1994, explained his predicament.

> Honestly, at that time, we did not have any kind of tax policy. . . . We had to identify our priorities and then the laws were changed one by one. First we had to figure out how to write a budget. Later the officials could think about how

to stimulate the economy. But at first we just had to create and define taxes such that we could fill the budget.[7]

Inexperienced tax officials received a significant amount of help from external bodies, like the Organization for Economic Cooperation and Development (OECD), the European Community, and most of all, the IMF, to transform and educate the tax bureaucracies. Local officials from transition countries traveled abroad to participate in seminars on taxation. The OECD in conjunction with the IMF organized an early series of four seminars for bureaucrats from transition countries. In 1990 and 1991, about thirty representatives from Yugoslavia, the Soviet Union, Bulgaria, Czechoslovakia, Hungary, Poland, and Romania gathered to attend workshops led by IMF and OECD tax specialists. The stated objective of the meetings was to "promote a better understanding of the principles which underlie tax systems in market-oriented economies and of the 'international rules of the game' which the OECD Committee on Fiscal Affairs has helped to develop" (OECD 1991, 11). To promote this end, the OECD founded the Center for Co-operation with European Economies in Transition in March 1990. Officially, the purpose of the center was "to provide technical advice, to undertake policy dialogue, and, in a few cases, to train officials in the context of a programme of activities that is designed and reviewed annually" (5). The OECD asserted that it formed the center to provide a service to tax officials in postcommunist Europe who sought advice. According the center's early literature, the center's "technical advice and policy dialogue take numerous forms and cover a wide range of subjects. . . . Training of government officials involved in implementing market-oriented policies is being carried out" in a limited way. However, the OECD became quite active in providing technical support in fiscal reform, in collaboration with other multilateral institutions. The OECD's involvement in advising and training tax officials in Eastern Europe was not only coordinated with the other major international financial institutions. Quite curiously, the OECD notes, "the experience of the business community is also called upon where appropriate" (1991, 5).

In addition to providing training abroad for several hundreds of tax officials, the major international financial institutions sent envoys to each country to advise on tax reform. Foreign specialists, often under IMF contracts, moved to Eastern Europe to train officials from the finance ministries to design new budgets and tax codes. Aleksandrov again describes his early experience leading the Bulgarian Ministry of Finance.

> All the new laws and changes [in Bulgaria] were discussed with tax specialists from the IMF and the EC. . . . There were discussions between our specialists and theirs but no specific orders. We created a structure that is typical in Europe. . . . We needed to adopt EC standards of accounting. We measured production differently. We had no GDP before 1991. We had our methods of measuring profit and GDP, if you can call it that. We had to update our statistics.[8]

Often with the financial contributions from the OECD and the European Community, consultants hired by the IMF's Fiscal Affairs Department analyzed the needs of governments and provided classified reports to the minister of finance and the prime minister of each country. The ministers could then ignore the report or follow some of the suggestions—but there was no obligation to heed the advice. The technical advisers gained some leverage if a country had taken a loan from the IMF since the Article IV mission in charge of the loan might pressure the government to reform its tax system. That said, Vito Tanzi, the longtime director of the IMF's Department of Fiscal Affairs, insisted that linking technical assistance to lending conditionality formally violated IMF rules. Tanzi adds that, even on a practical level, it was hard to delay a loan payment when a government failed to follow technical advice.

> There would be a long list of structural changes as part of the lending arrangement; but then when it came time to release the next tranche, there would be waivers. We would say, they did this change or that change, and so let's ignore this other one [that was not done]. Plus sometimes you did not know what was going on.[9]

When the IMF sent technical assistance missions to the countries to provide advice on setting up new fiscal institutions, it staffed these missions largely with outsiders rather than with the IMF's permanent staff. According to Tanzi, outside specialists were needed because the regular staff, although technically and theoretically sophisticated, was "not really prepared for advising about the nuts and bolts of introducing, for example, the VAT, which requires about a hundred steps. So we found officials working in governments in countries with functioning systems and sent them to spend a year [in a country] to give technical assistance."[10] The IMF drew its advisers from countries with strong fiscal institutions. In Eastern Europe, advisers from Brazil and Australia were used effectively, which is why, Tanzi explained, the treasuries in Russia and Hungary bear a strong resemblance to that of Brazil.[11]

When training tax bureaucrats, IMF advisers emphasized the standard goals of fiscal design like simplicity, efficiency, equity, and neutrality (Shome 1995, 1). In general, the IMF was conservative in its advising, discouraging novel experimentation and alternative fiscal approaches (Bonker 2007, 50). For example, when the flat-tax experiments became popular in the region for the Baltic countries in the mid-1990s and for many other countries in the 2000s, the IMF discouraged them, as chapter 5 discusses more fully. In promoting mainstream fiscal systems, the IMF provided rather specific suggestions about the relative weights of various revenue forms appropriate for transition economies. Reflecting its past advice, the IMF published its recommendations for the design of tax systems for developing and transition countries (Shome 1995). The OECD similarly published a set of articles outlining the existing tax structures in OECD members. The OECD volume resembles the IMF tax handbook in its focus and emphasis (OECD 1991).

Publishing a collection of articles identifying best practices within taxation suggests that a one-size-fits-all mentality prevailed in the IMF and the OECD in the area of tax reform. To some extent, this impression is warranted since the East Europeans were presented with a unified front on tax reform due to the coordination of tax assistance (Easter 2009). The way in which technical advice was presented certainly gave the impression that a consensus had formed and that fiscal reform should be technical rather than political. That said, the OECD did not expect tax reform to happen in a political vacuum. The involvement of the business community and trade unions in the OECD's conferences suggests that special interests were considered (even if only superficially) in the technical determination of a "best practices" model of taxation. The bodies consulting in the OECD tax reform efforts in postcommunist countries included IBM Europe, Nestlé, Renault, and Shell on the business side; and some of the trade union organizations invited to the early workshops came from France, Czechoslovakia, Poland, and the United States (OECD 1991, 454–55).

Nonetheless, the tax handbooks published by the OECD and IMF did present tax reform as a technical matter that should follow the experience of advanced industrialized countries (OECD 1991; Shome 1995) rather than political constraints in postcommunist countries. The scholarship on transition has often warned against simply superimposing institutions from one country onto another and expecting them to function the same elsewhere, despite different cultural and political arenas (Rose 1993; Jacoby 2000; Fukuyama 2004). Indeed, given their different institutions and histories, local interpretations of the basic market institutions varied significantly from country to country.[12] Moreover, the decades of a command economy in Eastern Europe importantly shaped the basic attitudes and assumptions about taxation. For example, many observers have noted that East European officials did not necessarily accept the idea that tax rates and enterprise obligations had to be accepted as fixed. Quite commonly, postcommunist leaders wanted to continue using the tax system as a flexible instrument to keep people employed and enterprises afloat, simply allowing a firm to pay wages instead of taxes as the need arose. Not only did the early tax system often take the place of the plan as the tool for economic and social policy, as Tanzi and Tsibouris argue (2000, 16); the early postcommunist system of taxation continued to function with much of its same ad hoc and post hoc flexibility. The practice of the discretionary renegotiation of tax rates both prior to and following a tax period remained common. The renegotiation of tax rates in the 1990s prolonged the "soft budget constraints" that Hungarian economist Janos Kornai wrote so famously about in the 1980s in his descriptions of command economies (1986, 1990). The flexibility of the early tax obligations also created room for the manipulation of the system for personal gain (Ganev 2007). In short, for tax systems to function effectively within the new capitalist system, government officials and the tax bureaucracy had to adjust their expectations of the relationship between the tax state and taxpayers.

## Creating Compliant Taxpayers: Experience, Perceptions, and Conceptions of Justice

Besides writing new laws and training new bureaucracies, another crucial step in postcommunist tax reform involved reconditioning ordinary taxpayers and changing their attitudes—attitudes toward revenue collection and state expenditures. As noted above, politicians understood they had to bolster welfare protection in the short term while ultimately diminishing public expectations of the state's responsibility in the long term. This was a fundamental reorientation required in the transition from communism to capitalism. In other words, one major difficulty for postcommunist fiscal reformers lay in satisfying the citizens' expectations resulting from years of living under communism, while gradually reducing popular demands for extensive, state-based welfare protection in the medium and long run. This required governments to make their citizenry aware of the costs of high welfare protection (Csontos, Kornai, and Tóth 1998). As Haggard and Kaufman note, after citizens had grown accustomed to living under a paternalistic system, they became afflicted by a potent version of what they and others[13] call a "tax illusion," meaning that citizens expect or even "insist on the provision of services without realizing the extent to which these reduce net earnings" (2001, 5).

The problem of a tax illusion in Eastern Europe was especially acute, hindering tax collection efforts. Under the planned economy, personal contributions to federal budgets were largely hidden, and citizens rarely paid taxes directly. As many political economists have noted, given that the state did not previously rely on a personal income tax for much revenue at all, there was a lack of "tax consciousness" among ordinary people (Kornai 1997; Vámosi-Nagy, Kocsis, and Alvaro Sanchez 1997; Bonker 2007). Again, under communism the state appropriated what it needed out of the national income—income that was mainly generated by public enterprises. Personal tax contributions were exceptional and then only minimal. For example, a wage tax (separate from a payroll tax) existed in the Czechoslovak command economy on income from self-employed activities and cultural production. But this was relatively minor, with at least 85 percent of national taxes coming from enterprise surpluses, payroll taxes, and turnover taxes (Heady and Smith 1995, 20). Although the amount of government revenue from personal income taxes was quite a bit larger in Hungary (about 30 percent of public revenues) given the greater private sector, most people living under communism had no experience with income taxes (Vámosi-Nagy, Kocsis, and Alvaro Sanchez 1997, 480). In the Soviet Union under Brezhnev's leadership, only about 8 percent of total revenue came from taxes on personal income (Kornai 1992, 137, quoted in Torgler 2003, 358). Since labor taxes were deducted from the employer's payroll, the majority of workers had no personal experience in directly paying taxes and thus had little sense of how much tax they actually contributed. Under the new regime, citizens needed to assume responsibility for the cost of public goods.

This lack of experience in paying taxes had an important influence on taxpayer attitudes and ultimately their tax compliance. The vast scholarly research on tax compliance investigates a large range of institutional, experiential, and cultural factors to explain levels of taxpayer compliance across societies. There appears to be very little consensus in the literature over the determinants of tax compliance in general or in transition countries in particular. Some of the early theoretical work on tax compliance takes a utilitarian approach emphasizing the calculations of taxpayers who weigh the benefits of evasion against the risk of penalty (Levi 1988; Slemrod 1992). The recent scholarship on tax compliance in transition countries instead emphasizes the taxpayers' personal experiences interacting with tax officials (Mitra and Stern

2002, 37; Stepanyan 2003, 10), their perceptions of their government's performance (Pommerehne and Frey 1992), and/or their perceptions of the compliance levels of their fellow citizens (Berenson 2006, 127; Alm and Torgler 2003; Torgler 2003). Several studies on transition countries contend that the strong mistrust that arose between tax officials and taxpayers due to the inefficacy of, or the harassment by, tax authorities lowered tax compliance in postcommunist countries (Mitra and Stern 2002, 37; Stepanyan 2003, 10). Other theorists consider tax compliance within the larger institutional structure of a country. For example, some theories of compliance and tax morale in Eastern Europe identify a citizen's trust in the legal and political system and even a taxpayer's ability to participate in referenda (on tax and nontax matters) as important explanatory variables (Torgler 2003; Frey 2002; Frey and Feld 2002).

Particularly interesting are the tax compliance studies that take a constructivist approach. They privilege norms, ideology, and values to explain tax compliance levels (Putnam 1993; Webber and Wildavsky 1986; Hull 2000). These values are not directly responding to government efficacy or action but instead are products of taxpayers' convictions and perceptions of distributive justice (Wenzel 2003). Students of tax morale have examined different values, like perceptions of fairness and national pride, as shapers of tax morale (Wenzel 2003). Torgler finds strong evidence in postcommunist countries that pride in one's country along with demographic factors (especially the age and gender of a taxpayer) positively correlates with tax morale (2003).

## Distributional Implications of Postcommunist Tax Reform

It is difficult to weigh these various factors contributing to relative levels of tax compliance in transition countries. First, the data on tax compliance are imprecise. Since the level of compliance must be estimated by proxy (using survey data on individual perceptions of *other* people's tax evasion) or through indirect measures, like the amount of electricity used relative to changes in tax revenues, comparative data across multiple countries are unreliable. A second challenge in making broad pronouncements about the factors contributing to tax compliance and morale during postcommunist transition stems from the rather heterogeneous pattern of tax compliance across the region. That is, not only do levels of compliance and tax morale vary but so do the trajectories. Tax morale improves in some countries over time (like Poland and Bulgaria) but declines in others (like the three Baltic countries and Russia) (Torgler 2003, 362, table 3).

Even if compliance levels do not follow one pattern, there does seem to be a common pattern in the way governments used the tax system for achieving distributional ends, which may be related to expectations about taxpayer compliance. Simply put, the common practice of using the tax system to redistribute income in the early part of postcommunist transition suggests that governments may have worried how citizens' perceptions of distributive justice would affect levels of tax compliance and the efficacy of the tax system overall. One pattern is clear: postcommunist taxation begins in a much more progressive fashion, but the progressivity of taxation erodes over time. In other words, the tax burden on poorer taxpayers (as a proportion of the taxpayer's resources) increased as the country transitioned to capitalism over time.

Under communism the income tax system had little or no distributional impact on individual welfare. As noted, the wage tax was small, and the taxes on income from self-employment, literary or artistic activity, or private agriculture were more intended to encourage or discourage particular economic activities than to redistribute income (Heady and Smith 1995, 22). In addition, the payroll tax in command economies was a flat rate levied on the aggregate payroll, with very few exceptions. Thus, in contrast to a market economy, the flat rate did not bear distributional consequences for the individual citizen since, in the command economy, there was no unemployment and a central administrative process determined the wage structure (22). Distributional objectives could instead be achieved through the system of administered wages and job creation programs (24).

Political officials responsible for postcommunist tax reform initially opted for some redistribution in the new capitalist tax structures. For example, in creating the main consumption tax, the multitiered value-added tax (VAT) held important distributional implications for all countries. A value-added tax is a type of sales tax that is based on the value a producer adds to a product over the course of its production.[14] For the consumer, it is a sales tax that is incorporated into the price of any good or service. The governments in the Czech Republic, Poland, Hungary, Slovakia, Russia, Ukraine, Moldova, Estonia, Lithuania, and Latvia, among others, applied a reduced or a zero VAT rate for food and other necessities, like medicine, home heating, repairs, and children's items in some instances. The standard rate is the rate that applies to the vast majority of goods and services, whereas the reduced rate covers a limited defined set of goods. In particular, the Czech Republic in 1993 introduced a standard VAT rate of 23 percent, with a reduced rate of 5 percent. Slovakia in

1993 introduced a 25 percent standard VAT rate and a 6 percent reduced rate (Heady and Smith 1995, 25). Hungary introduced its first VAT in 1989 with three rates: 0 percent, 15 percent, and 25 percent, with the zero rate applying to about 40 percent of household goods, with very few goods taxed under the 15 percent rate (Bonker 2007, 105). Then in 1992, tax reforms replaced the two lower rates with one reduced rate of 6 percent, until a fiscal shortfall led the government to raise it to 10 percent the following year (105). In Poland, instead of the 22 percent standard VAT rate, a 7 percent reduced rate applied to many types of food, to energy, and to children's goods. The Russian standard rate in 1993 was 20 percent, and the reduced rate was 10 percent for certain necessities (Stepanyan 2003, 27).

Over the course of the 1990s, however, many governments removed or reduced the exemptions and preferential tax arrangements for low-income citizens. For prospective EU members, tax harmonization typically required an increase in the taxes on food and other items as part of the EU accession process, as discussed in the following chapter (Stepanyan 2003, 14).[15]

Following a similar pattern, income taxes were initially more beneficial to low-income taxpayers but lost a degree of progressiveness over the course of the capitalist transition. That is, all postcommunist governments initially introduced a progressive income tax structure that included various exemptions, for example, for families with children and special needs. Once again, the progressive tax structure and the redistribution favoring the poor diminished over time. For instance, in the Baltic countries, the first postcommunist tax reforms set multiple tax brackets with rates ranging from 15 to 35 percent. In the mid-1990s, Estonia, Latvia, and Lithuania replaced their progressive income tax rates with a unified flat tax and a significant reduction in exemptions (Stepanyan 2003, 16). In Russia, the initial 1992 system established three tax brackets: 12 percent, 20 percent, and 30 percent. In 2001, a single-rate structure replaced the multirate structure, and the three brackets converged at 13 percent. More striking, in 1994 Ukraine's personal income tax relied on eight brackets, with the top rate reaching 90 percent. By 1995 the top rate was reduced to 60 percent (with seven brackets) and by 1996 to 40 percent (with six brackets) (Stepanyan 2003, appendix). Romania stands out with fifteen initial tax rates on personal income (Torgler 2003, 359). By 2008, single rates had replaced the many-tiered, progressive rates in the Czech Republic, Slovakia, Bulgaria, Romania, Albania, and Macedonia, among others. In short, the principle of progressive taxation dominated tax design in the early postcommunist tax systems, but by the late

1990s and the 2000s, income taxes and value-added taxes flattened substantially, in some cases abandoning almost entirely the principle of progressive taxation and wealth redistribution through taxation.

It bears mentioning that the decline in progressive taxation coincided with the growth of economic inequality throughout the region. Inequality grew under capitalism—perhaps not unsurprisingly—as seen in the change in Gini coefficients reported in table 4. Some might view the growth in inequality unproblematic during the shift from communism to capitalism, in particular if this inequality resulted from the enrichment of the most innovative, productive, or hardworking East Europeans in society. Yet the concentration of wealth may have occurred as much from the distortions and corruption within the privatization programs as from successful entrepreneurship. As Tanzi and Tsibouris write, the inequality in the postcommunist region increased in many transition countries not because wealth was created by the new rich but because wealth was "raided from the government, at times with the implicit connivance of the government" (2000, 5). Few would deny that corruption in the privatization of state-owned companies contributed significantly to wealth concentration in the region (Goldman 2006).

## Conclusion

How should we interpret the declining progressiveness of the tax system (both in direct and in indirect taxes) in the light of the general level of politicization of taxation in the region? The main argument of this book is that domestic

**TABLE 4. Gini Coefficients in Postcommunist Countries**

| Country | 1987 | 1994–96 | 1997–99 | 2000–2003 | 2004–6 |
|---|---|---|---|---|---|
| Bulgaria | 23 | 25.8 | 26.4 | 31.9 | 29 |
| Czech Republic | 19 | 25.4 | — | — | 25 |
| Estonia | 23 | — | 37.6 | 37.2 | 36 |
| Hungary | 21 | — | 24.4 | 26.9 | 27 |
| Latvia | 23 | — | 32.4 | 37.7 | 38 |
| Lithuania | 23 | — | 32.4 | 36.0 | 36 |
| Poland | 26 | — | 31.6 | 34.5 | 34 |
| Romania | 23 | 28.2 | — | 31.0 | 31 |
| Russia | 24 | — | 48.7 | 45.6 | 40 |
| Slovakia | 20 | 25.8 | — | — | 26 |
| Ukraine | 23 | — | 29.0 | 28.1 | 28 |

*Source:* UN Development Report 2001, 2003, 2004, and 2006; World Bank, World Development Indicators 2006, Washington, DC; Tanzi and Tsibouris 2000, 8.

politics has had a surprisingly weak effect on the evolution of the tax system and on tax policy-making. In this regard, the weak public response to the declining progressiveness of the tax system in a time of increasing income inequality reaffirms the larger findings of this study.

That is not to say that the public's attitudes and perceptions did not matter at all. As noted, government leaders and fiscal specialists may have anticipated public attitudes toward distributive justice when initially designing the tax system, to preserve political stability in a time of great political flux. Moreover, perceptions of fairness may have shaped overall compliance levels. There seems to be some limited evidence of this in survey research, as seen in the case of Poland (Berenson 2006). However, it is certainly ironic that the transition away from authoritarianism and the deepening of democracy did not coincide with a higher level of popular input in taxation—the topic for the remainder of this book.

As difficult as it is to understand the motivations of policymakers, bureaucrats, and taxpayers, one conclusion about the early transition to capitalist taxation is unambiguous: the early period of tax reform occurred in an economically tough and politically challenging environment. Economic conditions were inhospitable to revenue generation. The early transitional recessions, the large shadow economies, the incomplete monetization of the economies, the understaffed and underresourced bureaucracies, and inexperience among taxpayers presented significant challenges for revenue generation. Despite substantial input from the international tax policy community, developing capitalist tax systems faced tremendous hurdles. The uncertain political environment, the fear of electoral backlash, and the prevalence of tax illusion confounded the institution building required for a functioning tax system.

In order to appreciate more fully the impact of politics on taxation, this book now turns to the development of specific tax structures. For the following chapters, the focus is to uncover the role of politics in the evolution of particular tax forms, with the aim of identifying those tax areas that remain politicized and those that essentially lie beyond domestic political debate.

## CHAPTER 3

# Ceding Control: European Integration and Consumption Taxes

As the postcommunist governments began to devise their tax systems in ways that were compatible with and supportive of their democratic and capitalist transformations, they paid close attention to the tax forms in Western Europe. In part, the East Europeans were searching for solutions to fiscal problems. They also, however, began quickly to fuse their domestic economic transformations with their geopolitical goal of deepening ties to the West and severing ties to the East. It is striking just how early the postcommunist leaders adopted a pro-European rhetoric, with many politicians embracing the slogan of a "Return to Europe" in 1990 (Appel 2004). This rhetoric was not only part of winning elections and establishing a party's pro-European identity, it also became an early trope for discussing the country's political and economic future. Shortly after the fall of communism, governments deliberately designed their new institutions to integrate with the European Community. The emulation of laws and structures took on a new meaning, though, as actual EU membership became a realistic goal. Tax policy-making, like many areas of economic policy-making, began to reflect and ultimately mirror the tax structures required by EU legislation.

This chapter examines the powerful influence of European integration on the evolution of consumption taxes in postcommunist Europe. Perhaps more than any other area of taxation, consumption taxes reflect the demands of regional integration and the loss of policy-making authority within newly sovereign countries. The chapter begins with some background on the importance of consumption taxes for budgetary revenues in postcommunist Europe. It then turns to the scope of EU regulation in this area, focusing especially on the value-added tax (VAT). The chapter then examines the import of European tax institutions through the accession negotiation process in order to demonstrate how little influence leaders or their constituents had in negotiation outcomes. Due to the requirements of tax harmonization, East European governments relinquished their control over consumption taxes in broad and specific ways for the sake of becoming EU members, weakening public participation and denigrating legislative deliberation in the process.

## Consumption Taxes in Eastern Europe

In Eastern Europe today, consumption taxes constitute one of the largest portions of tax revenue.[1] Indirect taxes include export and import duties, excise duties on products like alcohol, fuel, and tobacco, and the value-added tax on virtually all other products and services. As noted in chapter 1, a value-added tax is a type of sales tax that is based on the value a producer adds to a product over the course of its production.[2] For the consumer, it is a sales tax that is incorporated into the price of any good or service. Excise duties on specific goods are paid by the producer but indirectly passed on to the consumer. These duties typically serve to discourage the consumption of goods that the state deems undesirable or to pay for externalities associated with the consumption of a good. The tariffs on imports and exports in the European Union are paid by companies and applied to goods produced outside the European Union, although certain non-EU countries have negotiated favorable terms through programs like the Euro-Mediterranean Association Agreements[3] and, more recently, the European Neighbourhood Policy.[4]

Indirect taxes are crucial for budgetary revenues in Eastern Europe. Already in 1995, taxes on goods and services constituted 33.9 percent of total taxes in the Czech Republic, 42.8 percent in Hungary, 38.3 percent in Poland, and 36.0 percent in Slovakia (*Eurostat 2008*). Just over one decade later, indirect taxes constituted 30.9 percent of total taxes in the Czech Republic, 41.0 percent in Hungary, 42.8 percent in Poland and 39.6 percent in Slovakia (*Eurostat*

**TABLE 5. Tax Revenue as a Percentage of Total Taxation in 2006**

| Country | Indirect Taxes | Direct Taxes | Social Contributions |
|---|---|---|---|
| Bulgaria | 56.5 | 20.1 | 25.5 |
| Czech Republic | 30.9 | 24.4 | 44.7 |
| Estonia | 44.0 | 23.0 | 32.9 |
| Latvia | 43.3 | 27.9 | 28.8 |
| Lithuania | 38.9 | 32.6 | 28.6 |
| Hungary | 41.0 | 25.3 | 33.6 |
| Poland | 42.8 | 22.2 | 36.1 |
| Romania | 44.5 | 21.4 | 34.2 |
| Slovakia | 39.6 | 20.4 | 40.0 |

*Source: Eurostat 2008*, 237, 239, 247, 255.

*2008*). Tables 5 and 6 report the contribution of consumption taxes in nine postcommunist European countries in 2006 and 1995 to total tax revenues, juxtaposed with other tax areas. Table 7 reports the percentage that the VAT contributes to overall revenues for eleven postcommunist countries for 2006.

The simultaneous processes of European integration and postcommunist transition encouraged a greater reliance on indirect taxes for several reasons. Consumption taxes are hard taxes for individuals to shirk and thus are a relatively reliable source of revenue (Heimann 2001; Eurostat 2004, 243). Given the existence of large shadow economies in the aftermath of communism and given the weak tax-collecting capabilities of new states, the VAT's relative reliability was valuable (EC-OECD 1998, 12). However, even if leaders had not considered the VAT an appealing form of taxation, they would nevertheless have had to adopt it in order to pursue their foreign policy goal of joining the European Union. Ukraine presents an interesting example of a country where the VAT has not been perceived as a reliable revenue source due to corruption within its implementation in the second half of the 2000s. In this particular case, the unreliability of the VAT led Ukraine's prime minister, Yulia Tymoshenko, to suggest replacing the VAT with a simpler sales tax. This would have helped recover revenue that was being lost due to distortions and corruption in the implementation of the VAT. However, the premier retreated from this position since it was inconsistent with recent trade agreements with the European Union. Thus, even as the prospects of EU membership diminished in the 2008–9 economic crisis (just a few years after its peak in 2004 and 2005 following the Orange Revolution), the government accepted that deeper European integration fundamentally constrained Ukraine's ability to abandon a VAT for a simpler sales tax.[5] It was a realization that the central European countries had made more than a decade earlier.

**TABLE 6. Tax Revenue as a Percentage of Total Taxation in 1995**

| Country | Indirect Taxes | Direct Taxes | Social Contributions |
|---|---|---|---|
| Bulgaria (2000) | 46.2 | 21.7 | 33.8 |
| Czech Republic | 33.9 | 26.5 | 39.6 |
| Estonia | 36.6 | 28.9 | 34.5 |
| Latvia | 42.4 | 21.5 | 36.1 |
| Lithuania | 43.5 | 30.4 | 26.0 |
| Hungary | 42.8 | 21.3 | 35.9 |
| Poland | 38.3 | 31.6 | 30.5 |
| Romania (2001) | 41.0 | 21.9 | 37.1 |
| Slovakia | 36.0 | 26.5 | 37.4 |

*Source: Eurostat 2008*, 237, 239, 247, 255.

## Consumption Taxes in the European Union

The deference of policymakers in Eastern Europe to EU tax codes is evident in all areas of consumption taxes. Simply put, leaders had to accept the regime in toto if they wanted to join the EU. In some respects, the East Europeans' deference to customs duties, and perhaps even excise taxes, is rather intuitive given their intent to participate fully in the European trading area. Not surprisingly, old EU member states harmonized customs duties before they harmonized value-added taxes. The subsequent deference to regulations concerning value-added taxes is less intuitive, however, since they are less directly related to free trade than customs duties are. Moreover, the VAT is more politically sensitive, as consumers usually experience changes to VAT rates fully and directly. Nevertheless, even in this one area where we might have expected some countries to opt out of certain aspects of the model, we see a full adoption of the European VAT law in the new member states. This section focuses further on VAT harmonization, within the harmonization of indirect taxes, since it is the closest version of the "hard case" in indirect taxes.

When initially designing their VAT laws, the new postcommunist policymakers usually borrowed from or broadly emulated the VAT model in West European economies (Kiss and Szapary 2000; Heady and Smith 1995; Tanzi 1991). This model was evolving in the decades prior to EU enlargement. All West European member states had been required to adopt a value-added tax as the main form of consumption tax after 1970, when the First and Second VAT Directives replaced the diversity of production and consumption taxes across member states in the European Economic Community. An important step was taken in 1977 when the Sixth VAT Directive (77/388/EEC) created a common VAT system for all member states (Keen et al. 1996, 380). By harmonizing the tax base across countries, the Sixth VAT Directive required the VAT be applied to the same transactions in all member states in order to create a common assessment basis.[6]

Since the harmonization of the base in 1977, new laws have extended the EU's regulatory reach. The current EU requirements for the VAT can be found in the 414 articles of the Council Directive 2006/112/EC of November 28, 2006.[7] Exemplifying the increased scope of VAT regulations at the EU level, the EU now requires the minimum standard VAT rate for member countries to be at least 15 percent and the reduced rate for a small set of enumerated goods to be at least 5 percent (Keen et al. 1996, 381).[8] Both the regulation concerning the tax base and the establishment of a minimum threshold became highly constraining features of the EU's VAT legislation. The harmonization of the base meant that governments could no longer identify politically sensitive goods to tax at a lower rate. Similarly, the minimum rates constrained tax policy in new member states in that they could not compete for consumers with lower tax rates. Furthermore, although states could impose a higher rate, the elimination of fiscal frontiers discouraged governments from setting the national VAT rate too high. Those governments that set a high VAT rate could lose revenues to a country with a lower VAT rate when a private person chose to buy a good elsewhere in the EU. Most likely, the EU will determine a narrow range, or even a fixed rate of VAT, as VAT harmonization deepens in the future. Since price incentives are widely thought to undermine fair competition in the common market, the current status of varying VAT rates across EU countries is formally deemed "transitional."[9] This deepening level of harmonization is consistent with the trajectory of value-added taxes over past decades.

What advantages led the European Economic Community to switch to a value-added tax and to require it of new and existing member states? First, the VAT avoids many tax complications in the import and export of goods across member states (and third-party trading partners) that plague other indirect tax structures. Second, the VAT is considered neutral with respect to domestic production and distribution, and thus the VAT causes less distortion than other tax forms. Third, the VAT is a particularly flexible and stable source of revenue because it taxes *all* types of income regardless of whether the income is earned in the formal or the informal sector. For example, income stemming from an illicit activity like drug trafficking is not taxed when it is earned, whereas it *is* taxed when it is spent on goods and services through the VAT. The VAT is also a predictable revenue generator. A broad-based VAT with few exceptions is expected to generate about 0.4 percent of GDP for every 1 percentage point of the standard rate (EC-OECD 1998, 10). Moreover, after the initial implementation period, the VAT seems practical and easy to administer (although the Ukrainian Tax Administration would likely disagree).

From a political perspective, one of the main drawbacks of the VAT is that a uniform tax rate on consumption imposes a larger burden (as a percentage of disposable income) on low-income households than it does on high-income households. Applying a lower rate on certain goods mitigates these effects only somewhat. Adjustments through income taxes or income transfers can, however, offset the effects on the consumption of low-income households.

## Harmonization of Consumption Taxes in Eastern Europe

Hungary, an early reformer with a large shadow economy, was the first to impose a value-added tax in 1988, followed by Lithuania in 1992 and Estonia, Romania, Slovakia, the Czech Republic, and Poland in 1993. Other early VAT reformers include Latvia in 1988 and Russia in 1991, both introducing a VAT before achieving full sovereignty from the Soviet Union.[10] Table 7 reports the year the VAT was introduced in eleven countries, along with rates and percentage of contributions to total revenue.

Although the initial VAT on select goods (with a social impact) was low, it increased steadily throughout the 1990s, achieving levels consistent with EU averages. By the end of the decade, most of the EU candidate countries had set their standard VAT rate similar to the average VAT rate in existing EU member states. Specifically, by 2003 the average VAT standard rate in the candidate countries was 19.1 percent, only .02 points below the EU average (Martinez-Serrano and Patterson 2003, 11). In the case of excise taxes, most East European states at the end of the 1990s had also achieved EU levels for all products except tobacco (Vazquez-Caro et al. 2001; Martinez-Serrano and Patterson 2003, 11). By the end of 2009 even tobacco products were taxed in Eastern Europe at the same rate as in Western Europe.

In most countries, the adoption of EU tax structures began simply as a practice of general emulation. In some cases tax emulation was even a matter

**TABLE 7. Introduction of Value-Added Taxes**

| Country | Year Introduced | Standard Rate (1995) | Standard Rate (2007) | 2006 VAT (% of revenue) |
|---|---|---|---|---|
| Bulgaria | 1994 | 22 | 20 | 36.3 |
| Czech Republic | 1993 | 22 | 19 | 18.1 |
| Estonia | 1993 | 18 | 18 | 29.6 |
| Hungary | 1989 | 25 | 20 | 20.4 |
| Latvia | 1988 | 18 | 18 | 28 |
| Lithuania | 1992 | 18 | 18 | 25.7 |
| Poland | 1993 | 22 | 22 | 24 |
| Romania | 1993 | 18 | 19 | 27.1 |
| Russia | 1991 | 28 | 18 | 18.5 |
| Slovakia | 1993 | 23 | 19 | 25.1 |
| Slovenia | 1999 | — | 20 | 22.1 |

*Source:* EC-OECD 1998; U.S. Council for International Business 2007; Eurostat 2007; Mertens and Tesche 2002.

of identity politics. For example, a top official in the Hungarian Ministry of Finance explained that even if membership in the EU (or then the EC) was not on the horizon in 1988, the Hungarians were looking at European models in developing their own tax structures, in part as a way to use economic reforms "to differentiate themselves" as much as possible from the Soviets and the system of central planning.[11]

Over time, though, the prospect of EU membership became the motivation behind adopting specific tax structures and rates.[12] Indeed, when asked directly, one leading Czech politician, Václav Klaus, explained that tax codes were not dictated to him as the federal finance minister in the spring of 1992, the period when consumption taxes were under design. However, the prospect of integrating economically with Western Europe was still the decisive factor in introducing a VAT and several other forms of consumption taxation (referring specifically to fuel and tobacco taxes). He noted that in the early 1990s, initial discussions on consumption taxes included a consideration of an American-style sales tax, but informal pressures existed already at that time to adopt a VAT to join the European Community. Klaus contends that while these "pressures were only implicit . . . and were not written down. . . . if you wanted to join the EU, you had to adopt a value-added tax."[13]

Further external pressure for adopting a value-added tax stemmed from the policy recommendations of the International Monetary Fund. The IMF was active in disseminating policy advice in the region, in particular in fiscal matters, as discussed in the previous chapter. While the IMF did not make the adoption of the VAT a strict condition of borrowing, it strongly encouraged a broad-based VAT framework in developing countries, and in fact it had been recommending to countries in Latin America and Africa to rely more heavily on VAT revenues (and less on trade taxes) for decades (Fjeldstad and Moore 2008, 235; Mahon 2004, 3).

While the external pressure to adopt a VAT began somewhat informally, a reference framework was soon made explicit in the European System of Integrated Economic Accounts (ESA95) in order to help states harmonize tax structures and rates (Kiss and Szapary 2001). Once governments began actively to pursue EU membership, the VAT became a mandatory fiscal structure, and the methods of calculating the tax base became explicit. Therefore, although some states adopted the VAT since the IMF encouraged it, and since it would reorient the country away from the East and toward the West (or rather away from communism and toward capitalism), many leaders quite early understood that the VAT was required for integration in Europe (Tait 1992; Newberry 1995).

By the start of EU accession negotiations, not only was the general form of excise duties and the value-added tax written down in the *acquis communautaire* and required for membership, the rates themselves were laid out for candidate countries in the form of EU directives for both excise duties and value-added taxes on tens of thousands of goods and services. "Tax harmonization," as it is called, was mandatory prior to accession. As former Czech premier Vladimír Špidla described it, "Harmonization of VAT rates was one of the admittance tickets to the EU." Without it, you could not enter (*Právo*, March 11, 2004).

## Tax Harmonization and EU Accession

Harmonization of consumption taxes worked as follows: In order for a candidate country to become a full EU member, it had to complete a series of accession negotiations. The negotiations themselves were broken into policy chapters, one of which was exclusively devoted to consumption taxes (Chapter Ten). Each country set up a Chapter Ten negotiating team staffed primarily from the Ministry of Finance. A small part of this team resided in Brussels, but most members remained in the capital cities to meet regularly with the local delegation of the European Commission. Negotiations occurred in writing between the local negotiating team and Brussels.[14] Every year, the commission published a report detailing a country's progress in aligning its laws with the *acquis*.

Each candidate country had to implement the necessary fiscal legislation to transform the tax codes according to the *acquis communautaire* in order to close the chapter and advance in the accession process. All chapters had to close for the accession negotiations to end and for EU accession to proceed. In the case of tax harmonization, the commission specified a minimum percentage of taxation that must be imposed on a good. Areas under the auspices of Chapter Ten included everything from taxes on food, medicine, children's clothing, school textbooks, gasoline, cigarettes, housing construction materials, financial services, homemade spirits, agricultural inputs, restaurants, home heating oil, telecommunications, and many thousands of other goods and services.

Toward the end of the accession process, most governments determined whether they could implement the *acquis* in absolutely all areas before the date of accession. If a candidate country concluded it needed to postpone a particular tax change, its representatives could try to negotiate special terms that included a derogation or a transitional period. For example, one of the greatest tensions in the Chapter Ten negotiations for nearly all countries concerned excise duties on cigarettes. According to one Chapter Ten negotiator, in order to meet the EU stipulation of a 57 percent tax minimum, the cost of cigarettes for the most popular brand would increase by about 85 percent in his country.[15] Adding to the challenge of harmonizing taxes on cigarettes, the commission increased the tax requirements for tobacco over the course of the accession process, which confounded the closing of the Chapter Ten negotiations.[16] Fearing a public backlash, numerous East European governments fought hard to win a special arrangement for taxes on cigarettes. For example, Slovakia lobbied hard to extend the transitional period for taxes on cigarettes. These new tax rates would be destabilizing, and the government had hoped to limit the shock to the smoking population. Government officials and local fiscal specialists also worried about the budgetary impact of the new tax regime on cigarettes. Ironically, some feared that a significant hike in the excise duty might negatively impact the budget, with governments expecting the sale of legal cigarettes to drop and the domestic consumption of smuggled cigarettes to rise (Michonski 2002, 139). But older member states like Germany and Austria also strongly resisted compromise on this issue given fears of unfair competition and the illegal trafficking of tobacco across their borders from the east. By the end of the negotiations, very limited transitional periods for cigarette taxes were granted for nine of the ten postcommunist countries. Only Slovenia did not make cigarette taxes a priority in the negotiations. In the nine cases, the transitional period typically phased in tax increases over a three- or four-year period.

Another tense tax issue that rankled due to a conflict of interests concerned the duty-free shops that existed at border crossings. The Austrians demanded that the Czechs change the tax regulations on duty-free shops along their borders since businesses on the western side of the border were losing consumers to businesses on the eastern side of the border. It was clear that these border shops could not survive after accession because no economic border would remain. But existing EU members did not want to wait until 2004 for their elimination. The Austrians in particular were frustrated that the Czech government was not quicker in implementing new laws on border shops. Actually, successive Czech leaders tried to close the shops, but Czech parliamentarians did not accept the idea that the closures had to occur in advance, and they rejected a bill that would have revoked the operating licenses three years before accession. Each year the commission's reports criticized the Czech Republic's lack of progress in this area. Even as late as 2003, the commission report highlighted the Czech Republic's failure to shut down duty-free shops at land borders.[17] Unabashedly privileging the interests of existing members over potential members, the report insisted the shops be closed immediately (rather than, say, on the date of accession) (Commission Report CO2003-SEC2003). However, the Czech shop owners stood to benefit from the prolongation of the existing system and pressured parliamentarians to resist the government's efforts. Although the shops closed shortly before the borders disappeared, the commission tried to use its position in the accession negotiations to anticipate this reform to the advantage of the Austrian businesses. In the case of duty-free shops, only the realization of EU membership (and the disappearance of the tax border) transformed the existing arrangement.

Poland and Slovakia were repeatedly criticized in their annual reports for failing to raise the level of their VAT rates. Poland fought hard to maintain low tax rates on newspapers, books, and magazines published in Poland, arguing that they were crucial for the survival and development of Polish culture. In addition, in Poland the rates on food and agricultural items (like livestock, plants, and seeds) were also below the rate allowed in the *acquis*, and disagreements over the taxation of agricultural goods similarly delayed the accession negotiation process.

In a similar vein, reforms to the taxation of alcohol were politically sensitive in most of the acceding countries. The annual reports often criticized the low taxation of beer (like in Slovakia), wine (in Hungary), and spirits (in Slovakia, Hungary, and Bulgaria among others). Indeed, a common area that the East European negotiating teams focused on was the tax for fruit growers who produced spirits (like *slivovice*) for small-scale or personal consumption. Ultimately, five postcommunist countries obtained special tax arrangements for this type of product. Several countries asked for special tax treatment on locally published books; but the commission granted only Poland a transitional period for taxes on books in the final moments before closing the chapter.

The number of exceptions allowed for each country at the closing of the Chapter Ten negotiations did not vary significantly. The number of transitional periods or derogations ranged from 3 in Lithuania to 9 in Poland, and the average number of exceptions per country in the Chapter Ten negotiations for the 2004 and 2007 rounds together was 5.5. The derogations and transitional periods for each new member country are listed in table 8. The granting of a derogation or transitional period within the chapter negotiations suggests that, at least in principle, a candidate country enjoyed some degree of negotiating power and, by extension, some policy autonomy. Such autonomy, however, is easy to exaggerate. Indeed, the discussion of the negotiated transitional periods on a few goods above may leave the wrong impression about the degree of flexibility within the negotiations. First, the number of derogations and transitional arrangements was paltry in the tax negotiations and all of the chapter negotiations. In taxation, the country with the highest number of special arrangements was Poland. It obtained nine temporary exceptions but agreed to different tax arrangements for *tens of thousands* of goods and services in adopting all of the other Chapter Ten directives.

**TABLE 8. EU Negotiations: Chapter Ten Derogations**

| Country | Transitional Arrangements and Derogations |
|---|---|
| Bulgaria | • Turnover threshold to exempt SMEs from VAT set at about €25,000<br>• VAT exemption for international passenger transport<br>• Special excise regime for fruit growers' distillation for personal consumption<br>• Lower excise duty rates on cigarettes until December 31, 2009 |
| Cyprus | • Turnover threshold to exempt SMEs from VAT set at €15,600<br>• Zero VAT rate on foodstuffs until December 31, 2007<br>• Zero VAT rate on pharmaceuticals until December 31, 2007<br>• Reduced VAT rate on restaurants until December 31, 2007<br>• VAT exemption on building land<br>• VAT exemption on international passenger transport |
| Czech Republic | • Turnover threshold to exempt SMEs from VAT set at €35,000<br>• Reduced VAT rate on heating until December 31, 2007<br>• Reduced VAT rate on construction until December 31, 2007<br>• Lower excise duty rates on cigarettes until December 31, 2007<br>• Special excise regime for fruit growers' distillation for personal consumption<br>• VAT exemption on international passenger transport |
| Estonia | • Reduced VAT rate on heating until December 31, 2007<br>• Turnover threshold to exempt SMEs from VAT set at €16,000<br>• Lower excise duty rates on cigarettes until December 31, 2009<br>• Full alignment to the parent-subsidiary directive until December 31, 2008<br>• VAT exemption on international passenger transport |
| Hungary | • Reduced VAT rate on heating until December 31, 2007<br>• Turnover threshold to exempt SMEs from VAT set at €35,000<br>• Reduced VAT rate on electricity, gas for one year after accession<br>• Reduced VAT rate on restaurants until December 31, 2007<br>• VAT exemption on international passenger transport<br>• Special excise regime for fruit growers' distillation for personal consumption.<br>• Lower excise duty rate on cigarettes until December 31, 2008 |

TABLE 8.—*Continued*

| Country | Transitional Arrangements and Derogations |
|---|---|
| Latvia | • Turnover threshold to exempt SMEs from VAT set at €17,200<br>• Lower excise duty rates on cigarettes until December 31, 2009<br>• VAT exemption on international passenger transport<br>• VAT exemption on royalties<br>• Reduced VAT rate on heating until December 31, 2004 |
| Lithuania | • Turnover threshold to exempt SMEs from VAT set at €29,000<br>• Lower excise duty rates on cigarettes until December 31, 2009<br>• VAT exemption on international passenger transport |
| Malta | • Zero VAT rate on foodstuffs until December 31, 2009<br>• Zero VAT rate on pharmaceuticals until December 31, 2009<br>• VAT exemption on water<br>• VAT exemption on new buildings and building land<br>• VAT exemption on inland passenger transport and domestic interisland sea passenger transport<br>• Turnover threshold to exempt SMEs from VAT set at €37,000 (for enterprises for which the economic activity consists mainly in the supply of goods), 24,300 (for enterprises for which the economic activity consists mainly in the supply of services with a low value added), and 14,600 (all other cases) |
| Poland | • Zero VAT rate on books until December 31, 2007<br>• Reduced VAT rates on restaurants until December 31, 2007<br>• Turnover threshold to exempt SMEs from VAT set at €10,000<br>• Lower excise duty rate on cigarettes until December 31, 2008<br>• Reduce excise duties on ecological fuels until one year after accession<br>• Reduced VAT rate on construction until December 31, 2007<br>• Super-reduced VAT rate on agriculture inputs, excluding machinery, until April 30, 2008<br>• Super-reduced VAT rate on foodstuffs until April 30, 2008<br>• VAT exemption on international passenger transport |
| Romania | • Turnover threshold to exempt SMEs from VAT set at about €35,000<br>• VAT exemption for international passenger transport<br>• Special excise regime for fruit growers' distillation for personal consumption<br>• Lower excise duty rates on cigarettes until December 31, 2009 |
| Slovakia | • Reduced VAT rate on heating until December 31, 2008<br>• Reduced VAT rate on construction until December 31, 2007<br>• Reduced VAT rate on electricity, gas until one year after accession<br>• Turnover threshold to exempt SMEs from VAT set at €35,000<br>• Lower excise duty rates on cigarettes until December 31, 2008<br>• Special excise regime for fruit growers' distillation for personal consumption<br>• VAT exemption on international passenger transport |
| Slovenia | • Reduced VAT rates on construction until December 31, 2007<br>• Reduced VAT rates on restaurants until December 31, 2007<br>• Turnover threshold to exempt SMEs from VAT set at €25,000<br>• VAT exemption on international passenger transport |

*Source:* Author's summary from European Commission, http://europa.eu.int/comm/enlargement/negotiations/chapters/chap10/ (accessed September 20, 2004).

Moreover, it is striking to note that many chapter negotiations allowed absolutely no special arrangements. In nine of the thirty-one chapter negotiations, no exceptions or transitional periods were granted for any of the ten countries joining the EU in the first wave, including the chapters on Industrial Policy, Economic and Monetary Union, Education and Training, Science and Research, Culture and Audio-Visual Policy, Consumers and Health Protection, External Relations, Common Foreign and Security Policy, and Financial Control (European Commission 2003). Given the complexity of these areas and the diverse political and economic environments of the acceding states, the lack of any country-specific arrangements within these chapters is remarkable.

In fact, even referring to the preaccession meetings between the commission and the representatives of the applicant countries as "negotiations" is highly misleading. In the accession process, candidate countries had to adopt the *acquis* in full, and that condition was nonnegotiable (Vachudova 2005, 110, 123, 131). Although the existing member states at times have opted out of parts of the *acquis*, the applicant member states in the 2004 and 2007 rounds could not opt out of any part of the *acquis* (Boruta 2002, 64). The only room for "negotiation" was *when* the states would fulfill the requirements. As one Polish negotiator explained, the candidate countries were made to understand that a permanent exemption to any part of the *acquis* was a nonoption (Boruta 2002, 61). In the area of taxation, all harmonization had to occur by the date of accession except for those few goods with transitional periods. In these exceptional instances, the transitional periods for the Chapter Ten negotiations all expired by 2009, including for the countries in the 2007 round of enlargement.

In the Chapter Ten negotiations specifically, Brussels was not especially generous or sympathetic to the special tax preferences or the political circumstances of a country that might lead its representatives to request alternative arrangements. For example, Hungary fought hard but unsuccessfully for a zero or even a reduced tax rate on prescription medicine and schoolbooks—products whose lower tax status Americans might take for granted. But the commission refused these and many other requests.[18] As other EU scholars have noted, the bargaining power of a candidate state was almost nil in light of its unambiguously stated, overarching goal of full and immediate EU membership (Holmes 2003). Thus, given that Brussels had to approve all derogations for the chapter negotiations to close, and given that all chapters had to close for a country to be eligible for full membership, the consequences of refusing to adopt even a small part of the tax *acquis* were enormous. As a member of the Polish negotiating team, Irena Boruta, explained, the only freedom that a candidate country had in the accession process was to postpone accession or not to accede to the treaty. Barring those two options, the *acquis* had to be accepted in full. In a Ministry of Foreign Affairs publication, Boruta writes, "In Poland's case the non-negotiability . . . derives from the fact that it (Poland) does not, basically, have any alternative to joining the Union. If there were any rival treaty to which Poland might plausibly accede, we would be better placed to drive hard bargains on our EU obligations" (2002, 62). But this was not the case.

If there were any areas where the European Commission could have shown slightly more flexibility, it was in those tax areas that would not interfere with competition in the internal market, such as taxes on restaurants, construction, and home heating. In older member states, sometimes exceptions were granted. Tax advantages in these areas do not unduly privilege local producers in competition with foreign providers. Yet even in these instances, the new members could not necessarily obtain special consideration. For example, the Czech government fought for a lower VAT rate on restaurants during the Chapter Ten negotiations to no avail. Restaurants were an important sticking point in the Hungarian negotiations as well. The reason that restaurants were politically sensitive for some postcommunist governments was that many kinds of eating establishments fell under the category of "restaurant"—like canteens in factories or school cafeterias. Therefore, several candidate countries opposed the higher tax status for restaurants. Hungary and two other postcommunist countries obtained a transitional period of taxes on restaurants, but the Czech Republic closed this chapter without managing to obtain a special arrangement. Even after accession, the Czech Republic continued to push for lower restaurant rates, enlisting the support of France in its efforts.

During accession, the tax harmonization process left the EU candidate countries powerless in accommodating various interest groups affected by the changes, in particular in areas concerning the internal European market. As a former Czech finance minister explained, this was as true for large, powerful interest groups like telecommunications and tobacco producers, who lobbied against EU demands, as it was for mass groups like smokers or the elderly who are large consumers of cigarettes or pharmaceuticals.[19] Whereas some domestic economic groups benefited and others lost from tax harmonization, the legislative changes reflected not the balance of power among these groups but rather existing EU law. In sum, the goal of EU membership curtailed the autonomy of East European states to set their own tax policy and limited the ability of government officials—willingly or unwillingly—to respond to those domestic interest groups standing to lose from tax harmonization.

Leaders on the ground were well aware of the loss of policy sovereignty and at times publicly lamented their lack of control over the terms of accession. Moreover, on a sociocultural level, some prominent postcommunist leaders found ceding policy-making control to Brussels to be hauntingly reminiscent of the Communist past. One of the more vocal Euroskeptics in the region, Czech president Václav Klaus, expressed his frustration with yielding authority to EU bureaucrats along these lines. Klaus explained, "It is particular to our history," referring to having been dominated by the Hapsburgs, the Nazis, and then the Soviets.

> We want to govern ourselves now. We do not want to be governed by Brussels. We want to make our own decisions. We already know what it is like to have our policies dictated from the outside. . . . We are an integral part of Europe, we want to participate in the European integration process, but we want to be nothing more or nothing less than a self-governing nation in the European Union.[20]

Klaus was not alone in drawing parallels between his country's deference to Brussels and its past deference to Moscow. Similar concerns emanated from the Polish right. And certainly leaders who were fully supporting accession grew tired at times of the asymmetrical power that older member states enjoyed relative to new states (*Economist,* April 21, 2001). An exasperated Viktor Orban, Hungary's prime minister during the accession process, told journalists following a series of EU meetings that "there is life outside the EU," complaining of Hungary's treatment during the accession negotiations (*MTI Hungarian News Agency,* February 3, 2002). Given that these countries only achieved a meaningful level of national sovereignty with the collapse of the Soviet Union, it is hardly surprising that East European officials felt leery of ceding authority to EU bureaucrats and privileging external over internal considerations in setting economic policies.

## Tax Harmonization, Policy Autonomy, and Democratic Development

A tremendous amount of legislative action was required to harmonize indirect taxes and close the Chapter Ten negotiations, not to mention the other twenty-eight substantive chapters. How did the postcommunist European governments adopt the legislation required for tax harmonization? The legislation to harmonize tax rates and tax structures typically passed through the national legislature using fast-track procedures with little parliamentary discussion or public debate. This reality is captured well by an observation by Kopstein and Reilly, who report that during Hungary's June 1999 parliamentary session, 152 of the 180 laws that were passed "were not subject to any debate because they were part of the *acquis communautaire*."[21] The former Czech finance minister, Bohuslav Sobotka (CSSD), noted the lack of parliamentary involvement in tax policy-making. He explained the constraint as follows.

> [Setting] individual rates is limited by EU rules; there is quite a strict regulation in this area. It tells the newcomers clearly what items can be exempted from tax and it also clearly says that the standard rate must not be lower than 15 percent. Therefore, we cannot exempt certain items simply based on our Parliament's decision. (*Právo*, December 4, 2003)

Fast-track procedures to pass EU legislation are not limited to postcommunist candidate countries. They exist in older member states as well. Although tax harmonization occurred in Western Europe too, the loss of policy-making power in taxation is all the more remarkable in postcommunist Europe in three important ways. First, the sheer scope of EU legislation that had to be adopted by the 2004 and 2007 entrants was much greater than in past rounds of enlargement. The postcommunist candidates had to meet the requirements set out in a much larger body of law without meaningful public discourse or parliamentary debate. Second, older members had more time to review and digest these changes, and many changes occurred piecemeal. Third and most important, older member states that use fast-track procedures to adopt new EU legislation on taxation participated in the drafting of these laws. That is, nationally elected officials helped to generate and contribute to the content of the new EU tax codes. In contrast, the East Europeans inherited them in full (Cameron 2003, 227). Speaking to this issue, David Cameron explains, "It is not an exaggeration to say that on accession, the new members will be recreated as states, committed to processes of policy-making and policy outcomes that in many instances bear little or no relation to their domestic policy-making processes and prior policy decisions but reflect, instead, the politics, policy-making processes, and policy choices of the EU and its earlier member states" (25).

Reflecting on the political implications of EU membership, many scholars have highlighted the effects of the elite-based accession process on the democratic development of East European countries (Holmes 2003; Cameron 2003;

Grabbe 1999). Quite apart from enlargement, the European Union has long been criticized for its democratic deficit, and for the disproportionate role European elites play. Yet during the accession process, the democratic deficit was widened even further, with critics asserting the "process has evolved in a purely elitist and technocratic fashion with little involvement of the public at large" (Ekiert and Zielonka 2003, 15). In Eastern Europe the problem of a democratic deficit exists on two levels: The elites are not involved in the generation of laws they adopt, with national legislatures adopting extensive tracts of legislation without debate or detailed review, *and* the East European citizenry, like the West European citizenry, is minimally involved. Citizens can only vote in a national referendum whether to join the multilateral organization or exist outside of it. The public is not consulted on parts of *acquis* but only on the overarching choice of EU membership. In short, the democratic deficit for Eastern Europe stems from the limited input from both the mass public and from the national leadership. As a result, large policy areas—such as the entirety of indirect taxes—are dictated by an outside body. As Vachudova eloquently writes, "At no time in history have sovereign states voluntarily agreed to meet such vast domestic requirements and then subjected themselves to such intrusive verification procedures to enter an international organization" (2005, 108).

What can be concluded with certainty is that larger and larger areas of taxation moved beyond democratic debate for postcommunist states as a result of European integration. The extent to which this occurred during the accession negotiation process is striking. The absorption of tax codes governing the treatment of nearly all goods and services, the lack of derogations, and the paltry number of transitional periods (all of which expired a few years after accession) demonstrate more than anything the loss of control over fiscal policy-making.

The harmonization of indirect taxes—involving the comprehensive adoption of legislation evolving from a process outside the domestic political sphere—raises important questions about democratic development in the region. Does the weakening of domestic policy autonomy mean that European economic integration undermines the quality of democratic governance? As important as the EU was for promoting democratic practices, its export of tax codes to Eastern Europe with limited to no input from the mass publics or local leaders paradoxically weakened democratic development. Indeed, when governments are compelled to set policy in response to the directives of a non–popularly elected body like the European Commission rather than according to the preferences of domestic constituents, public participation and hence democracy are eroded.

As noted in chapter 1, it is quite ironic that the development of the tax system, in particular consumption taxes, is associated with the weakening of democratic development. The literature on historical institutionalism often associates the development of the tax system with the rise of representative government in Western Europe, drawing heavily on the English and Dutch experiences. In particular, scholars have argued that representative institutions evolved out of the ruler's need to secure a reliable tax base and satisfy its revenue imperative (Levi 1988; North and Weingast 1989; Mahon 2005; Bräutigam 2008). The ruler entered into a contractual relationship with taxpayers (creating the "fiscal contract") as a way to collect revenues more effectively and reliably. The bargaining between state actors and domestic groups, which creates the "fiscal contract" in the West European context, led to more consensual tax relations between the ruler and the ruled. In Eastern Europe, however, this bargaining was absent as economic and societal actors missed the opportunity to negotiate with rulers over many tax areas.

The governments' loss of policy autonomy in developing indirect taxes was great. Indeed their ability to respond to domestic pressures by adjusting consumption taxes diminished considerably with European integration. This loss is sustained by the fact that all EU law takes precedence over national law. Indirect taxation provides an unambiguous example in which states forfeited their control over developing their tax institutions, and they are unlikely to regain meaningful control any time soon. In addition, along with other external factors, regional integration also impacts the development of direct taxes in Eastern Europe. It is useful to now turn to the ways in which governments are losing policy autonomy over income taxes due to both regional and global integration.

## CHAPTER 4

# The Race to the Bottom? Corporate Taxes and the Competition for Capital

European economic integration has required leaders in Eastern Europe to adopt a specific consumption tax regime. It has also generated pressures and constraints on how governments tax corporations. The competition for investment within Europe, when combined with restrictions posed by European law, has limited the flexibility of leaders in taxing the business sector. As a result, East European leaders on both the right and the left of the political spectrum profess the need to lower corporate tax rates in order to remain competitive regionally and globally. Indeed, the globalization of finance and the international competition for foreign direct investment have prompted governments in many parts of the world to lower corporate tax rates as part of a range of strategies to attract foreign investment and prevent local investors from seeking out more favorable environments.

The diminished reliance on corporate taxes in Eastern Europe leaves governments with limited options: they can cut expenditures, rely on deficit spending, or shift the tax burden onto less mobile revenue sources, like labor and consumption. The first option, cutting spending, may appeal to some governments, and certainly many governments have tried to reduce public spending. However, as noted in chapter 2 of this book, the need for high welfare protection emerged early in postcommunist countries and has persisted due to the social dislocation brought about by the uneven transition to a capitalist economy. The option of borrowing money to compensate for lower corporate taxes is limited in these countries as well due to EU stipulations and preparations for adopting the euro. Candidate countries sought to make the conditions of the Maastricht treaty, the conditions for entering the euro zone, their own fiscal targets, first, in order to prove their readiness and worthiness of full EU membership and, later, in order to meet their obligations to enter into the single currency zone. Beyond delaying monetary union, high deficits carry other costs since growing indebtedness can depress domestic investment. Furthermore, after the financial crises of 2008 and 2009, the cost of credit has grown significantly for East European countries, in particular for those outside the euro zone. The final option—shifting the tax burden onto less mobile sources of revenue—has its own negative domestic political and economic repercussions. The cost of labor is already high, and increasing the tax wedge exacerbates unemployment. Moreover, higher personal income taxes and consumption taxes are unpopular moves and might destabilize a weak government. Nonetheless governments enjoy little flexibility and are increasingly turning to noncorporate sources of tax revenue.

This chapter examines the evolution of corporate taxes in postcommunist Europe in order to assess the impact of external and internal factors. The chapter begins with an overview of trends in corporate taxation in eleven postcommunist European countries, comparing them with corporate tax trends in Western Europe. After presenting the regional trends in corporate income tax levels, the chapter turns to the experiences of four countries in postcommunist Europe: Poland, Hungary, the Czech Republic, and Slovakia. While all four countries joined in the first wave of EU accession, they vary along several dimensions. Each had its own challenges reforming its tax-incentive program to comply with EU codes, with the Czech Republic facing the greatest challenges in the harmonization of competition policy during the accession process.

These four countries also have displayed different attitudes toward competing for foreign direct investment. Hungary welcomed foreign investors and created favorable conditions for foreign investors immediately, whereas the Slovak government under Vladimír Mečiar discouraged foreign participation in the economy. Indeed the Slovak leadership only in the 2000s began to welcome foreign corporations and aggressively competed for their investment with their tax system and other business-friendly programs. Despite this variation, the brief case studies elaborate and reconfirm the trend demonstrated for the region as a whole. In all four country cases, the politics surrounding corporate income tax policies illustrates clearly the near irrelevance of traditional left-right divisions in shaping leaders' choices in shifting the tax burden away from the business sector and onto other revenue sources. The greatest political tensions surrounding the fiscal treatment of the business sector seem to appear at the supranational level, where corporate tax rates and investment incentives generated heated exchanges and diplomatic tensions among leaders in old and new EU member states. This chapter argues that postcommunist leaders undertook a particular strategy when taxing business, not to please their own constituents or to position themselves within the political arena at home. Rather their strategy stemmed from their efforts to reconcile the competing demands of regional and global economic integration.

## Regional Tax Trends

Despite some limitations in the data on taxation, it is evident that corporate tax rates in Eastern Europe have been falling since the early 1990s. This is seen most dramatically with the reduction of statutory corporate income tax (CIT) rates. Figure 4 charts the fall in corporate tax rates for eleven postcommunist countries relative to older EU member states (the EU-15); figure 5 charts the average statutory CIT rate of the eleven postcommunist countries alongside the average for the EU-15.

As the data on nominal rates reveal, several countries imposed a rather high corporate tax rate in 1995 more or less on par with the average CIT rate in Western Europe. For example, Poland's, Bulgaria's, and Slovakia's rates were slightly higher at 40 percent, and the Czech Republic's rate was 41 percent in 1995. In Romania, the corporate income tax rate was equal to the EU-15 average in 1995, which was 38 percent. By 2000, the EU-15 mean had fallen to 35.3 percent. However, the drop in postcommunist European countries was even more substantial during these five years. Poland's, the Czech Republic's, and Slovakia's rates had fallen to 30 percent, 31 percent, and 29 percent respectively, approaching the lower rates in the Baltic states. The corporate income tax rates in the Baltic countries were already comparatively low: Estonia's rate was 26 percent in both 1995 and 2000, Latvia's rate was 25 percent in both 1995 and 2000, and Lithuania's rate fell from 29 percent in 1995 to 24 percent in 2000. Hungary had led the downward trend in low corporate tax rates, as will be detailed below, by cutting its rate from 36 to 18 percent beginning in 1995. Ukraine's CIT rate remained consistently below the EU mean rate during the 1990s and 2000s: After holding at 30 percent from 1995 until 2004, the corporate tax rate fell to 25 percent in 2005. However, by 2006, Ukraine's nominal corporate tax rate was one of the highest in postcommunist Europe. Several countries reduced their CIT to a rate slightly below 25 percent. Russia's corporate tax rates fell from 37 to 24 percent in 2003. The Czech Republic's rate stood at 24 percent in 2006, while Slovakia's rate fell to 19 percent. Romania's and Hungary's rates fell to 16 percent, and Latvia's, Lithuania's, and Bulgaria's rates stood at 15 percent. In the late 2000s, the downward trend continued. By 2008, the CIT rates dropped to 21 percent in Estonia and the Czech Republic, 19 percent in Slovakia and Poland, 16 percent in Romania, 15 percent in Lithuania

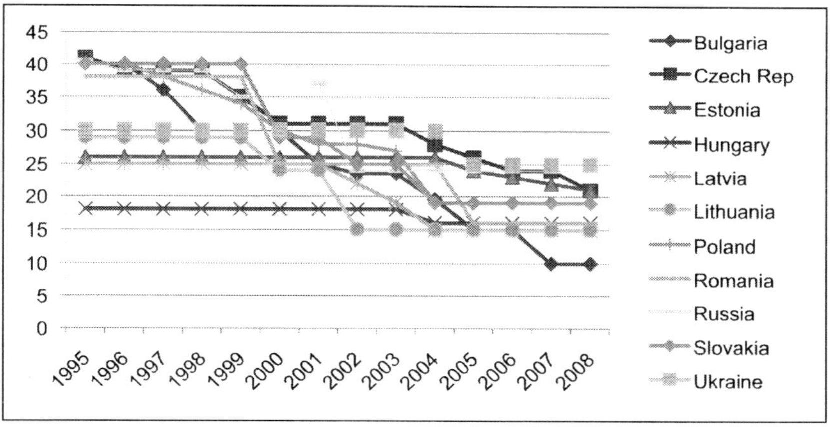


Fig. 4. Statutory CIT rates in postcommunist countries. (Data from OECD Tax Database; KPMG data; and other sources.)

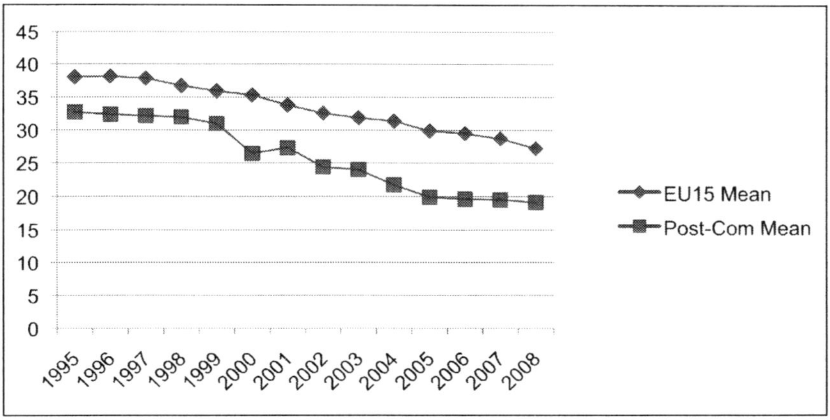


Fig. 5. Statutory CIT rates, EU-15 and postcommunist average. (Data from OECD Tax Database; KPMG data; and other sources.)

and Latvia, and 10 percent in Bulgaria. Some rates are even lower in practice. Most notably, Estonia levies no tax on corporate profits that are reinvested.

The decline in nominal corporate tax rates is a phenomenon that extends beyond postcommunist countries and the older members of the European Union. According to a 2007 OECD report, there has been a sharp reduction in statutory rates over twenty-five years. For seventeen OECD countries, the average CIT rate fell from 50.9 percent in 1982 to 37.6 percent in 1994 to 30.8 percent in 2006 (OECD 2007a, 21). Other taxes on capital fell as well. The statutory tax rate on dividend income has decreased during the 2000s. In a study of thirty countries, the average dividend tax rate fell from 50.2 percent in 2000 to 43.8 percent in 2006 (OECD 2007a, 23–24).

These rates are nominal tax rates rather than effective tax rates. Effective corporate tax rates (also known as implicit tax rates) are the ratio of corporate tax revenues to the corporate tax base. Effective tax rates hold advantages over other measures (like taxation as a function of GDP, or corporate tax rates as a percentage of total revenues) for assessing the trends in the total tax burden, since they take into account the effects of the size of the tax base.[1] After all, the drop in statutory rates for the East European countries discussed above could have been offset by changes in calculating the base. Thus, it is hard to speak definitively about trends in the overall corporate tax burden since nominal rates ignore movement in deductions, exemptions, or depreciation schedules, which may significantly increase or decrease a corporation's overall tax burden.

Yet, according to OECD data, the trends in effective corporate tax rates for advanced economies in the manufacturing sector reflect the trends of declining statutory tax rates (OECD 2007a, figs. 1.1, 1.2, 1.7). Effective tax rates are available for only a few postcommunist members of the European Union and OECD due to the complexities of computation.[2] Eurostat has published its calculations of implicit CIT rates for some postcommunist countries for some years, which are included whenever available in the specific country discussions below. In 2011, the available data were still limited. However, since the reductions in corporate tax rates in postcommunist countries occurred as part of a stated, deliberate strategy to attract and encourage investment, one would expect the downward trend in nominal corporate taxes to be reflected in implicit rates for most (if not all) countries, had they been available. At best, only some of the benefits of a lower nominal rate would be offset (or augmented) by changes to depreciation schedules, exemptions, and the like. In the countries where these data are partially available, the implicit rates also reflect the downward trend found in statutory rates, as reported below.

Lightening the tax burden on corporations has been one of the ways that countries stimulate domestic investment and compete with each other for foreign investment. In Eastern Europe, politicians from all over the political spectrum sought to lower corporate tax burdens. A focused analysis of the domestic political environments in Poland, Hungary, Slovakia, and the Czech Republic illustrates how global integration trumped partisan politics when it came to developing the corporate tax regime.

## Reforming Poland's Direct Taxes

Poland has revised its corporate income tax (CIT) rate over forty times in the first decade of fiscal reform.[3] The most striking trend to evolve from the frequent revision of Polish direct taxes was the substantial drop in corporate tax obligations. Poland's first elected government initially set the nominal corporate income tax rate at 40 percent in 1989. By the end of the decade the rate had fallen to 34 percent. Due to the successful policy efforts of Leszek Balcerowicz, former deputy prime minister and repeat finance minister, the parliament passed new legislation to lower corporate taxes even further. As part of the comprehensive 1999 Buzek-Balcerowicz tax bill, the Polish corporate tax rate was lowered from 34 percent in 1999, to 30 percent in 2000, to 28 percent in 2001, and it was structured to fall at set intervals until it reached 22 percent in 2004. In 2003, the parliament passed legislation lowering the CIT rate even further to 19 percent, a rate that stands in 2008. The implicit corporate tax rate in Poland in 1995 was 46.8 percent (the earliest year reported by Eurostat for Poland) and fell to 37.7 percent in 2000 and to 22.4 percent by 2005 (Eurostat 2008, table D.3.1.1).

The decreases in Poland's statutory and implicit rates are substantial. Corporate taxes have clearly fallen, and dramatically so, relative to other forms of taxation.[4] Even prior to the Balcerowicz reforms, data from one study show that corporate income taxes—as a share of total taxation—have dropped from 12.0 percent in 1992 to 7.7 percent in 1999, despite the growth of the corporate sector.[5] By 2005, corporate income taxes fell to 6.1 percent of total taxation (OECD 2007b, 81).

While successfully advocating decreases in CIT rates, Balcerowicz as Poland's deputy premier simultaneously pushed for dramatic declines in personal income taxes. However, in 1999 President Aleksander Kwaśniewski chose to veto the part of the bill concerning personal income taxes (PIT), and the government did not have sufficient parliamentary support to override the veto. The proposed PIT legislation called for a decrease in the marginal rate of the top tax bracket from 40 percent in 1999 to 28 percent by 2002, which in turn would have collapsed the two top tax brackets into one. The lower two brackets (out of three overall) would have changed only slightly, with the lowest bracket declining from 19 percent to 18 percent. Many thought this proposal excessively favored a small core of wealthy Poles, since well over 80 percent of Polish households were located in the lowest of the three tax brackets.[6]

Given the prevalence of tax reform in the political debates of 2004 and 2005, substantial income tax reform was expected to follow the September 2005 elections, when the two main parties on the right won the most parliamentary seats. However, strong divisions between the Law and Justice Party (led by Jarosław Kaczyński) and the Civic Platform Party (led by Donald Tusk), precisely over tax reform, prevented them from jointly forming a government and pursuing tax reform (*New York Times,* September 27, 2005).

The election victory of the economically liberal Civic Platform in October 2007 again suggested that tax cuts were pending. Civic Platform had pledged to set one low single rate of 15 percent for both personal and corporate income taxes (*Rzeczpospolita,* September 28, 2007). However, major tax reform was put on hold. In 2009 the corporate tax rate remained set at 19 percent. While the government did reduce the number of brackets and lowered personal income taxes for 2009 (with two rates of 18 and 32 percent replacing the multiple rates ranging from 19 to 40 percent), Prime Minister Tusk signaled that he would postpone flat-tax reform until after the Polish presidential elections in 2010 (*Polish News Bulletin,* September 9, 2008).

The recent history surrounding personal income tax is politically more complex (and dealt with again in the next chapter). However, the story of Polish corporate taxes is much more straightforward. Parties on the left and the right have supported falling corporate tax rates, whereas falling taxes on personal income stem from the Right's control of the government. Indeed, the impetus behind the decline in CIT rates came as much from left-of-center governments as from right-of-center governments. Following the Buzek-Balcerowicz tax reform, Leszek Miller's left-of-center government lowered tax rates for corporations even further than proposed by Leszek Balcerowicz, the right-wing economist and former liberal finance minister. Not only did Miller's government lower the corporate tax rate to 19 percent in 2004, this same left-of-center government turned to ordinary Poles to grapple with its deficit problems. First the government broke with the annual practice of adjusting tax brackets for inflation (preventing bracket creep). Miller declared the moratorium on readjusting brackets as a measure specifically to cope with the growing deficit (*Poland Business Review Newswire,* November 5, 2001; *Rzeczpospolita,* November 25, 2002). In a similarly unpopular move, the government imposed a new tax on personal savings accounts. Both the increase in personal income taxes due to bracket creep and the additional revenue from individual savings accounts occurred alongside the elimination of several important exemptions and deductions from personal income tax obligations, most notably the deductions related to housing and home investment (*Financial Times*, January 25, 2002). At the same time, consumption tax rates rose due to EU commitments.

Since the early 1990s, Poland's parties have been divided over personal income taxes, but they have been unified in keeping corporate taxes at low levels or reducing them further. The contrast between the increase in taxes on ordinary Poles, as wage earners or as consumers, and the decrease in taxes on corporate profits is surprising given the political power of Polish unions. One might have expected the powerful Polish unions and the predominance of the Left in government to diminish the tax burden on working Poles at the expense of corporations—and not the reverse. After all, a simple interest-group approach would suggest that the distribution of the tax burden should reflect the demands of the most powerful groups in society. Yet, Poland does not depart from the general regional trend of reducing the corporate tax burden. This is true despite the fact that Polish labor was remarkably influential in policy-making, especially in the 1990s, with Polish trade unions achieving a moral authority in the debates over the design of the new polity and economy (Levitsky and Way 1998). One Polish daily explains it this way.

> There is no other country in Europe in which union activists are the core of executive and legislative power. . . . The unions have [even] demanded the right to give opinion on the state budget, which would be a clear interference in the prerogatives of the Sejm. Authorities, and not only the current Solidarity group, seem to be intimidated by the power of the unions. (*Politiyka*, December 12, 1998)[7]

The evolution of the tax structure in Poland seems to defy political logic. But the pattern of shifting the tax burden away from corporations was neither a temporary aberration nor a phenomenon limited to Poland.

## Hungary's Corporate Taxes

Like the Poles, the Hungarians have frequently revised their income tax rates since their new tax system was first decreed in 1988. Moreover, the pattern in tax policy-making is similar: From 1991 to 1998, personal income taxes have increased from 15.8 percent to 16.7 percent as a share of total taxation, whereas corporate income taxes have decreased from 9.1 percent to 5.5 percent.[8] In 2000 and 2005, CIT as a percentage of total tax revenues remained low at 5.7 percent of total taxation.[9]

The most dramatic legislated shift from corporations to individuals occurred when Gyula Horn's left-of-center government halved the corporate tax rate on reinvested profits (from 36 to 18 percent) starting in 1995. When the radical tax cut first took effect, it included a supplementary tax of 23 percent on distributed profits in addition to the 18 percent tax on profits. However, in one year's time the supplementary tax was removed, thereby setting the nominal tax rate on corporate profits to the lowest level in the region at that time: 18 percent.[10] Considering that Hungary's rate was combined with favorable arrangements on accelerated depreciation and numerous exemptions, an economist at the Hungarian National Bank estimated informally that when the nominal rate was 18 percent, the implicit corporate tax rate was about 11 percent.[11] The minister of economics and transport, Istvan Csillag, estimated in a press interview that the implicit rate was only about 10 percent when the nominal rate was 18 percent (*MTI Hungarian Newswire,* July 14, 2003). Implicit CIT rates were not published for Hungary at the time of writing in 2010.

In 2004, the government led by the Hungarian Socialist party (MSZP) under Peter Medgyessy lowered the corporate tax rate further to 16 percent and lowered the personal income tax rates, also by 2 percent (for all brackets), while increasing the VAT (to 15 percent for the lowest rate and 25 percent for the standard rate). That same year, government officials announced the intention to lower the CIT rate to 12 percent in the near future (*BBC,* April 19, 2004). Yet these intentions could not be realized, given the high budget deficit in 2005 of 6.1 percent of GDP (Economist Intelligence Unit, Country Profile: Hungary, 2006a). Instead the Socialist-led government introduced an austerity reform package that added a 4 percent "solidarity tax" to the nominal rate of 16 percent, thereby creating a temporary corporate tax rate of 20 percent in 2006 (*Financial Times,* August 11, 2006). For 2009, the Socialist government sought to reduce the nominal rate to 18 percent, but the global financial crisis derailed this plan. In 2009, Prime Minister Ferenc Gyurcsany announced his intent to lower corporate taxes to 19 percent, which he achieved (*MTI Econews,* February 17, 2009, and July 26, 2010).

This brief 4-point CIT rate increase in isolation suggests a break with the overall pattern of the Left participating actively in lowering CIT rates. Yet it must be recalled that this same left-of-center party was responsible for 20 percentage points of reductions prior to the 4-point increase. Moreover, when evaluating the Hungarian Socialist Party's stance on taxing the business sector, it is necessary to note that the same left party (led by Gyurcsany) the very next year introduced small favorable tax cuts for business, despite continuing deficits. For example, in November 2007 the government doubled the proportion of pretax profits that companies could place into tax-exempt development funds, and it introduced special tax breaks for companies that raise capital for investments by listing their shares on the Budapest Stock Exchange (*MTI Hungarian Newswire*, November 13, 2007; November 16, 2007).

To compensate for the low corporate tax rate since 1994, Hungary's personal income taxes and labor taxes rose. Most strikingly, PIT rates for the poorest taxpayers increased substantially with the reform of the tax system. In 1995 the Socialist government brought all individuals into the tax net by replacing the zero income-tax rate with a 20 percent rate for the lowest income bracket. The most important factor generating the increase in PIT revenue, though, stems from the state's infrequent adjustment of the tax brackets for inflation (*MTI Hungarian Newswire*, November 13, 2007; November 16, 2007). This has created the remarkable situation in which the average Hungarian taxpayer finds himself in the highest tax bracket.[12] This contrasts with Poland, in which over 80 percent of taxpayers fall in the lowest tax bracket.[13] By way of further comparison, the highest tax bracket in Hungary in 2003 (with a rate of 40 percent) affected taxpayers with an annual income exceeding 5,300 euros, whereas in Poland, the highest bracket (also 40 percent) applied to incomes exceeding 16,400 euros. In the Czech Republic, the top bracket (32 percent) applied to incomes above 10,400 euros.[14]

The relative increase in the tax burden on consumers and wageworkers in Hungary follows from other factors as well. For a period, Hungary's indirect taxes accounted for over 41 percent of all federal tax revenues due to a high VAT rate (Eurostat 2008, 237). Although the VAT nominal rates have fluctuated, indirect taxes still remain a large part of total tax revenues, hovering around 40 percent of total taxation since 1995.[15]

## Corporate Income Taxes in the Czech Republic

A similar trend in corporate income taxes is found in the Czech Republic. Corporate income taxes as a share of total taxation equaled 16.5 percent in 1993 and 12.2 percent in 1995. It fell to a low of 10 percent in 2000, and in 2005, it stood at 12.0 percent.[16] By comparison, personal income taxes in 1993 as a share of total taxation equaled 8.9 percent. In 1998 it reached 13.6 percent, lowering slightly to

12.7 percent in 2004.[17] The implicit corporate tax rate in 1995 was 47.2 percent (the earliest year reported by Eurostat for the Czech Republic) and fell to 26.2 percent in 2000 and 23.4 percent by 2006 (Eurostat 2008, table D.3.1.1). The right-of-center coalition government under Václav Klaus reduced corporate income taxes steadily throughout the 1990s, and its center-left opposition, the Social Democrats, continued this pattern after winning office in 1998. The right-wing government pushed through legislation lowering the statutory corporate tax rate gradually from 45 percent to 42 percent in 1994 and further to 35 percent for 1998 (Easson 1998, 193). Under the Social Democrats, the trend continued due to tax reforms in 2000 that lowered the nominal corporate tax rate to 31 percent (on top of new legislation in 1999 that shortened depreciation schedules for calculating tax obligations) (Bronchi and Burns 2000, 17). Then in July 2003, the Social Democratic government lowered the CIT rate further to 24 percent over three years. The Social Democrats' important constituents, the trade unions, called for a less steep drop (to 26 percent), but the 24 percent rate proposal prevailed (*Právo,* March 11, 2004; *Prague Post,* September 18, 2003). In 2004 a Finance Ministry spokesman from the same center-left government acknowledged plans to lower the CIT rate to 21.5 percent by 2006 to compete with Slovakia's new low rate (*Prague Post,* October 21, 2004).

The substantial decline in the statutory rate does not fully capture the reduction in Czech corporate tax contributions, due to the rise in exemptions and deductions, especially the deductibility of interest income and the application of a lower (and still declining) tax rate on distributed earnings (Bronchi and Burns 2000, 21). Since the election of the center-right government in 2006 and the passage of the tax reform legislation in 2007, the decline of corporate income taxes, and income tax rates generally, continues. In 2008, the CIT rate fell to 21 percent, and in 2010 fell further to 19 percent.[18]

## Corporate Income Taxes in Slovakia

In Slovakia the downward trend in corporate income tax obligations is also apparent. As in the cases above, corporate income taxes as a percentage of total taxation fell throughout the 1990s and 2000s. In 1995, corporate income taxes contributed 15 percent of total taxation, but by 2000 corporate taxes contributed only 7.7 percent. Despite the growth of the corporate sector following an influx of foreign investment in 2004 and 2005, the contribution of corporate income taxes as a share of total revenue was 8.7 percent in 2005. The implicit corporate tax rate in 1997 was 42.0 percent (the earliest year reported by

Eurostat for Slovakia), and it fell to 21.6 percent by 2005 (Eurostat 2008, tables D.3.1.1, A.2.2_T).

Governments from all over the ideological spectrum in Slovakia have lowered the nominal corporate income tax rate, and no government has increased it. The first important reduction of nominal CIT rates from 45 to 40 percent occurred in 1994. Vladimír Mečiar's populist government did not lower nominal rates further during his tenure in office (1994–98), but his government did lighten the tax burden on the corporate sector by introducing important tax incentives to companies that invested in depressed regions or at a high level. The Mečiar government also offered tax breaks to individual entrepreneurs, which, along with tax evasion, led to much lower corporate tax revenues in his final years in office (Matthes and Thode 2001, 26).

In the hopes of reintegrating Slovakia into European and transatlantic organizations, the Slovak electorate voted Mečiar out of office in 1998. The formation of a new government required the cobbling together of an ideologically diverse coalition, which included parties ranging from former communists to promarket conservatives, as well as the conservative Catholic Party and the Slovak nationalists. This left-right coalition government in 2001 lowered the corporate income tax rate from 29 to 25 percent. In 2003, a new ideologically unified, right-wing coalition government that was led by Premier Mikuláš Dzurinda lowered the CIT rate to 19 percent starting in 2004 as part of a larger tax-reform program. The program also introduced other tax reductions favorable to business. For example, Slovakia's 2004 tax reform eliminated the dividend tax, which proved to be a boon for smaller domestic companies. (Foreign companies could already avoid paying taxes on dividends according to EU laws by establishing parent companies in the Netherlands.) Moreover, business leaders, with their higher than average salaries, saw their income taxes halved due to the larger tax reform program. In short, Slovakia's fiscal environment became more favorable to businesses and entrepreneurs despite a wide range of parties holding power.

Slovakia's favorable tax system for business remained intact when the Right lost the 2006 elections. Despite the campaign rhetoric that aggressively criticized Premier Dzurinda's overhaul of the tax system, the left-wing *Smer* government did not increase Slovakia's 19 percent CIT rate after it came to power. Only minor changes came about with the change in Slovakia's government in 2006. For example, the government reintroduced a lower VAT rate on certain medical items only—but left untouched tax rates on foodstuffs, books, or children's products, which in the past had been taxed at a lower rate.[19] Despite its campaign rhetoric the *Smer* government kept its tinkering with the tax system to a minimum, limiting itself to symbolic gestures in the few areas where the government had some room to maneuver. For example, the left-of-center government altered the allowance at which income remained untaxed for the wealthiest income earners (*ČTK Business Newswire*, December 6, 2006). Interestingly, the expected political dividend behind the introduction of this so-called millionaire's tax did not materialize once the members of parliament found a way to exclude their own incomes from this tax (despite earning a level of income that qualified them) (*Slovak Spectator*, October 1, 2006).

## Investment Incentives

In addition to competitive slashing of corporate income taxes, a separate and even more direct fiscal technique to attract foreign investment that deserves consideration is the use of investment tax incentives. Indeed, the competitive pressures that depressed corporate tax rates also motivated the creation of a broader set of investment tax benefits (Vámosi-Nagy et al. 1998, 483). The Hungarian, Polish, Czech, and Slovak governments have all employed generous tax holidays for large investors in order to encourage large-scale foreign investment. Like low corporate tax rates, tax holidays have not been politically sensitive in the domestic political realm, although they have raised problems during EU accession at the elite level. Investment incentives were intended to attract investors in a global investment environment, but the decision to curtail them stemmed from formal EU rules on acceptable forms of state aid.

Poland and Hungary offered tax investment incentives throughout the 1990s, initially with little regard for the practices in existing EU member states. For example, Poland and Hungary both allowed firms up to ten years of tax-exempt status when certain conditions were met. Slovakia developed similarly beneficial tax holidays in the late 1990s. While such tax-incentive packages were formally available to domestic firms, for the most part they were limited to multinational corporations that could afford the initial start-up investment conditions. Apart from the standard legislated conditions, large companies could negotiate even better conditions with local and federal officials on a case-by-case basis. The details of these firm-specific arrangements are commercial secrets.

The 2004 accession countries had to renegotiate the terms of the incentives to comply with EU competition policy, which links the maximum allowable amount of the tax break to the cost of the initial investment and the relative economic conditions of the region for any state aid granted after 1994. Without changing the terms, it was not possible to close the chapter on competition policy (Chapter Six) during the accession negotiation process. Striking a compromise proved difficult since Mario Monti, the commissioner for competition during the first wave of accession, was particularly rigid. He wanted candidate countries to cancel their tax-incentive programs prior to the date of accession.[20] However, foreign companies were promised tremendous tax incentives, and the new EU countries feared the long-term consequences of reneging on the contracts. Would the affected companies simply move further east if they violated these contracts? Would this undermine their credibility in future negotiations with foreign investors?

The European Commission found the concessions from Slovakia, Poland, and Hungary to be unacceptable. For example, since 1994 Poland had used tax breaks to encourage investment in Special Economic Zones, zones typically located in regions with high unemployment. While the terms could vary, the 1994 decree stipulated that firms could be exempt from paying corporate taxes for the first ten years of the investment. For the second ten years, firms could pay as little as half the corporate tax rate. Certain investment conditions had to be met relating to the size of the investment and the number of jobs created (OECD 2000, 158–59).[21]

In Hungary, tax incentives were also used to attract especially large investors (over ten billion forints, around forty million U.S. dollars) and to direct investment to priority development districts. If the investment occurred in an area where the unemployment rate was higher than 15 percent, the investment could be up to 33 percent lower than the ten billion forints otherwise required.[22] When these conditions were met, firms could be exempt from paying corporate taxes until as late as 2011. Hungary had other tax-incentive programs (say, to promote hotel development or to hire unemployed workers) to encourage foreign investment.

In Slovakia during the Mečiar period, the business environment was relatively unattractive to foreign investors, due to limitations on foreign ownership, insecure property rights, and political uncertainty. As a result, the level of foreign investment in Slovakia was about one-sixth the level of investment in Hungary and the Czech Republic in the 1990s. Due to delayed efforts to attract foreign investors with state aid, the transition to EU rules was less cumbersome. That said, Slovakia did have to reform its fiscal aid program to comply with EU rules. Like Hungary, large investments had qualified for ten-year tax holidays if certain qualifications were met. The investment minimum to qualify for a tax-incentive package was 4.5 million euros for production companies, and even less for some service industries and companies established in districts with over 10 percent unemployment. The government also offered beneficial customs arrangements for construction and the import of machinery for large investors as well as grants for job creation and job training. As a result of the accession treaty negotiations, special tax-incentive programs had to be phased out by 2009 in Slovakia and 2011 in Hungary and Poland, although particular industries were given additional time to restructure, in particular the steel industries in Poland and the Czech Republic.

The unacceptability of these long-term benefits in Slovakia, Poland, and Hungary to the European Commission posed a serious dilemma. The tax holidays had been in place for several years and were not set to expire until many years after the date of accession. It was especially difficult to renegotiate the terms of these tax-incentive programs with companies since offering other forms of compensation (apart from tax breaks) would still violate the provisions of the EU's competition policy. According to Polish tax specialist Hanna Litwinczuk, Poland could only use the standard parameters as set by EU directives to try to satisfy their commitments to investors. While existing EU policy allows tax breaks for investment in regions where the GDP per capita equals 75 percent of the EU average, these deductions are limited to one-half the value of the full investment.[23] This is a far cry from the one- and two-decade-long tax breaks many of these companies had expected to enjoy. Ultimately, Slovakia, Poland, and Hungary had to cease their investment programs and harmonize future programs with the *acquis communautaire*. Individual negotiations occurred with corporations to try to keep them from relocating, yet the negotiated terms themselves again were constrained by the transitional arrangements granted for acceding countries. Moreover, postaccession tax-incentive programs also required approval from Brussels. For example, when the Hungarian parliament approved the government's proposal in 2007 to double the proportion of pretax profits that companies could place into tax-exempt development funds, it required approval of the European Commission to take effect (*MTI Hungarian Newswire*, November 13, 2007; November 16, 2007). In general, any new fiscal aid program requires the strict review and final approval of the European Commission. As a document on the postaccession state aid rules summarizes, "The State aid laws in the Candidate Countries will cease to apply and the State aid offices will lose their competence to review aid. This Centralised review by the European Commission is designed to ensure that government financial assistance is scrutinised more vigorously."[24]

The Czech Republic also developed an investment incentive program, primarily through the leadership of the Social Democrats. As elsewhere in the region, large investors could benefit from generous tax holidays, further decreasing the proportion of tax revenues contributed by the corporate sector. In a return to a short-lived practice of tax holidays in the early 1990s, the Social Democrats actively supported extensive investment incentives for foreign greenfield investments over ten million dollars, rendering reinvested profits tax exempt for ten years.[25] Not only did the left-of-center government bring momentum to the investment incentive programs for corporations, it repeatedly thwarted efforts by the right-wing opposition to eliminate the incentive programs (on the basis of discrimination against smaller and typically domestic investors) (*Právo*, March 18, 2005; *Mladá Fronta Dnes*, July 11, 2005).

The Czech Republic seemed to be in a different position from its neighbors when negotiating and closing the chapter on competition policy with the European Commission. At first the negotiations went much more smoothly, and it appeared that the goal of European integration would not impinge upon the Czech investment incentive program. On the surface it appeared that the Czechs had more autonomy in developing investment tax incentives than Poland or Hungary. However, this seeming autonomy was explained, at the time, as a function of the early foresight of CzechInvest, the governmental organization in charge of attracting foreign capital. According to a former Czech minister of finance, Pavel Mertlík, CzechInvest reformed the country's investment incentive program with constant input from EU officials, precisely to avoid the kind of problems the Hungarians, Poles, and Slovaks later faced. As Mertlík explained, when the investment program was being developed, the people at CzechInvest "knew very well the European legislation . . . and they were very frequently going to Brussels and saying 'here are the next couple of paragraphs [of the draft legislation], are they okay like that?' " When asked directly, "Why write your laws, paragraph by paragraph, with the approval of Brussels?" this was Mertlík's reply:

> Because we know it is a sensitive issue from Brussels' point of view. They are very sensitive to everything that relates to competition policy. If they finally find out that the investment incentives law is not fully in accordance with their respective directives of the EU, it will be a serious problem for [us] the negotiating country.[26]

What is remarkable about the former finance minister's attitude, especially as a leading official in the tax negotiations, is the ease with which policy-making authority was ceded to Brussels. Ultimately, the CzechInvest program ran into problems with the commission. The Social Democratic government unexpectedly found itself having to renegotiate the deals CzechInvest had made after accession, since the deals were later found to violate the EU's competition policy.

## The Decline in Corporate Tax Obligations: Possible Explanations

The Slovak, Czech, Hungarian, and Polish examples illustrate the common pattern of shifting the tax burden away from corporations regardless of which party is in power. Other postcommunist countries display similar behavior by political parties in which both the Right and the Left decreased corporate taxation. For example, Bulgaria's right-wing government under Simeon II lowered corporate income taxes repeatedly from 28 percent when he was elected in 2001 down to 15 percent in 2005, when he left office. When Prime Minister Simeon II was replaced by the Bulgarian Socialist Party leader, Sergei Stanishev, the government continued the cuts. Left-wing Stanishev formed a coalition government with right-wing Simeon II's party and the centrist Turkish minority party, and extended the downward trend quite significantly. The Socialist-led coalition lowered the CIT rate to one of the very lowest in the region: 10 percent.

Why are corporate tax obligations falling? Clearly these patterns are not the product of right-wing governments pursuing a particular partisan approach or catering to a specific constituency. Indeed, in none of these countries does the reallocation of the tax burden away from businesses follow traditional party lines. According to the statistical analysis presented in chapter 7, if anything the Left is more responsible for the declines in corporate income taxes. As the case studies above reveal, the Left has not undone the gains for corporations achieved by the Right, and in fact many advantages for corporations arose or were augmented during the Left's tenure in office (most notably under premiers Horn in Hungary, Miller in Poland, and Zeman in the Czech Republic). In short, regardless of whether the Left or the Right dominates, the direction of reform remains the same: a decline in statutory corporate tax rates and an increased reliance on personal income taxes and/or consumption taxes.

Labor appears ineffective in blocking this trend. Even though labor is stronger in Poland, workers have been no more influential in diminishing their tax burden than their counterparts in Hungary or the Czech Republic. In fact, Polish labor suffered—at a time when Solidarity was at its strongest—when the dreaded *popiwek* was in force—a tax designed to stifle wage growth.[27] If anything, labor in Poland has suffered from a slightly higher tax burden than its counterparts in Hungary and the Czech Republic, where labor is weak.[28] Moreover, in Poland the workers were the first to feel the consequences of the Miller (left-wing) government's budgetary shortfalls due to the government's moratorium on automatic adjustments of income tax brackets for inflation. In a similar vein, the Czech Social Democrats did not heed the calls to slow the decline of CIT rates (*Právo,* March 11, 2004). Contrary to the demands of trade unions, the direct tax policies of left-wing Czech and Polish parties suggest a greater interest in attracting and maintaining investment than in catering to traditional domestic constituencies.

Why is the corporate tax burden falling? Given that the drops result from deliberate national legislative action and not from European legal requirements, could these reforms reflect domestic concerns first and foremost? It does not seem likely. The explanations of national officials certainly suggest that external concerns are driving the downward movement of CIT rates. References to regional and global competition dominate the formal statements for CIT reform. Time and time again, leaders have justified lowering corporate tax rates by pointing to the need to remain competitive, especially vis-à-vis other EU states. For example, in 2004 the Czech Social Democrats' finance minister, Bohuslav Sobotka, celebrated the decline of CIT rates along with new accelerated depreciation schedules for machinery and equipment, noting that the effective rate will fall "roughly [to] 17% as of 2006" and should "guarantee the Czech Republic's competitiveness within the framework of the European space and will enhance investors' interest" in the country (*Mladá Fronta Dnes,* May 21, 2004). The same finance minister later that year explained to Czech reporters, "We have to take changes in the neighboring countries into account. This is why I am glad that we managed to push through the decrease of the corporate income tax despite the opposition's pressure. Investors perceive that we have a certain plan to cut down this tax. The curve is clear and it will certainly help more foreign investments to flow into the Czech Republic" (*Právo,* December 4, 2003). In Hungary, where corporate taxes long enjoyed a comparatively low level, leaders still worried about how to maintain the country's relative advantage. In 2003 the Hungarian minister of economics and transport, Istvan Csillag, stated that "it was worth looking at how Hungary could hold its position compared to Slovakia or the Czech Republic for instance, where a wave of tax cuts is underway" (*MTI Hungarian Newswire,* July 14,

2003). Dariusz Rosati, the Polish foreign minister at the time of EU accession, stated, "Low taxes are a way, at least partly, to neutralise that competitiveness gap" (*Polish News Bulletin*, June 9, 2004).

Ironically, this competitive use of corporate tax cuts in Eastern Europe created tensions with the older EU members, who have long bemoaned the shift of the tax burden away from corporations to workers and consumers—or from more mobile to less mobile actors. In the twenty years preceding the first Eastern enlargement of the EU, the effective (implicit) tax rate on capital decreased, while the effective tax rate on labor increased (see figure 6).

This tax trend, at least in part, is the consequence of the increasing tax competition among European countries following the gradual removal of barriers to the mobility of capital in Europe. This shift in the tax burden has troubled European authorities for some time, as was made explicit in the October 1997 Communication from the European Commission to the European Council, in which the commission concluded unequivocally, "This trend in tax structure should be reversed."[29]

Around the time of accession of the first wave of postcommunist states, West European concerns about tax competition and factor mobility among EU leaders surfaced repeatedly. West European leaders voiced their fears of the flight of businesses in pursuit of lower taxes in the East. For example, in 2004, leaders in Germany chastised the new member states for setting corporate tax rates too low, accusing them of "tax dumping" (*Der Spiegel*, April 26, 2004). Former German chancellor Gerhard Schroeder began advocating the harmonization of corporate taxes in the days leading up to EU accession, and Schroeder's push for tax coordination quickly gained momentum in Finland, France, and Sweden (*Der Spiegel*, April 26, 2004; *Munich Focus*, April 26, 2004; *Baltic News Service*, June 1, 2004). Despite having tolerated Ireland's low CIT rate, the larger EU countries appeared anxious about the prospects of multiple countries in the common market offering much lower corporate tax rates. Reaffirming the German chancellor's position, former Frenczh premier Jean-Pierre Raffarin threatened that the countries that are "trying to attract capital through low taxes might have a difficult time acquiring all [of the available] subsidies," insinuating that East European members would be denied structural funds if they insist on keeping corporate taxes low (*Hospodářské noviny*, May 17, 2004).

East European leaders responded angrily to proposed restrictions on tax competition, insisting that low corporate taxes were necessary to level the playing field of the EU and to attract foreign investment. To illustrate, former Slovak finance minister Ivan Mikloš stated unequivocally, "We are strictly against

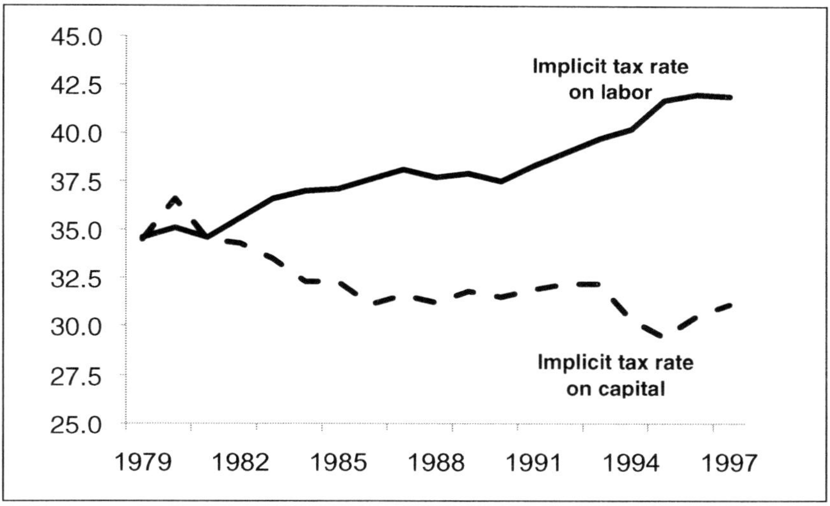


Fig. 6. EU tax rates. (Data from *Eurostat 2000*.)

harmonisation of direct taxes." Czech president Václav Klaus similarly responded, "Those who argue along these lines must know whether they want free markets, or whether they would rather have broad harmonization. I thought it was almost unbelievable what I heard about this from the German chancellor or the Swedish prime minister" (*ČTK*, June 3, 2004; *Hospodářské noviny*, April 27, 2004). Dariusz Rosati, the Polish foreign minister at the time, explained, "Tax rises would have to be accompanied by cuts in wages, which today do not amount to even a quarter of average German wages. In this context, speaking of fiscal dumping is improper" (*Polish News Bulletin*, June 9, 2004). In a similar vein, Polish prime minister Marek Belka at the time responded to calls to raise Polish corporate taxes by stating that Poland might be prepared to consider raising corporate income taxes when it reached Germany's economic status (*Polish News Bulletin*, May 28, 2004).

The East European finance ministers felt low taxes were crucial to compete in a globalized economy, and it was the West European countries that needed to adjust their tax policies to remain competitive. The former Slovak finance minister explained, "Tax and other competition from new EU member countries only highlight the structural and policy shortcomings in the preparedness of many of the old EU member countries to face severe global competition" (Mikloš 2008, 70).

Despite their admonishments, the older EU members failed to change the tax policies of new member states. Instead, the reverse occurred. Subsequent leaders in Germany, Great Britain, Spain, and Austria began to advocate lower CIT rates in their own countries in order to compete with the tax regimes in the new member states. Governments dominated by the Right in Great Britain and Germany lowered the CIT rate by 2 and 9 percentage points respectively. Even French president Nicolas Sarkozy, who had spoken out against low corporate taxes in Eastern Europe as finance minister a few years earlier, promised to cut corporate tax rates by 5 points after his election in 2007. Moreover, the left-of-center governments in Spain (under Zapatero) and Italy (under Prodi) similarly called for significant cuts in CIT rates at home (*International Herald Tribune,* May 29, 2007). In fact, in 2008 Italy lowered its CIT rate by 5.9 percentage points. Indeed, the trend that the European leaders warned against has gained momentum from the energetic efforts to attract and retain investment with a low corporate tax regime in postcommunist Europe. In the European Union, the average statutory corporate tax rate fell from 38.0 percent in 1995 to 31.4 percent in 2004.[30] Hence, an acceleration of the downward trend in corporate tax rates and the shift of the tax burden away from business seem to be spreading to Western Europe from Eastern Europe.

In sum, the response of the East Europeans to the pressures of globalization troubled many West Europeans who felt obligated to follow suit. Curiously, in corporate taxation, the East Europeans are leaders rather than the followers in the spread of the corporate tax paradigm—a paradigm that presents low corporate taxes as a crucial strategy to attract investment and speed economic growth. According to one East European leader, the West's initial reaction to low corporate taxes in the East proved quite convenient on one level—it unified support for slashing corporate taxes. As governor of the National Bank of Poland Balcerowicz commented, "The pressure from some of the EU member states for us to raise our direct taxes was completely absurd from an economic point of view. The benefit is that today even the greatest populist will not dare propose raising the corporate income tax. I only wish France and Germany also called us to raise the personal income tax, as that might have had a mitigating effect on the politicians. Instead, the parliament has recently passed a new, 50-percent PIT rate" (*Rzeczpospolita,* November 5, 2004).

## Academics versus Politicians: Evidence and Rhetoric

Although policymakers speak openly about the external pressures on tax policy-making and its consequences for setting tax rates, academics are much less unified on whether the international competition for investment has threatened tax policy autonomy. Curiously, while European policymakers have long acknowledged the shift of taxes away from highly mobile revenue sources (capital and business) to less mobile sources (labor and consumers), academics are somewhat less unified in their interpretations of the phenomenon.[31] That is, despite the calls of distress from European policymakers, some scholars argue that global finance has not led to tax competition among advanced economies or declining tax revenues from mobile sources (specifically, capital and business)—at least not prior to 1997. The curious discrepancy between the foreboding statements of policymakers and the reassuring findings of some academic scholars on the fiscal policy autonomy of states has led one prescient political scientist to ask whether the politicians "suffer from 'false consciousness' or whether scholars look at the wrong data or draw the wrong conclusions" (Genschel 2002, 246).

No consensus has emerged on the question of globalization and taxation for Western Europe where the data are more reliable and effective tax rates are more available. The impact of globalization on taxation in postcommunist Europe is even harder to determine, where data are incomplete and effective rates—the best measure—are not available. Until effective rates are available, it will not be possible to conclude definitively that the burden has shifted. The Ministries of Finance of these countries have not made available their formal estimates of effective tax rates in most cases, and the comparative data are spotty. However, even without the full data, we can easily discern, first, that these governments have repeatedly lowered corporate tax rates and provided tax incentives to attract and motivate investment. Second, the public statements of leaders across the region indicate they are paying attention to the tax rates set by their counterparts abroad, and they intend to compete for investment with lower CIT rates. Surprisingly, there seems to be very little domestic political pressure on East European governments to redirect the downward trajectory of CIT rates. In the Czech Republic, for example, the union leaders did not call for the government to cease or reverse the trend but just to slow it down (*Právo,* March 11, 2004). While corporate tax policy is a controversial issue among European elites, it is not a hot-button issue domestically.

By its very nature, it is difficult to explain why a particular trend has *not* become politically salient. Are citizens unaware of the trend? Are they indifferent to or perhaps even silently supportive of the idea of corporate tax competition? That is, do citizens accept the logic of the reform—namely, that it is necessary to lower corporate taxes to compete for investment? Why not consider other strategies? After all, cutting corporate income taxes is only one of the many tools governments can use to raise foreign investment levels.

The Czech, Slovak, Hungarian, and Polish experiences with reformulating tax-incentive programs to attract corporations underscore the influence of regional and global factors in tax policy, especially corporate income tax policy and tax investment incentives. Much of the downward pressure on corporate tax rates comes from multiple levels of competition: with neighboring postcommunist states and older EU members, as well as developing countries in Asia and Africa. Some of the limitations on investment tax incentives derive from regional constraints related to EU membership. The motivation to offer tax incentives came from the common pressure to appear attractive within the global competition for investment.

The implications of tax reform in Eastern Europe reach beyond the study of postcommunist transition. The corporate tax policies in postcommunist EU countries paint a vivid picture of the evolving nature of domestic policy-making within increasingly integrated regional and global economies. Many scholars have identified a similar pattern in the developing world, in which the competition for international investment occurs through the lowering of wage and nonwage labor costs, the provision of special tax holidays for foreigners, and the relaxing of environmental and employee safety standards (Shields 1995).

It has been problematic for any state, postcommunist or otherwise, to impose a high tax burden on business and capital. What makes the East European cases particularly striking is that they have ceded enormous control over tax policy-making owing to regional *and* global imperatives. *Both* indirect and direct taxes are in large part externally constrained. And while there are still some tax areas in which the standard left-right political divide can influence the positions of leaders on taxation—like the setting of personal income tax brackets, as discussed in the next chapter—these areas are also showing signs of international influences as well.

In highlighting certain areas in which East European taxation is substantially externally driven, this study does not argue implicitly that external coercion is involved or that ordinary citizens have necessarily suffered from the tax shift away from lower corporate taxes. First, in the area of consumption taxes, it would be overly simplistic to argue that because the EU requires specific fiscal arrangements, the organization coercively imposed its will on otherwise unwilling East European leaders. Some national policymakers used the accession negotiation process to advance tax reforms that they already wholly supported.[32] For example, when asked about the role played by the prospect of EU accession, Balcerowicz responded to a *Rzeczpospolita* interviewer, "Simplifying things, you can say that when the reformers were in power, that prospect played a relatively small role, because they wanted to make reforms anyway. But because not all cabinets were reformist, the prospect of EU accession played a very favourable role in some periods" (*Rzeczpospolita*, November 5, 2004). One way to interpret Balcerowicz's observation is that a liberal economic approach to taxation would have prevailed anyway, that is, regardless of the international pressure, when the Right held power. The real shift that occurred was when the Left controlled the government, since it adopted what might be interpreted as a traditionally right-wing approach to taxation on business. Leaders on the left of the political spectrum broke with traditional divisions and alignments, perhaps due to a perception of inevitability. It is necessary to turn to personal income taxes to see how the traditional partisan divisions still impact the tax regime.

## CHAPTER 5

# Politics and Personal Income Taxes

Thus far this book tells a story in which domestic political logics do not seem to matter much for taxation. Consumption taxes, even if they irritate or offend the public at times, are beyond political bargaining in most East European polities due to the way EU accession and membership have been managed. Furthermore, the shift away from corporate responsibility for tax revenues is uncontroversial and does not reflect existing partisan divides. Still, some areas of direct taxation remain politically sensitive on the level of the voting publics. Different aspects of the personal income tax remain highly politicized, including deductions for families with children and taxes on small businesses and the self-employed. Most important, political parties still go to battle over the distribution of the personal income tax across income brackets and economic groups. Recently, one of the main debates over the division of budgetary responsibility across the rich and the poor concerns the merits of progressive taxation versus flat taxation. Flat taxation applies a single rate to the earned income of all taxpayers (usually above a certain basic threshold) regardless of whether the taxpayer's income is low or high. There are many countries in which flat-tax proposals led to heated public debates and became strongly politicized.

Given the controversy surrounding flat taxation, the speed with which the flat tax has spread is truly remarkable. Over a dozen postcommunist countries have adopted it, including Estonia, Lithuania, Latvia, Russia, Ukraine, Georgia, Slovakia, Romania, Macedonia, Bulgaria, Albania, the Czech Republic, and Serbia.[1] In 1994, Estonia's economically liberal government became the first to implement a flat tax, followed shortly thereafter by Lithuania and Latvia. After Russia introduced a 13 percent flat tax in 2001, many other postcommunist governments followed suit. In 2003, Serbia introduced its own type of flat tax at 14 percent, Ukraine matched Russia's 13 percent rate in 2004, and Slovakia set its flat-tax rate to 19 percent starting that same year. The Georgian legislature, with a vote of 107 to 11, overwhelmingly approved a flat-tax rate of 12 percent beginning in 2005. Following the election of President Trajan Basecu, Romania also enthusiastically adopted a flat tax, with the new government introducing a flat tax on its second day in power in January 2005. The flat tax continued to sweep the region in 2007 with Macedonia adopting a 12 percent flat tax and Albania a 20 percent flat tax (which Albania then halved to 10 percent the next year). In 2008, Bulgaria and the Czech Republic were next to implement a flat tax (of 10 percent and 15 percent, respectively), and Hungary's parliament voted to introduce a 16 percent flat tax in 2011.[2]

The preponderance of examples adds both credibility and momentum to right-wing parties that advocate flat taxes in Poland and Slovenia. Economically liberal parties in Germany, Spain, Finland, Greece, and Great Britain are also contemplating the possibility of a flat tax seriously (although not necessarily realistically). Moreover, this flat-tax fever is spreading to smaller countries outside of Europe and the former Soviet bloc, with several governments considering it, like Panama, Costa Rica, Guatemala, and El Salvador, and several governments adopting it, like Paraguay and Trinidad and Tobago in 2006, Iceland in 2007, and Mauritius in 2009.[3]

Enthusiasts often treat the flat tax as a panacea, and the idea of the flat tax continues to titillate many promarket, liberal politicians who hope to have the opportunity to embark upon this fiscal experiment in their own economies. It is difficult to know whether the flat-tax revolution in postcommunist Europe deserves all of the enthusiasm and hype it currently generates among its many champions. First, some analysts note that most of the East European countries did not implement true flat taxes, at least not in the form outlined by Robert Hall and Alvin Rabushka, two American economists widely revered by flat-tax enthusiasts. The primary aim of the flat tax is to simplify taxation. However, simplification requires not only (and not even primarily) the collapsing of all rates into one; it also requires governments to simplify how they calculate the tax base. That is, a single rate without the elimination of complicated deductions, exemptions, and loopholes violates the spirit (and, most likely, the revenue advantages) of the flat tax.

Second, other analysts question whether it is appropriate to credit the implementation of the flat tax per se with the positive economic outcomes when other concomitant factors were also important (Gaddy and Gale 2005; Ivanova, Keen, and Klemm 2005). Consider the Russian example. Flat-tax enthusiast Alvin Rabushka revels in the fact that in the seven years after Russia implemented its 13 percent flat tax, the revenues from personal income taxes tripled (once corrected for inflation) and the GDP grew over 6 percent on average per year.[4] Certainly these are powerful selling points for the advocates of the flat tax (Mitchell 2003; Laar 2005; Belien 2005). But as arguments for the flat tax go, they are gross simplifications since many other reforms could also have contributed to the increase in tax revenues and the growth of the Russian economy. After all, the flat tax was part of a broader tax reform program. At the same time as the flat tax took effect, the Russian government issued taxpayer identification numbers, eliminated ceilings for overdue taxes, increased significantly the legal authority of the tax administration, and bolstered the state apparatus (Gaddy and Gale 2005). Social insurance taxes were lowered, and there were changes to corporate taxes and later energy taxes, a topic returned to in the following chapter. Given the simultaneity of reforms, scholars have found it nearly impossible to calculate the effect of the flat tax on revenue or growth.

Moreover, while many accept the possibility that the flat tax created some sort of supply-side effect—that is, a Laffer effect[5]—in Russia,[6] the question still remains just how much new economic activity resulted directly from the single tax rate. Even in Russia's celebrated flat-tax reform, scholars have shown that the productivity response was quite low (Gorodnichenko, Martinez-Vazquez, and Sabirianova Peter 2009). Furthermore, sophisticated analysts have had a hard time isolating the effect of tax reform from factors related to Russia's energy boom (Ivanova, Keen, and Klemm 2005). Certainly a large portion of the growth in GDP and income tax revenues can be traced to the surge in gas and oil prices. For example, speaking to the efficacy of the Russian tax reform, the IMF's representative in Moscow attributed 80 percent of the increase in Russian revenues in 2001 to the strength of the oil and gas sector (Kwon 2003).

Third, seldom do the proponents of flat taxes consider that in the majority of cases, personal income tax revenues fell after the adoption of the flat tax, thereby undermining the promise of more revenue overall due to increased compliance or improved incentives to work. According to IMF calculations in 2006, personal income taxes as a percentage of GDP increased only in Latvia, Lithuania, and Russia in the year immediately following the reform.[7]

What do the adoption of the flat tax and the battles over income taxes generally reveal about the politics of taxation in postcommunist Europe? To what extent has the design of personal income taxes resulted from domestic political battles? Do personal income taxes represent the final bastion of national tax politics, or does the sudden adoption of the flat tax across numerous countries over a short period of time suggest once again the dominance of international factors? This chapter focuses on the politics surrounding the adoption of the flat tax in order to illustrate the ways in which personal income taxes remain one of the few surviving tax areas beholden to domestic politics. An analysis of regional trends and a fuller discussion of Estonia and Slovakia and, more briefly, Ukraine and Bulgaria demonstrate the importance of political struggles and electoral outcomes for the adoption of the flat tax. Although the reason to focus on each case is elaborated below, these cases together elucidate the importance of domestic politics and the role of the political Right for the flat tax, even when the Right is engaged in power-sharing agreements with the Left. The empirical evidence demonstrates that domestic politics still determines whether the proponents of the flat tax can see their policy agenda succeed. After analyzing the regional pattern in electoral politics and the specific efforts of right-wing politicians and parties to promote the flat tax in the case studies, the chapter concludes with an analysis of the flat tax as a transnational policy trend and introduces some caveats about the likelihood of the continued politicization of personal income taxes in Eastern Europe.

## Regional Trends in Personal Income Taxes

With over a dozen countries having adopted the flat tax, a key pattern has emerged. Assuming that an approximate left-right political spectrum exists (and it essentially does in the vast majority of flat-tax countries), we can see that the flat tax becomes law through the efforts of right-wing parties and politicians in coalition governments. Although this may seem intuitive on one level, it is a stark departure from other tax areas where tax patterns do not reflect partisan changes within or across political systems. The regional trend suggests that for the flat tax to be adopted in postcommunist polities, the right wing of the political spectrum must gain power since left-wing parties, and their main constituents, are not pursuing the same personal income tax agenda as right-wing parties.

It is possible to identify which party in power has been the driving force behind the adoption of the flat tax in each country. When a left-right ideological spectrum exists, as is clearly the case in the new EU member states, it is the party on the right who introduced and drove the adoption of the flat tax. For example, in Estonia it was Pro Patria Party, in Latvia the Latvian Way party, in Lithuania the Conservative Party, in Romania the Justice and Truth Alliance, in Georgia the National Movement-Democrats, in the Czech Republic the Civic Democratic Party, in Slovakia the SDKÚ-DS, in Macedonia the VMRO-DPMNE, and in Bulgaria the NMS2. Table 9 provides an overview of the parties that were in the coalition government at the time of adoption and provides information about those parties outside of the government. In nine cases, the parties responsible for the reform occupy the right of the ideological spectrum and were members of the coalition government. The importance of the Right is especially clear for those former communist countries that have joined the European Union.

In some instances, especially non-EU members, the ambiguity of where parties fall on the left-right spectrum complicates the story. That is, the dominant parties do not fall clearly within the conventional left-right ideological spectrum, in which more economic liberalism is associated with parties on the right and more state intervention in the economy is associated with parties on the left. The main reason that parties are harder to identify is that salient noneconomic issues determine the dominant party cleavages. In postwar Serbia when the flat tax was adopted, the main issue dividing political parties was a party's attitude toward Slobodan Milošević. In Serbia the ruling DOS coalition was composed of seventeen parties united only in their opposition to Milošević. These seventeen parties spanned the ideological spectrum. The two largest parties in the coalition were the Democratic Party (a social democratic party) and the DSS (an economically liberal party), and both supported the flat tax.

In Russia, the most powerful political party at the time of the flat tax, Unity, does not fall easily into a traditional political category. Unity and later United Russia were the parties of power that were defined primarily by their support of President Vladimir Putin. The flat tax was part of the overhaul of the tax system by Putin's early administration when Unity dominated the legislature. Although Putin's prime minister and team of economic advisers in 2000 were decisively liberal, they were not members of the economically liberal, opposition parties, like Yabloko or Union of Rightist Forces. Despite these complex cases of Russia and Serbia, the pattern remains within postcommunist Europe that right-wing politicians are behind the introduction of the flat tax. Electoral outcomes influence whether and when the government manages to move away from progressive taxation. Table 9 captures the importance of electoral patterns. The domestic political context and traditional partisan divides remain crucial to the development of personal income taxes, and international pressures from regional or global integration are not overpowering the political realities on the ground. What this table shows, and what the case studies below will flesh out, is that the emergence of the flat tax depends largely on domestic politics. The statistical analysis in chapter 7 lends further support to this argument.

## Estonia's Introduction of the Flat Tax

How is the flat tax a consequence of the national political environment? To better understand the importance of domestic politics and the role of the political Right, it is useful to begin with the first postcommunist country to introduce a flat tax, Estonia. Since Estonia was the first East European country to experiment with a flat tax, and since the major international financial institutions and advisers discouraged its adoption, there is little reason to question whether the flat tax was a product of external or domestic factors. Despite the IMF's powerful position in Eastern Europe in the early 1990s, its advice was dismissed in this area of reform. Moreover, Estonia at this time was freer from EU influences than it would be later in the decade during accession negotiations.

In Estonia, a coalition government, led by Mart Laar of the Pro Patria Party (Isamaa), pushed through the parliament the new flat-tax system in December 1993, in time for it to be put into force in 1994. This young government that formed in September 1992 contained right-wing and centrist parties including Laar's Fatherland Party (with 30 of 101 seats in the parliament), the Estonian National Independence Party (10 seats), and the Moderates Party (12 seats). The flat-tax program was part of the government's larger promarket approach to dealing with the country's economic challenges. In addition to the flat tax, Estonia eliminated all tariffs on trade, unilaterally opening its borders to foreign goods and exposing domestic firms to international competition. Estonia was the first former Soviet Republic to abandon the ruble and establish its own fully convertible currency. It also adhered to a strict monetary policy and pursued a swift privatization program (Grennes 1997, 9–17).

According to Laar, adopting a flat tax posed a major political challenge. First, his government had a very thin, one-vote majority. Second, there were no other foreign exemplars adding credibility to the proposal. Prestigious Western bodies like the IMF opposed a flat-tax model. Laar states, "We had a lot of advisors and everybody said it was impossible." Lowering the tax rate to 26 percent and making it flat would cause great fiscal imbalances. At home, the idea was highly unpopular, Laar explains, and there were "protests inside the parliament and outside the parliament."[8] The opposition, including major parties on the left like the Estonian Center Party, vowed to overturn the flat tax once it took power.

The controversy surrounding the new Income Tax Act led to a three-month delay and several compromises before the parliament passed the act. The proposal to link the amount of exempt income to the number of children

TABLE 9. Parties in Power during Adoption of the Flat Tax

| Country | First Year in Force | Party with Most Seats in Parliament | Parties in Coalition | Parties out of Government | Parties in Coalition Government Favoring Flat Tax | Parties in Government against Flat Tax | Parties out of Government against Flat Tax |
|---|---|---|---|---|---|---|---|
| Estonia | 1994 | "Isamaa" Pro Patria | Pro Patria, National Independence Party, Moderates (center-right) | Coalition Party, Royal Union, Estonian Center Party, Royalist Party, Estonians Citizens Union | All | — | Center Party |
| Latvia | 1994 | Latvian Way | Latvian Way, Latvian Farmers Union, Christian Democratic Union (center-right coalition) | Latvian National Independence Movement, Harmony for Latvia, Equal Right, Union for Fatherland and Freedom, Democratic Centre Party | All | — | |
| Lithuania | 1997 | Conservative Party | Conservative Party, Christian Democrats | Labor Party (LKDP) | Conservative Party, Christian Democrats | — | Labor Party (LKDP), Lithuanian Social Democratic Party (LSDP) |
| Russia | 2001 | Unity (President | Unity (controls executive | Communists, Union of | Unity | — | Communists |

| | | | | | | | |
|---|---|---|---|---|---|---|---|
| | | Vladimir Putin) | branch) | Right-Wing Forces, Yabloko, FAR, LDP | | | |
| Serbia | 2003 | Democratic Party (PM Zoran Djindjic, a social democratic party) | Democratic Opposition of Serbia (DOS; 17 parties that range from left to right) | Democratic Party of Serbia (DSS), Socialist Party of Serbia (SPS), Serbian Radical Party (SRS), Party of Serbian Union (SSJ) | Democratic Party and most members of DOS | New Serbia (NS), Democratic Center (DC), Democratic Alternative (DA) | SSJ, SRS, SPS and others (DSS eventually supports Budget) |
| Ukraine | 2004 | For a United Ukraine (Centrist, PM Yanukovych, of Party of the Regions) | 11 parties including Agrarian Party, European Choice, People's Choice, People's Democratic Party, Regions of Ukraine, and Working Ukraine-Industrialists and Entrepreneurs | Our Ukraine Bloc (Yushchenko), Tymoshenko Bloc, Socialist Party, Communist Party (Right) | Some members within For a United Ukraine | Agrarian party, members of For a United Ukraine | Socialist Party, Community Party |
| Slovakia | 2004 | SDKÚ-DS | SDKÚ-DS, KDH, the Party of the Hungarian Coalition (SMK), and the Alliance of the New Citizen (ANO) | HZDS, the Slovak National Party (SNS), the Party of the Democratic Left (SDL') | SDKÚ-DS, KDH, the Party of the Hungarian Coalition (SMK), and the Alliance of the New Citizen (ANO) | — | HZDS, the Slovak National Party (SNS), the Party of the Democratic Left (SDL') |

(continued)

TABLE 9.—*Continued*

| Country | First Year in Force | Party with Most Seats in Parliament | Parties in Coalition | Parties out of Government | Parties in Coalition Government Favoring Flat Tax | Parties in Government against Flat Tax | Parties out of Government against Flat Tax |
|---|---|---|---|---|---|---|---|
| Georgia | 2005 | National Movement-Democrats (center-right) | National Movement and United Democrats | Rightist Opposition | National Movement-Democrats (almost unanimous) | (1 no vote/20 abstain/37 absent among coalition) | Rightist Opposition |
| Romania | 2005 | Justice and Truth Alliance (PM Traian Basescu, right-wing) | National Liberal Party and Democratic Party, Romanian Humanist Party, Hungarian Democratic Union in Romania | Social Democratic Party (progressive, originally offered failed flat-tax proposal) | Justice and Truth Alliance | — | SDP and Greater Romania Party |
| Macedonia | 2006 | VMRO-DPMNE (PM Nikola Gruevski, right-wing) | Internal Macedonian Revolutionary Organization-Democratic Party of Macedonian National Unity (VMRO-DPMNE), Democratic Party, of Albanians (DPA), New Social Democratic Party (NDSP), | Social Demo-cratic Alliance of Macedonia (SDSM), Democratic Union for Integration (DUI), Internal Macedonian Revolutionary Organization-People's Party (VMRO-Narodna). | All; a coalition campaign promise | — | Social Democratic Alliance of Macedonia, the Liberal Democratic Party, and the Democratic Union for Integration |

| | | | | | | | |
|---|---|---|---|---|---|---|---|
| | | | Democratic Renewal of Macedonia (DOM), Party for a European Future (PEI), Party for Democratic Prosperity (PDP) | Social Democratic. | | | |
| Bulgaria | 2008 | Bulgarian Socialist Party (BSP, PM Sergei Stanishev) | "Coalition for Bulgaria": Bulgarian Socialist Party (BSP), the National Movement for Stability and Progress (NMSP), and the Movement for Rights and Freedoms (MRF). Right-wing parties | United Democratic Forces, Democrats for a Strong Bulgaria, Bulgarian People's Union, Ataka Coalition + 10 independents | Stanishev cabinet of BSP | United Democratic Forces, Democrats for a Strong Bulgaria, Bulgarian People's Union | Other members of the BSP |
| Czech Republic | 2008 | Civic Democratic Party (ODS, PM Mirek Topolanek) | ODS, Christian Democrats (KDU-CSL), Greens | Social Democrats (CSSD), Communists (KSCM) | ODS, KDU-CSL | Greens | Social Democrats (CSSD), Communists (KSCM) |

*Source:* Author's determinations.

proved an especially sensitive issue that had to be revised in the final version of the flat-tax bill passed December 8, 1993 (Laar 2002, 271–77). Moreover, the bureaucracy did not support the idea, especially officials from the Ministry of Finance who feared budgetary shortfalls. Indeed Laar proposed the flat tax under very poor macroeconomic conditions. When Laar's government came to power, Estonia suffered from high unemployment and inflation. In 1992, inflation exceeded 1,000 percent, over one-quarter of the workforce had lost their jobs, and trade with the East was collapsing (World Bank 1996, 174). Laar's main economic adviser, Ardo Hansson, notes that the flat tax seemed too radical at the time, and there were few who clearly supported it. "It probably couldn't be pushed through the same way today. But it was possible then."[9]

Despite a rather aggressive program of shock therapy, the government's economic policies were not the main factors that forced the first liberal reformers out of office or that destabilized the coalition's unity. Instead, controversies over the political rights of the large Russian minority living in Estonia seriously weakened the government's grip on power (not to mention its good standing abroad). Laar himself lost a vote of no confidence in September 1994 (having survived a previous vote of no confidence) due to his alleged involvement in the secret transfers to secessionists in the Russian Republic of Chechnya in 1992. (Laar was replaced by Andres Tarand, who briefly served as the caretaker prime minister until general elections were held in March 1995.) Laar remained deeply involved in Estonian politics despite the scandal, shuttling between public and academic life and reemerging as prime minister a second time from 1999 to 2002.

Despite the Right's thorough defeat in 1995, subsequent Estonian governments left the flat tax in place. Initially, the Left promised to rescind the flat tax once in power. However, the flat tax gained more support over time, in part due to the revenue growth that followed. Personal income tax revenues increased from 1,832.1 million Estonian kroons in 1993, to 2,388.2 million kroons in 1994, to 3,593.1 million kroons in 1995, to 4,353.7 million kroons in 1996, with the real upward trend in personal income tax (PIT) receipts continuing for many years (Eurostat 2005).[10] Decades later, Laar has become a kind of icon of the flat-tax movement. He remains an enthusiastic and vociferous advocate of the flat tax, and Laar credits the flat tax with not only Estonia's spike in tax revenues but also declining unemployment and increasing economic activity.[11] Laar's right-wing party maneuvered deftly and aggressively to realize this reform, in the face of strong opposition from leftist parties and IMF officials. Given the timing and lack of precedent, there appear to be no external forces accounting for the adoption of Estonia's approach to personal income taxes. Despite strong opposition and significant delays, Estonia's main leaders and party on the right propelled the introduction of the flat tax.

## Slovakia's Flat Tax

Slovakia is an important case in the flat-tax revolution, in that it is widely considered a clear success case. It served as an example for future proponents of the flat tax in the region, a topic returned to below. Slovakia is also a case where electoral outcomes and the collaborative efforts of parties on the right led to flat-tax reform. That does not mean that the adoption of the flat tax in Slovakia was simple. Slovak partisan politics was complicated by nonmaterial party cleavages similar to Serbia's. That is, a broad coalition came to power in 1998 united only by each party's opposition to a former antidemocratic leader. What is crucial here, however, is that the flat tax came about only after the 2002 elections, when the coalition shed its parties on the left, so that compromise with the Left was less necessary. Slovakia was also the first postcommunist country in line to join the European Union when it adopted the flat tax. The Slovak case helps to underscore the irrelevance of the EU in its move away from progressive taxation. Instead, the Slovak case demonstrates the importance of domestic political conditions.

Slovakia's tax reforms came about in 2002 when four right-of-center parties formed a coalition government and aggressively pursued a broad liberal economic agenda. When Mikuláš Dzurinda, the leader of the largest right-wing party, Slovak Democratic and Christian Union–Democratic Party (SDKÚ-DS), extended his tenure as prime minister into a second term, he was free from many of the constraints of his first term when his coalition government lacked ideological coherence. During the first term from 1998 to 2002, Dzurinda led a left-right, umbrella coalition with parties ranging from the former communists to promarket conservatives, as well as the conservative Catholic party and the Slovak nationalists. As noted, they were united only in their opposition to Slovakia's previous leader, Vladimír Mečiar, and in their desire to end Slovakia's international isolation and exclusion from multilateral organizations. As Haughton writes, the goals of NATO and the EU membership were the only glue binding Dzurinda's diverse coalition together (2003).

With a more homogeneous coalition government and a short-lived three-person majority in the parliament after 2002, Dzurinda's second government was able to pass far-reaching structural reforms in the areas of taxation, pension reform, social welfare benefits, and health care. In a very short period of time, the retirement age rose to 62 (from 55 for women and 60 for men). The government introduced co-pays for medical treatment, scaled back unemployment insurance, and linked child social benefits to the employment of one parent. In addition the government extended the privatization of strategic enterprises and added greater flexibility to the labor market. Most important for this study, a flat tax replaced a more progressive tax system. All of these programs required a dramatic revamping of existing codes. During this brief window, the government managed to achieve the speedy passage of politically sensitive legislation across multiple areas of reform, despite a string of presidential vetoes and despite quickly losing its majority in the parliament.

As a result of Dzurinda's reforms, Slovakia's new tax system became extraordinarily simple, taxing virtually all income and consumption at 19 percent.[12] Thus, all levels of personal and corporate income were taxed at 19 percent, and the government set the value-added tax at 19 percent. According to Ivan Mikloš, the former finance minister credited with the Slovak tax reform, the design of the new fiscal regime aimed to simplify and neutralize the existing system and sought to shift more of the tax burden from income onto consumption.[13] To simplify the tax codes, the reforms not only created one rate for all income levels above a newly raised tax-exempt allowance, it eliminated existing deductions and exemptions to a degree not seen in other flat-tax systems in the region. Nearly all of the 90 exemptions, 19 sources of untaxed income, 66 tax-exempt items, and 37 items with special rates were eliminated (Goliaš and Kičina 2005, 3).

It is extraordinary that Slovakia was able to introduce so many austerity programs and radically overhaul the fiscal system, health-care system, pension system, and labor protections all at the same time. Although the Dzurinda government failed to see through its planned educational reforms, the overall legislative accomplishments of the government are striking. Any of these reforms was radical enough to derail a government in a stable political environment. In fact, attempts in other countries to pursue weaker reforms in just one of these areas, such as labor reforms in France in 2005, or pension reforms in Latvia in 1999, were met with protests and riots that derailed the reforms.

Certainly the Slovak government had good reason to expect strong resistance to the flat-tax reform. There was no evidence of popular support—on the contrary. Before designing the new legislation, a February 2003 poll ordered by the Ministry of Finance showed that 70.9 percent of the population favored progressive taxation. Only 21.6 percent favored a flat tax (Goliaš and

Kičina 2005, 12). Yet the new tax regime came into force the very next year. Why was this right-of-center Slovak government able to see through these politically daunting structural reforms, especially in taxation, when similarly enthusiastic parties and governments on the right elsewhere, such as in Poland or Slovenia, had tried but failed to implement flat-tax reform due to what can be described as normal political constraints? What does this experience suggest about the politics of Slovak taxation? To what extent did domestic political opposition really matter in the Slovak reforms? In order to answer these questions and to gauge the importance of Slovak democratic politics for taxation, special attention must be paid to Slovakia's electoral politics, the media, and nongovernmental organizations in the transformation of the tax regime.

## Electoral Politics and the Weakness of the Left

The election results of 2002 took many in Slovakia by surprise. The right-wing parties did not expect to be able to form a government without a left-wing, nationalist, or populist party's support. As noted, in 1998 several ideologically diverse parties were needed to form a government in order to overcome the stronghold of Vladimír Mečiar's party, HZDS, over the Slovak electorate. The Right managed to form an ideologically coherent government owing first to several extraordinary scandals from Premier Mečiar's tenure (such as Mečiar's blanket pardon of anyone involved in the kidnapping of President Kovac's son, which many interpreted as a kind of self-pardon). Second, among the mass publics, there existed a desire to enter the European Union in 2004 without risk or mishap. As a result, HZDS remained outside the 1998 and 2002 governments. Third, one of the main nationalist parties, the Slovak National Party (SNS), which attracted a following in earlier elections (5.4 percent in 1994, 9.1 percent in 1998, and 11.7 percent in 2006) and had a role in the previous coalition governments, split shortly before the 2002 elections into the Slovak National Party (SNS) and the Real Slovak National Party (PSNS) due to personal infighting (Deegan Krause 2003). As a result, both nationalist parties missed the 5 percent threshold required to obtain seats in the 2002 parliament, receiving 3.3 percent and 3.7 percent of the vote respectively. The proportional representation system enabled the Right to benefit from SNS's internal divisions and its forfeited block of votes. The main left-wing party, SDL', the Party of the Democratic Left, was also weakened by defection and failed to pass the 5 percent threshold (Haughton 2004). The position of SDL' was usurped by the newly formed left party, Smer. Its previous leader, Robert Fico, was a top member who defected from the SDL'. These shifts in parties allowed four parties on the right to capture a thin majority and to form a government.

The Left's disarray was not only critical for the Right to form a unified government, it also enabled the Right to make the most of its short-lived majority in parliament to pass major reforms. While populist and left-of-center MPs criticized the government's proposals, they were unable to offer counterproposals for serious consideration. Indeed, any opposition to proposed tax reforms from left-wing members of parliament (MPs) or their traditional constituents proved ineffective. According to one former Ministry of Finance official, the number of Slovak economists capable of analyzing and critiquing the reforms was limited. Many Slovaks with doctoral degrees in economics worked abroad, and those working in the country tended to rally behind the government's proposals.[14] It was repeated in author interviews with former members of Mikloš's Finance Ministry that Slovakia lacked strong economists on the left to provide intellectual or technical rationales for challenging Mikloš's tax reforms.[15] Martin Simecka, the editor-in-chief of *Sme*, the main Slovak daily, writes that the Dzurinda cabinet managed to create the sense that their reforms were infallible, unchallengeable, and in accordance with universal economic laws. Their approach undermined public discussion among even moderate critics (*ČTK*, December 27, 2005; Martin Simecka, *Respekt*, December 2005).

The civic and social groups most strongly opposed to Mikloš's reform were Slovak labor unions and Roma groups. The chairman of the Slovak umbrella labor union, the Trade Union Confederation (KOS), described the reforms as "horrific," arguing that the flat tax impoverished the poorest Slovaks (*ČTK*, September 14, 2004). Yet the unions were too weak to block reforms. First of all, Slovak trade unions lacked credibility. As explained by Grigorij Mesežnikov, the director of an influential Bratislava think tank, the Institute for Public Affiars (IVO), they were seen as excessively partisan, which was problematic given their commitment to political neutrality in the tripartite system. He explained that the unions were also perceived as serving the interests of labor bosses over Slovak workers.[16] Alone the unions could not alter the course of reform (Mathernová and Renčko 2006, 639). Neither could the Roma groups, which represented the constituency most hurt by the broad set of reforms. To no avail, the Roma groups demonstrated in protest and even began to riot and loot stores in eastern Slovakia (in the towns of Cierna nad Tisou, Trhoviste, Pavlovce nad Uhom, and Trebisov) in February 2004. These demonstrations defused quickly once the state dispatched two hundred Slovak state police and one thousand army troops in a show of force (*Warsaw Voice*,

March 7, 2004; *Radio Twist* February 22–24, 2004; *TA3*, February 21–24, 2004). Even the veto of the flat tax by President Schuster—one veto within a string of the president's preelection vetoes—was overturned in December, in time for the law to take effect the following month, January 2004.

The unions' most significant effort to block reforms took the form of a petition for a referendum, held in April 2004, calling for the government to hold early elections. Their goal was to take advantage of popular fears of reform and potentially high inflation following the implementation of the EU membership requirements (Bútora et al. 2004). This referendum was organized jointly by the unions and the opposition left-wing parties. In anticipation of the assault against its agenda, the government asked voters to boycott the referendum. The prime minister claimed the referendum was unconstitutional since there was no deadlock in government and thus no basis for new elections. The referendum required a 50 percent turnout to be valid. Despite the fact that the referendum was held the same day as Slovakia's presidential elections—and 47 percent of the population voted in those elections—insufficient turnout for the referendum (36 percent) invalidated it (*ČTK*, April 4, 2004). The referendum's failure enabled the flat tax to be adopted as designed.

## The Slovak Media and Think Tanks

Most civic organizations and interest groups did not pose a barrier to the overhaul of the tax system. On the contrary, Slovak think tanks, the media, and Slovak business tended to lend support to the Mikloš tax reform. As a legacy of the Mečiar period, Slovakia's nongovernmental organizations (NGOs) were generally pro-Western and proreform. In the past, the Slovak NGOs and think tanks played an important role in organizing mass opposition to the Mečiar government and worked to end Slovakia's exclusion from NATO and the EU. In the 1990s, this sector served as the holding space for many talented pro-Western intellectuals and politicians. Mikloš came from the ranks of Slovakia's NGO sector, as did many of his colleagues pursuing economic and social reforms in the Dzurinda government. With government encouragement, the think tanks and NGOs became a support base for, rather than a source of neutral analysis of, the liberal reforms. Scholars of Slovak politics emphasize the relationship between ministers and the groups of experts working in (and funded by) the NGO sector in designing and implementing reform projects.[17]

Economists in the NGO sector used the major Bratislava newspapers, most notably *Sme* and *Pravda*, as publication outlets to express support for reforms.

Fisher, Gould, and Haughton (2007) highlight the supportive role played by the mainstream media in supporting Dzurinda's reforms. They describe journalists as "active participants in policy making" and identify particular journalists with former government experience as especially important for the process, like Robert Žitnansky, Miroslav Beblavý, and Vladimír Tvaroška (Fisher, Gould, and Haughton 2007, 992). Mikloš's adviser, Martin Bruncko, had frequent contact with the press, and he acknowledged that the government could easily manipulate and persuade the young journalists. Due to years of media repression under Mečiar's tenure and under communism, the journalism profession in the early 2000s was still in its infancy. Even journalists at the major Slovak newspapers tended to be in their early and mid-twenties. Bruncko found that the young journalists were impressionable and rather quick to accept the logic of the reforms.

Nor did the Slovak business sector prove to be an obstacle to tax reform. According to Mikloš, lobbyists from various industries failed to protect the continuation of favorable loopholes or special exemptions for enterprises. He explained their failure: "We knew we could not make any exceptions for any one company, or else another company would use it to try to get its own exception."[18] As expected, winning the support of industry never posed a significant challenge to the tax reform package since the local business sector would benefit from the lower corporate tax rates and the elimination of the dividend tax. The lifting of the dividend tax as part of the tax reform package was a boon primarily for smaller domestic companies.[19] Moreover, business leaders, with their (much) higher than average salaries, were the obvious beneficiaries of the flat tax. After all, the wealthiest Slovaks saw their personal income tax obligations essentially cut in half overnight with the flat-tax program.

The substantial benefits of the flat tax for the wealthiest Slovaks were intended to encourage and reward additional productive activity. Dzurinda nonetheless sought to reduce the negative financial impact of the tax reform on the poor, especially since the lowest statutory rate would leap from 10 percent to 19 percent (Moore 2005, 4). First, the tax-exempt allowance (setting the level at which income became taxable) increased from SKK 38,760 to SKK 80,732 (19.2 times the monthly living minimum). Second, the expenditure side of the budget was at times used to compensate those most hurt by tax reform. For example, pensioners received a lump sum transfer in 2004, and pensions became more favorably indexed to inflation and wages after 2005, thereby augmenting the after-tax real income for pensioners (Mikloš, Jakoby, and Morvay 2005, 57). Similarly, child benefits increased in 2004 as long as one parent was working. Real incomes grew by 3.5 percent in 2004, amid the austerity measures and tax reforms (57). According to Mikloš, Jakoby, and Morvay, the only group that saw no improvement to their net income from the tax reforms were single individuals with monthly gross income ranging from SKK12,000 to 20,000 (2005, 57). An independent think tank, INEKO, calculates that those with monthly incomes of SKK10,000 to 23,000 were the immediate losers of the reform, with the loss of about 2 percent of income (for singles without children) (Goliaš and Kičina 2005, 10–11). Those with children were compensated by other means.

Some of the social costs of the tax reform for the poor were milder than predicted in part due to fortunate timing issues. In particular, the reforms took effect the same year Slovakia became a full member of the European Union. Its membership contributed to its ability to attract foreign investment, which in turn helped to increase the tax base. Soon the growth of corporate tax revenues, despite the lower CIT rate, gave the government the resources to compensate the relative losers of the tax reform. Lower-than-expected inflation also helped budgetary balances (see tables 10, 11).

There were further positive effects from EU membership, dampening the social costs of reform. The new single 19 percent VAT rate should have brought about higher food prices because the tax on food increased from 14 to 19 percent. Since the poor spend a much larger percentage of their income on food than the rich, the new single VAT rate was feared to be one of the more unjust and politically disruptive measures. However, prices rose less than expected because the rate hike coincided with a fortuitous entry of several foreign supermarket chains into the Slovak market in early 2004. Increased competition and price wars kept food prices low and forced retailers to absorb much of the tax increase.[20]

The right-wing government did not survive the 2006 elections, despite a growing economy, the successful entry into the European Union, and the im-

**TABLE 10. Tax Revenues from 2003 to 2007 (in thousands of SKK)**

| | 2003 | 2004 | 2005 | 2006[a] | 2007[a] |
|---|---|---|---|---|---|
| Direct taxes | 80,839 (37.2%) | 73,961 (30.8%) | 82,703 (30.8%) | 92,913 (33.1%) | 102,336 (33.2%) |
| PIT | 39,680 (18.2%) | 35,122 (14.6%) | 39,310 (14.6%) | 42,215 (15.0%) | 46,046 (14.9%) |
| CIT | 32,016 (14.7%) | 33,164 (13.8%) | 39,538 (14.7%) | 45,839 (16.3%) | 51,268 (16.6%) |
| Indirect taxes | 136,378 (62.8%) | 165,919 (69.2%) | 185,981 (69.2%) | 188,126 (66.9%) | 205,708 (66.8%) |
| Total tax income | 217,217 (100%) | 239,880 (100%) | 268,684 (100%) | 281,039 (100%) | 308,044 (100%) |

*Source:* Ministry of Finance of the Slovak Republic, quoted in Mikloš 2008, 67, Table 3.4.
[a]The data for 2006 and 2007 are forecasts by the Slovak Ministry of Finance.

proved electoral performance of Dzurinda and Mikloš's party (SDKÚ-DS). In 2006 the left-wing party Smer formed a coalition government with the reunited SNS and the new HZDS. Given that Smer campaigned on an antireform platform, it was unclear what would happen to the Dzurinda reforms once the Right lost power (*ČTK*, June 13, 2006).

As in Estonia, the flat tax in Slovakia has (thus far) survived the system's partisan turnover.[21] Why is this? First of all, Smer's coalition partners did not similarly run on an antireform platform (*ČTK*, June 13, 2006). Second, the finance minister from Smer, Jan Pociatek, was especially pragmatic and even incorporated members of Mikloš's team into his own ministry, like Richard Sulik, the author of the flat-tax proposal. Hence, despite pledges by Smer's leader, Robert Fico, during the 2006 electoral campaign to reverse the tax reforms, once in office the prime minister proved unwilling to tinker much with Dzurinda's economic program. Thus far, any scaling back of the tax reforms is mostly symbolic. For all intents and purposes, the 19 percent flat tax and the new tax code remain intact (*ČTK*, June 13, 2006). Given the economy's impressive performance (table 11), Smer's caution is not surprising.

At the time of its inception, any opposition to the new flat tax from trade unions, industry, or the left-wing parties was weak and ultimately inconsequential. What does this experience suggest about the politics of Slovak taxation? The inability of the opposition to mobilize and affect the reform process does *not* mean that income taxes in Slovakia, broadly speaking, are or were apolitical or transcend ordinary politics. On the contrary, politics mattered crucially for the realization of the flat tax. The flat tax came about owing to the particular configuration of interest groups and power in society. The left-wing

**TABLE 11. Slovak Macroeconomic Indicators**

| | 2000 | 2001 | 2002 | 2003 | 2004 | 2005 | 2006 | 2007 | 2008 |
|---|---|---|---|---|---|---|---|---|---|
| Percentage GDP change | 1.4 | 3.4 | 4.8 | 4.7 | 5.2 | 6.5 | 8.5 | 10.4 | 6.4 |
| Inflation rate | 12.2 | 7.2 | 3.5 | 8.4 | 7.5 | 2.8 | 4.3 | 1.9 | 3.9 |
| Jobless rate | 18.8 | 19.3 | 18.7 | 17.6 | 18.2 | 16.3 | 13.4 | 11.1 | 9.5 |
| Average monthly salary (in koruna) | 11,430 | 12,365 | 13,511 | 14,365 | 15,825 | 17,274 | 18,761 | 20,147 | — |
| Budget deficit (as % of GDP) | −12.3 | −6.5 | −8.2 | −2.7 | −2.3 | −2.8 | −3.5 | −1.9 | −2.2 |

*Source:* Eurostat for all data except data on average monthly salary from International Labor Organization.

parties were in disarray, civil society groups opposing the flat tax were weak, and those supporting the flat tax enjoyed positions of strength. Most important, the victory of the Right in the 2002 elections allowed an ideologically unified, right-wing government to form and to carry out its policy agenda. Within the Slovak political arena, the Right taking power prompted the adoption of the flat tax.

## Ukraine and Bulgaria: Are They Exceptions?

At first glance, neither Ukraine nor Bulgaria seems to follow the pattern in which the right-wing politicians gain power through elections and then push this agenda through. In these cases, the condensed information in table 9 does not sufficiently capture the complexity of partisan alignments. After all, when the flat-tax legislation was introduced and adopted, neither the president nor the prime minister in either country was from a right-wing party. Although these countries stray somewhat from the pattern, the introduction of the flat tax nonetheless stemmed primarily from the efforts of right-of-center politicians and occurred when the parties on the left had not managed to create or sustain a coalition without major concessions to right and center-right parties. It is important to consider turnover, partisan loyalties, and indeterminate election outcomes in Ukrainian and Bulgarian politics to see the role of the Right in flat-tax reform.

In the case of Ukraine, a few specific details help to explain why the flat-tax legislation, which was adopted in March 2003, emerged under the For a United Ukraine government, a coalition of parties with few right-wing politicians. First of all, the alignments in Ukraine's party politics are ambiguous due to the personalization of politics. In much of postcommunist Ukraine, noneconomic cleavages have been extremely important in shaping the identities of political parties. The personalization of politics—especially when President Kuchma was in power—meant that parties came together and formed alliances in large part due to their support of a particular leader. Hence, what united the eleven parties constituting the For a United Ukraine Party was each party's support for President Kuchma rather than a common ideology. There were parties clearly on the left who were part of this coalition (like the Agrarian Party) and supported Kuchma; but there were also parties clearly on the left who were out of the coalition (like the Ukrainian Communist Party) who opposed Kuchma. Moreover, For a United Ukraine was highly factionalized, and party loyalty was relatively weak.

Second, Ukrainian parties have been divided over the geopolitical orientation of the country. Some parties were characterized by their position on whether Ukraine's foreign policy should lean east or west, rather than whether Ukraine's economic policy should lean left or right. As became well known prior to Ukraine's Orange Revolution, Viktor Yanukovich's Party of the Regions (a leading member of For a United Ukraine) favored somewhat closer ties with Russia, and Viktor Yushchenko's Our Ukraine Party favored closer ties with the West. These geopolitical cleavages caused members within the same party or party groupings to hold diverse views on the role of the state in the economy.

Yet if one is forced to assign a label to the eleven-party coalition in power, For a United Ukraine would be considered centrist or perhaps center left, but not right-wing. Does this mean that left-wing politicians were responsible for the flat tax in Ukraine? Not actually. The main left-wing parties in Ukraine (namely, the Communist Party and the Socialist Party) were not part of the eleven-party grouping and opposed the flat tax. The party from which the prime minister and the finance minister came, Party of the Regions, was economically centrist, if not liberal. That said, two other major parties, Our Ukraine and Yulia Tymoshenko's bloc, stood to the right of For a United Ukraine Party and were in opposition to the standing government. One would have expected the flat tax to have come from these parties.

In fact, these parties, despite being in the opposition, were essential to the introduction of the flat tax and were powerful actors in the parliament. Officials from Our Ukraine and Yulia Tymoshenko's bloc had power and legislative influence due to the power-sharing arrangements that emerged following the 2002 elections. The impetus for personal income tax reform came from actors within the opposition party, Our Ukraine, which held key posts in the parliament in 2002 and 2003. Opposition figures occupied important committee chairs because these parties and politicians actually fared quite well in the 2002 elections. Our Ukraine won more votes than For a United Ukraine but could not form a government due to elite infighting. In fact, For a United Ukraine only won 12 percent of the vote, surpassed by Our Ukraine, which won 24 percent of the vote, and the Communist Party, which won 20 percent of the vote. Because the opposition's numbers were so strong, For a United Ukraine was forced to share some power in order to get anything done. As a result, nineteen of the twenty-six parliamentary committee chairs were assigned to the opposition following the 2002 elections. For a United Ukraine had limited control of the committee focusing on tax reform, the Budget Committee.

Although it did have nineteen deputies (of thirty-nine total) on the Budget Committee, it did not hold the chairmanship, nor did it enjoy a majority. Specifically, nineteen members were from pro-Kuchma parties, seventeen were from the opposition parties, and three were not party affiliated.[22] Instead the chair was controlled by Our Ukraine, and thus Our Ukraine set the agenda. At the time, the Budget Committee was led by a deputy from Our Ukraine, Petro Poroshenko, who is widely seen as an economic liberal. Sergei Teryokhin, another known liberal from Our Ukraine, also sat on the Budget Committee, and Sergei Buryak, a member of the Yulia Tymoshenko party, drafted the 2003 tax bill. On tax reform they aligned with government officials from Party of the Regions, premier Viktor Yanukovich and finance minister Mykola Azarov, who also supported personal income tax reform.

In sum, given the strong performance of Our Ukraine Party in the 2002 elections and their control of the Budget Committee's agenda, one must be careful about identifying the ideological orientation of the actors behind personal income tax reform. Therefore, even if Ukraine does not follow the more straightforward pattern of a right-wing government driving the adoption of the flat tax, it still suggests that economically liberal politicians who were well placed in the parliament spurred the lowering and flattening of personal income taxes. In Ukraine the flat-tax legislation resulted from the efforts of economically liberal politicians who held powerful positions in the legislature due to the strong electoral performance of economically right-wing parties in the preceding election.[23] Of course, had the centrist party of power or President Kuchma strongly opposed the flat tax, the movement could have been stopped. However, the claims of Teryokhin that the 13 percent flat tax would bring more taxpayers into the tax net and reduce the shadow economy convinced many political elites at the time not to obstruct the bill, thereby allowing the legislation to pass with 352 out of 450 deputies supporting the legislation, despite the president's lukewarm support. Unfortunately for Ukraine's State Tax Administration, the promises of increased returns were not realized, as PIT revenues as a percentage of GDP fell. In 2003 (before the reform took effect), revenues equaled 5.1 percent of GDP. PIT revenues fell to 3.8 percent of GDP in 2004 and 4.1 percent of GDP in 2005 (World Bank 2006, 13, table 2.1).

## Bulgaria's Flat Tax

In a similar vein, Bulgaria is also a somewhat misleading case if one only looked at who led the government when the flat tax was introduced. It was

Bulgaria's *left-wing* prime minister who announced and assailed the 10 percent flat tax on July 30, 2007, surrounded by his ideologically mixed cabinet members. The announcement certainly took many by surprise. First, during the two years prior to the announcement, there appeared to be no political will to adopt a single personal income tax rate. The main party on the left, the Bulgarian Socialist Party, remained staunchly opposed to the flat tax and instead advocated increasing the top rate for the wealthiest Bulgarians from 24 percent to 28 percent just one year prior to the announcement (*Eastbusiness*, August 30, 2006). The parties on the right commented publicly about gradually diminishing the progressiveness of the personal income tax, rather than introducing a flat tax per se.[24] Suddenly the coalition government that came to power in 2005—composed of the BSP (Bulgarian Socialist Party), the NMS2 (National Movement for Simeon II, a center-right party), and the MRF (Movement for Rights and Freedoms, also known as the Turkish party)—reached an agreement to adopt a low flat tax during the peak of the summer holidays. The coalition government that brought the flat tax to Bulgaria was thus a Left-Right coalition, with the Socialists holding the most seats in the parliament and the cabinet, including the premiership. Even the finance minister, Plamen Oresharski, was formally an independent (although in the past he was linked to the right-wing party UDF) and was repeatedly on record opposing a flat tax (*Pari*, January 5, 2005; February 3, 2005). The minister of the economy was a member of the Bulgarian Socialist Party and had previously advocated higher taxes on the wealthy and opposed the flat tax. At the time of the announcement, however, he instead went on record supporting the flat tax. Does the Bulgarian case, in which a left-right coalition controlled the government, break with the standard pattern in the region? Did the flat tax as a policy innovation lose its right-wing political association? Why the sudden change in Bulgaria?

Indeed the regional pattern in which a right-wing party is responsible for introducing the flat tax in fact does hold in the Bulgarian case as well. The reason why the announcement and adoption occurred by a (minority) government with a Socialist prime minister is simply more complicated. A few factors were at work. Although the Bulgarian Socialist Party is ideologically mixed (and includes both some of the old guard with ties to business and some more modern politicians), the party's primary constituents are the pensioners, the poor, and rural voters. Clearly the flat-tax proposal was not intended to draw support from these groups. In order to serve these main constituent groups, however, the Socialists wanted to increase pensions more aggressively. In a deal with its right-wing coalition partner (NMS2), the Socialists agreed to adopt the flat tax as a quid pro quo for a sizable increase in pensions.[25] Thus, in 2007, the left-right coalition government voted to increase pensions by 21 percent. At the standard indexing of pensions to prices and wages, the 2007 increase would otherwise have been 8.5 percent.[26] Part of the deal may also have included the move to coordinate the introduction of the flat tax with the substantial increase (22.2 percent) of Bulgaria's minimum wage the same year (*Esmerk*, May 16, 2008; *Dnevnik*, May 16, 2008).

The quid pro quo coupled greater welfare spending with a tax cut. This raises several questions. How could the Bulgarian government afford this? Was this a problem for Bulgarian fiscal conservatives? The minister of finance, Plamen Oresharski, stated that the recent cuts in corporate income taxes and personal income taxes were affordable in that they were offset by the growth in indirect taxes (*SeeNews*, July 2, 2008). In 2007 interviews shortly after the announcement, members of the Bulgarian National Bank offered the interpretation that Bulgaria's fiscal conservatives need not feel troubled by the potential budgetary impact. In the short term, the Bulgarian government could manage to increase social expenditures while decreasing income taxes because the budget had been running a surplus[27] and the GDP had grown around 6 percent the previous year. Moreover, the Bulgarian government expected more revenues from other sources since it had committed to increasing excise taxes over the three following years in order to harmonize with EU tax standards. The government was even planning to accelerate the harmonization of excise taxes to front-load the inflationary pressures expected from rising fuel costs. The strategy was to cope with inflationary pressures sooner rather than later, so that Bulgaria would be better prepared to meet the Maastricht criteria on inflation when it began to actively prepare for monetary unification.

Even if the tax cut and pension increase seemed affordable, was introducing the lowest flat tax in the region *politically* affordable for the Socialists? That is, could the Socialists really afford the dramatic reversal of their positions? The answer to this question at the time was not clear, although one former Socialist Party government official responded to this concern by arguing that tax cuts are seldom unpopular, even if taxpayers benefit disproportionately.[28] To deal with the sudden policy reversal, Bulgarian politicians from many parties made reference to the programs in neighboring countries to explain their support for (or acquiescence toward) the flat tax. The adoption of the flat tax in neighboring Romania, Serbia, Macedonia, and Albania helped to lend support to the policy. As discussed below, the need to remain competitive permeated public statements on the merits of tax cuts.

To understand fully the relevance of domestic politics to the flat tax in Bulgaria, it is also important to mention that the coalition partners had an immediate and more local political reason to support the flat tax—to stem a challenge from a rising political star, Boiko Borissov. Borissov, the popular mayor of Sofia, had bolstered the popular standing of his new right-wing party (Citizens for the European Development of Bulgaria, GERB), in part by developing a platform based on tax cuts, and the 10 percent flat tax in particular. Borissov's party performed well in the May 2007 European parliamentary elections, and the coalition parties feared it would perform well in the October 2007 regional elections, which in fact it did. When the government announced the tax reform, the economist who was charged with setting the economic platform for Borissov's party accused the coalition of stealing his program—and, in essence, stealing the 10 percent flat tax was stealing Borissov's thunder. Curiously, the flat tax became a symbol of forward-thinking reform, and politicians from many camps were clamoring to receive credit for the idea. By announcing the tax cuts and the pension increase, the coalition may have succeeded in briefly weakening Borissov. The seemingly rushed announcement served to mute the opposition's criticism and to defuse temporarily the Borissov political threat.[29] Moreover, these considerations help explain the timing of the announcement. The first tax return affected by the flat tax occurred in April 2009 (for the 2008 fiscal year), which fell only a few months before the national parliamentary elections.[30] As it turned out, adopting one of Borissov's signature policies ultimately failed to thwart Borissov's ascent. Instead, Boiko Borissov became the subsequent prime minister, with GERB receiving the most votes in the July 2009 elections.

Domestic politics is crucial to understanding the emergence and the timing of Bulgaria's flat tax. Fiscal issues permeated the political debates, and parties went to battle over different approaches. Interviews with multiple Bulgarian policy specialists repeatedly suggest that the flat tax came about due to a negotiated deal between the pro-pensioner BSP and the pro–tax reform NMS2, and given the timing of the changes in social programs, these assertions are rather convincing. In other words, the flat tax emerged due to a political deal struck by parties who needed each other to stay in power, to ward off rising political competitors, and to offer tax relief a few months prior to a national election.

## The International Dimension

The existing literature on postcommunist taxation pays little attention to the political factors leading up to the adoption of the flat tax (Keen, Kim, and Varsano 2006; Gaddy and Gale 2005; Ivanova, Keen, and Klemm 2005; Moore 2005; Stepanyan 2003). The academic and policy research on the flat tax focuses primarily on the consequences of flat-tax reforms for the domestic economy. An important exception to this trend is Baturo and Gray's study of the flat tax in Eastern Europe. Baturo and Gray (2009) seek to identify those factors that best predict the adoption of the flat tax, considering several political and economic hypotheses, like the adoption of other (nontax) market reforms or the number of veto players in the political environment. They also seek to understand the effect of the accumulation of flat-tax experiences on a new country adopting a flat tax. The main purpose of their analysis is to shed light upon policy diffusion across countries. In analyzing this question the authors conclude that domestic ideological conditions matter significantly for the adoption of the flat tax. Based on a logit model for twenty countries in Eastern Europe and the former Soviet Union, the authors find an economically liberal ideology is "associated with statistically significant increases in the probability of flat tax adoption" (147). They show that when a right-wing party or coalition comes to power, the probability of adopting a flat tax increases, especially when other countries in the region have already adopted a flat tax.[31] The article concludes, "In the presence of the right ideological environment, rational policymakers learn from other countries' successes with the flat tax and move to adopt the reform themselves" (Gray and Baturo 2009, 150). Curiously, the former Slovak finance minister explains his government's adoption of the flat tax quite similarly. He credits domestic politics first but recognizes an international dimension. He stated when explaining Slovakia's tax reform, "Even when domestic politics dominate, the international environment shapes [the process]."[32]

Baturo and Gray's analysis raises an important point to consider: cross-national emulation and the bandwagon effect. Although personal income taxes still constitute an area driven by domestic politics, there is an international dimension to the adoption of the flat tax that must be recognized. After all, it is doubtful that leaders in a dozen postcommunist states developed their ideas and beliefs about the flat tax entirely independently from each other. Although the flat tax varies in detail from country to country, the repeated adoption of a unified rate of taxation for all income brackets across numerous countries with varying economic conditions suggests that the flat tax was not exclusively an individual discrete response to domestic political and economic concerns, but was also an interrelated international phenomenon (Ikenberry 1990). This raises the question of why a radical approach to income taxes—too radical to exist (thus far) in the mainstream of domestic politics in the advanced industrialized countries of Europe and North America—prevailed in so many postcommunist countries over a short period of time. What fueled the flat-tax trend in the region? The predominance of the Right is a necessary but not always a sufficient condition for the emergence of the flat tax. Did powerful international bodies promote a flat tax? What exposure did key actors have to tax policy experiments elsewhere? How important is observation and learning among reformers, a factor raised by Gray and Baturo (2009)? There are four potential international factors that deserve careful consideration: the role of Western public lenders and organs, the international networks of right-wing East European economists, the role of Western nongovernmental organizations (NGOs), and competitive pressures from global and regional integration. Each will be analyzed in turn.

Scholars of postcommunist structural reform have frequently emphasized the powerful influence of external actors on policy reform, especially the international financial institutions.[33] Many have shown that funding institutions such as the International Monetary Fund (IMF), the World Bank, the European Bank for Reconstruction and Development (EBRD), and the EU's PHARE program were active in postcommunist economic reform in many areas like the pension system, banking sector, and privatization (Johnson 2000; Orenstein 2008; Appel 2004). Others have focused on the proactive efforts of the European Commission and European Council to redirect national policies in postcommunist countries in human rights, minority rights, public sector reform, and a host of economic policy areas (Vachudova 2005; Grabbe 1999; Kelley 2004; Grzymala-Busse 2007). In other areas of taxation, especially consumption taxes, this study attributes the primary responsibility to the EU.

In the case of personal income taxes, however, it would be inappropriate to assign much importance at all to European bodies or the international financial institutions. Personal income taxes fall outside the competence of the EU.[34] The most relevant international body for this matter might be the IMF,[35] but it certainly did not promote the introduction of the flat tax. In the case of Slovakia, the IMF team-in-residence mainly assisted the Ministry of Finance in its calculations of the revenue impact of the proposed tax reform package. The IMF representatives at the time of Slovakia's Article IV Consultation in 2003 indeed worried about the budgetary impact of the flat tax and encouraged Slovakia to implement it over three years rather than one year.[36] In Estonia, the IMF outright opposed the idea of the flat tax. In Romania, the IMF also opposed any tax cuts given budgetary gaps and was actively promoting tax increases, especially in consumption taxes (Heath 2006, 97–98). The former head of the Fiscal Affairs Department of the IMF unambiguously opposed the flat tax. He explained that flat taxes were a poor policy choice in economies with great income inequality.[37]

Much more important than the international financial institutions were the cross-national contacts among Ministry of Finance officials and politicians on the right. As in many policy areas, local leaders were aware of other tax policy experiments occurring in the region. Direct observation and learning occurred, as Gray and Baturo's quantitative analysis suggests (2009). Exchanges between East Europeans over tax reform emerged on many levels. Sometimes top government officials served as spokesmen for fiscal reform. Slovak finance minister Ivan Mikloš traveled to Prague to speak at a 2005 flat-tax conference in Prague organized by ODS, the main Czech center-right party. In fact, Minister Mikloš and Premier Dzurinda made frequent public appearances at ODS's invitation, including at the 2006 ODS party meeting in Olomouc. ODS leader and prime minister Mirek Topolanek also organized meetings with conservative party leaders from Slovakia, Hungary, and Poland to discuss common flat-tax ideas (*ČTK*, January 25, 2005). The Slovak prime minister boasted that Poland's prime minister asked to see the entire plans for reform (Kandell 2004, 1). In addition, top Czech and Slovak politicians collaborated extensively during their nearly simultaneous parliamentary campaign seasons, with Topolanek and Dzurinda making a joint public endorsement of the flat-tax idea (Palata 2006).

These meetings were intended to lend political support, and they supplemented the transnational consultations that were more technical in nature. Finance ministers and ministry officials met face-to-face with each other to learn from each other's experience and to share materials.[38] The examples are many. For instance, Georgian premier Zurab Zhvania invited Mikhail Dmitriev, the deputy minister from the Russian Ministry of Economic Development and Trade, to advise on tax reform prior to Georgia adopting the flat tax (*Imedi TV*, Tbilisi, in Georgian, May 28, 2004, translated by *Financial Times*, May 28, 2004). Likewise, Ukrainian officials met with Russian government officials to discuss the flat tax. Ukraine's finance minister, Mykola Azarov, referenced his extensive discussions with Russia's tax minister, Gennadiy Bukayev, in September 2002, which shaped his revenue expectations from the flat-tax reform.

According to Azarov, Bukayev cautioned against expecting immediate revenue growth but posited gradual revenue growth as taxpayers emerged from the shadow economy (*Fakty i Kommentarii,* April 4, 2003, 6). Ludovit Odor, from the Slovak Ministry of Finance, went to Estonia to learn about its flat tax. Later, Odor himself served as a foreign flat-tax consultant in Slovenia, Serbia, Montenegro, and Albania, meeting with officials who had an interest in the flat tax for their own country. Likewise, Odor's colleague Richard Sulik, an author of the Slovak flat-tax proposal, also traveled to Estonia to meet with officials and learn about its flat tax. Later Sulik went to the Czech Republic to help Vladimír Tlustý of ODS write a full flat-tax proposal for the Czechs.[39]

Although it is not possible to prove in any definitive way that governments borrowed from each other's models, interviews with key politicians and consultants help illustrate leaders' attention to the fiscal policy experiments abroad. For example, when asked whether Slovakia considered other countries' experiences in designing the flat tax, Ludovit Odor replied this way.

> We looked at the different experiences with the flat tax. It was clear that we could not have the same effect as Russia since there was a lot of black money that came back to the country [and into the Russian formal economy] with the flat tax. I did not expect similar Laffer effects with the personal income tax. Instead, we looked at the Baltic countries [for effects on revenues].[40]

Odor's reference to the Baltic cases makes sense given he was sent to Estonia for training, if not enlightenment. The Czech adviser and proponent of the flat tax Petr Mach had a similar explanation.

> We proposed a flat tax not only because it is simpler or more just, but also because we could observe the [other] countries with a flat tax. They have higher growth. . . . We had [in the past only] theoretical reasons for why a flat tax is better, but now we also have some experience [from other countries]. . . . We can use them as examples, especially Estonia. Of course [for Czechs] we can point to Slovakia now.[41]

When asked whether Russia served as an example for Czech proponents of the flat tax, Mach shook his head.

> When we wanted to use these good examples of Estonia and Russia, even the Social Democrats said, "How can you refer to these Eastern countries?" It is not

> popular. . . . It works better to refer to Slovakia. I think Czechs believe that the growth is due to Mikloš's reforms. During the [2006 Czech parliamentary] campaign there was a lot of talk of Slovakia. Mikloš spoke a lot here. He was invited to write articles and he was willing to do so. Slovakia was in almost every article in the newspaper.[42]

Russia did serve as a positive and useful exemplar in flat-tax debates elsewhere, such as Bulgaria, as Bulgarian flat-tax advocate Gyorgy Angelov explains.

> Russia is a good example for many Bulgarians. Some Bulgarians do not like Western models so I used the Russia example to target this group—the older, left-wing Bulgarians. I also used this example because more Russians started to pay taxes once the rate was lowered. Most people do not expect more [Bulgarian] people to pay if the rate is lowered due to our culture. But we are close to the Russians. And if it could work for the Russians, then it can work for the Bulgarians.[43]

In addition to the dense consulting networks among East Europeans, other cross-border flows of information should be noted. American and West European proponents of the flat tax contributed to the literature and the debates over the flat tax. In interviews, bureaucrats and consultants repeatedly invoked Hall and Rabushka's book *The Flat Tax* (1995). This book could almost be referred to as the bible for flat-tax proponents in the region, if that did not verge on a form of blasphemy of the true deities of liberal economic reform in the region: Milton Friedman and Friedrich von Hayek.[44] Mart Laar, the former Estonian prime minister, who is credited with his country's adoption in 1994 of the flat tax and a number of other liberal reforms, muses about Friedman's influence on himself. Laar had announced quite famously that Milton Friedman's book *Free to Choose* was the only economics book he had read before becoming prime minister at age thirty-two (*Baltic News Service,* April 20, 2006).

> In the early 90s I set as Estonia's goal enacting a simple, transparent, and comprehensible tax structure that would encourage business and could ensure the collection of taxes. As a solution, I proposed the flat tax I had found in Milton Friedman's book, which my economic adviser Ardo Hansson deemed entirely reasonable. . . . All I can conclude fifteen years later is that we made an extremely good decision, whose consequences have been extremely positive and have been emulated in many other countries. The Baltics, who were first to go

> over to a flat tax, have developed far more quickly than their Eastern and Central European brethren who have remained faithful to progressive taxation. (*Stanford Review* 2006)

The East European economists on the right must be recognized as the impetus behind and the motors sustaining the flat-tax movement. However, in some instances and rather obliquely, American right-wing think tanks may have helped spread the flat-tax idea. For example, as noted earlier, members of Slovakia's team of reformers had spent much of the 1990s in think tanks, due to their exclusion from both the government and business sectors (Mathernová and Renčko 2006, 638). Mikloš in particular headed a conservative think tank in Bratislava from 1992 to 1998, named MESA 10 Center for Economic and Social Analyses. Martin Bruncko, Mikloš's adviser who also worked previously in the NGO sector, explained that the U.S. think tanks were important financial supporters of Slovak think tanks, exposing Slovak intellectuals to many conservative ideas and providing them with written materials from their institutions and published materials from the IMF and the World Bank.

> The NGOs played an important role in political change in Slovakia. Many in the government had spent the 1990s in think tanks. . . . The think tanks received money from these organizations, Heritage Foundation, CATO, and IRI [International Republican Institute], and there was a strong influence of Americans.[45] This affected people like Mikloš and others who came to believe that lower taxes were always better, the less state the better, and the more economic freedom the better.[46]

The flow of information and resources to Slovakia from the United States, Western Europe, and most important, from other postcommunist states sheds light upon the interconnectedness of countries and the relations among policymakers. These ties lead directly to the issue of policy diffusion, a topic of study of political scientists focusing on many regions of the world (Weyland 2005, 2007; Appel 2004; Simmons and Elkins 2004; Swank 2006; Brooks 2007). In just over a decade the flat tax spread across over a dozen countries in part because leaders felt the need to follow the example of seemingly successful neighboring countries. The study by Baturo and Gray (2009) mentioned above finds that as the number of countries with a flat tax rises, so does the probability that a new country will adopt a flat tax, given particular domestic conditions. Indeed, leaders on the right embraced the flat tax and were willing to bargain politically to enact it in response to apparent policy successes abroad. Baturo and Gray (2009) conclude, "Given the right ideological environment, the flat tax has taken off in Eastern Europe . . . [as a result of] policymakers rationally updating their beliefs about the tax's appropriateness for their own country" (131). Their findings also suggest that politicians gained confidence and their proposals gained credibility with the accumulation of flat-tax countries in the region.

In many instances, leaders raised the concern that their own country would fall behind others if it failed to adopt a flat tax. As the Czech senator who later became prime minister, Mirek Topolanek, stated, "We have no choice [to lower taxes] anyway because Slovakia has already gone ahead" (Kandell 2004, 1). Former Hungarian prime minister and leader of FIDESz party Viktor Orban stated, "We are considering it, the flat tax. We're losing our competitive advantage to countries with flat taxes" (*ČTK,* January 25, 2005). One Polish tax expert writes, "Nobody is hiding the fact that this [flat tax] is all about tax competition with other economies."[47] The West Europeans are feeling similar pressures, and certainly there is no shortage of statements by flat-tax proponents invoking the need to remain competitive.

## Conclusion

The transnational flow of policy ideas and the demonstration effect underscore the ways that the personal income tax partly resembles other areas of taxation in which external factors also contribute importantly to policy outcomes. This observation is not meant to detract from the larger point of this chapter, namely, that domestic political actors still bargain over the form of personal income taxes in their country. However, the motivation for certain right-wing actors to fight for the flat tax is linked to their observation of regional trends and their international associations with other politicians on the Right.

Two caveats related to the continuing politicization of personal income taxes must be raised as well. First, individuals or interest groups still go to battle over the allocation of the personal income tax across different income brackets and social groups. Rates and deductions are still strongly debated. While this leaves room for plenty of political noise, it concerns a small portion of the overall tax revenue. For example, the average contribution of personal income taxes to total tax revenues in 2004 for the ten new member states of the EU is 17.1 percent, whereas the contribution to total tax revenues in 2004 by consumption taxes is 41.6 percent (European Commission 2006, 217, 229). Specifically, as a share of total taxation in 2006, personal income taxes represent 13.6 percent in Poland, 18.1 percent in Hungary, 11.7 percent in the Czech Republic, 8.5 percent in Slovakia, 7.9 percent in Bulgaria, and 10.0 percent in Romania (Eurostat 2008, table A.2.1_T, 249). By contrast, indirect taxes, which are *beyond the realm of domestic political bargaining almost entirely*, represent a much higher proportion of total taxation in Poland (42.8 percent), Hungary (41.0 percent), the Czech Republic (30.9 percent), Slovakia (39.6 percent), Bulgaria (56.5 percent), and Romania (44.5 percent) in 2006 (Eurostat 2008, table A.1_T, 237). Even in Russia, a country not swayed by EU tax norms, the PIT never accounted for more than 10 percent of the total combined revenue for the federal and subfederal governments between 1994 and 2004 (Gaddy and Gale 2005). Because personal income taxes concern a rather limited portion of budgetary revenues, one must be modest in assessing the overall impact of domestic politics on taxation.

Second, the flat-tax approach, quite ironically, leads to the further depoliticization of the tax system in the medium and long term. In other words, even if implementing a flat tax is politically heated in the short term, the realization of the flat tax diminishes future tax debates all the more. After all, a flat tax, which taxes all households at one low rate, is made feasible usually by closing the exemptions, deductions, and loopholes of the kind that various groups fight for in the political arena. In short, the flat tax stands to make the tax system even less subject to domestic politics over time. For now, though, the debates over personal income taxes remain acerbic, passionate, and highly partisan.

Ultimately the political story behind flat-tax reform is very different from the apolitical story behind corporate taxes or consumption taxes discussed in the previous chapters. Neither the configuration of interest groups, the nature of social cleavages, the power of labor, or traditional partisan divides mattered for the downward trend in corporate tax rates across the region or for the strict adoption of EU codes in indirect taxation. In personal income taxation, however, the domestic political landscape matters crucially. In almost all cases, parties that can be identified as traditionally left-of-center have not introduced the flat tax. Rather, the flat tax is the domain of the Right, and parties and politicians from the Right have been responsible for its realization. Simply put, in the case of personal income taxes, it has mattered who won elections and who controlled the agenda for the flat-tax proposals to prevail.

# CHAPTER 6

# Politics and Taxation in Russia: The Case of an Oil Economy

Does taxation politics in Russia conform to the general pattern of taxation politics in Eastern Europe? What similarities are there between the development of the Russian tax system and those in postcommunist Europe? To what extent do external pressures constrain Russian tax policy given Russia's size and the structure of its economy? Is the geopolitical status of Russia or the size of its economy sufficiently different that a comparison to smaller countries undergoing a capitalist transformation after communism becomes irrelevant?[1]

Certainly Russia shares many important commonalities with its East European counterparts. As discussed in the previous chapter, the Russian experience with the flat tax is similar to and directly relevant to the flat-tax experiments that occurred across postcommunist Europe. Likewise, many of the challenges and problems that arose in the creation of postcommunist tax administrations in Eastern Europe, as discussed in chapter 2, appear in Russia as well. The question remains, however, to what extent have international considerations, relative to domestic political concerns, mattered for the evolution of Russia's tax system?

On the one hand, Russian tax policy differs from East European tax policy in that the former was highly politicized throughout the 1990s in numerous tax areas. Under President Boris Yeltsin, regional elites negotiated aggressively to alter their tax obligations. Powerful companies and well-connected elites maneuvered repeatedly and successfully to receive tax privileges. In addition, unlike much of Eastern Europe, there was no external multilateral body, and certainly no EU equivalent, requiring specific tax forms and minimum rates. Although the IMF provided technical advice in Russia and encouraged certain approaches to taxation, it had very little leverage in requiring specific tax reforms.

On the other hand, Russian taxation has begun to resemble the tax regimes in Eastern Europe in that it has also become less politicized over time—but for very different reasons. Over the course of the Putin presidency, Russia's oligarchs and regional leaders lost much of the influence they enjoyed in the Yeltsin years over the development and functioning of the tax system. Yet despite Russia becoming more integrated in the international economy in the 2000s, external constraints were not the main reasons for less politicized taxation. More important reasons were Vladimir Putin's consolidation of power and his forceful style of governance. This enabled his administration to see through major tax reforms and other structural changes that reduced the political influence of regional and corporate actors over taxation.

In order to account for the changing nature of Russia's tax politics, this chapter begins with a summary of tax politics under the Yeltsin presidency. It then turns to taxation under the Putin presidency in order to examine the process by which Russian taxation became depoliticized. This section considers the impact of Putin's governing style and consolidation of power, world oil prices, and Russia's greater participation in world commodity markets on the state's tax policy-making autonomy. The final section of this chapter analyzes the implications of the Russian case for the larger question of taxation, domestic politics, and international policy autonomy in the postcommunist region.

The larger goal is to explore whether the overall framework developed for postcommunist Europe applies to the Russian case. The following analysis suggests, first, that the international factors that dominate East European taxation are substantially less influential in shaping Russian tax policy and, second, that domestic political factors could, in principle, play a significant role in setting Russian tax policy. The fact that they did not during the Putin and early Medvedev presidencies was a function of the growing antidemocratic approach to governing Russia and the consolidation of power rather than external constraints posed by regional and global economic integration. This has an important implication for theories of globalization.

## Taxation after Communism

After the collapse of the command economy, the Yeltsin government, just like the other new governments in Eastern Europe, had to create a tax system that would function within a capitalist economy. Given the simplicity of taxation under communism, the tax administration during Soviet times was miniscule. Tanzi and Tsibouris note that this rather elementary tax administration managed to extract revenue levels that amounted to as much as 50 percent of GDP in the Soviet period (2000, 13–14). In comparison, much more complex fiscal systems, for example, in the United States and Japan, collected revenue equaling 32.9 and 32.8 percent of GDP respectively (1989 figures; OECD 2007, table 26, 264). Since it was no longer possible to appropriate and redistribute the profits from higher performing state-owned enterprises, the Yeltsin administration needed to create many new tax forms, such as a corporate income tax, a value-added tax, a personal income tax, new import duties, and reduced export taxes (Ebrill and Havrylyshyn 1999; Martinez-Vazquez and McNab 2000; Dobrinsky 2002). Several new laws were passed to set the foundations of a capitalist tax system, such as the *Law on the Fundamental Principles of the Budgetary System and the Budgetary Process* of October 1991, the *Law on the Foundations of the Tax System in the Russian Federation* of December 1991, and the *Law on the Foundations of Budgetary Rights and Rights to Form and Use Extrabudgetary Funds* in April 1993.

The speed with which major legislation was passed obscures the extraordinary difficulty of designing a tax system that would function effectively in the chaotic, uncertain postrevolutionary economic environment. It is necessary first to recognize the desperation of the Russian government to raise enough revenue to fulfill its basic responsibilities (Herrera 2005; Fish 2005). A fiscal crisis was mounting. Spending obligations far surpassed tax receipts, with budgetary deficits averaging 9.7 percent between 1992 and 1998 (EBRD 2001). Several factors confounded the government's attempts to bring in tax revenues. First, the Russian economy was in recession for much of the 1990s. In total, the gross domestic product contracted 42.5 percent between 1991 and 1998 (EBRD 2001). While the recession diminished the tax base, a shift from formal to informal economic activity further confounded efforts to extract revenues. The new formal economic activity that did emerge during the recession tended to concentrate in areas that were more difficult to tax, like services and small enterprises. Moreover, the complexity of the new economy made tax collection more challenging. Not only did the number and type of producers in the economy increase from the communist period, so did their methods of payment (Tanzi 2001, 54–55). In particular, nonmonetary interfirm payments and the growing use of barter in the Russian economy limited the state's ability to tax economic activity.[2] By some estimates, nearly half of all transactions in Russia in 1997 were nonmonetized (Gaddy and Gale 2005, 1591). Even transfers and remittances among multiple levels of government were often settled with noncash offsets and barter, which denied the federal budget cash revenues to pay public workers and pensioners and to meet other fiscal responsibilities (Woodruff 1999). Tax collection was especially challenging given that citizens were convinced of neither the fairness of the system nor the widespread compliance of their fellow citizens (Berenson 2007). Also, since the Russian citizenry had no experience paying taxes, there was no entrenched tax-paying habit.

Given these overwhelming fiscal challenges, one might expect the government to have rejected tax holidays, exemptions, and special privileges to well-connected economic and political actors. Due to the weakness of the state, however, the tax system was full of loopholes, special favors, and inconsistencies. While the general tax framework was set up in 1991 and 1992 and enshrined in Russian law, tax obligations were under constant negotiation and revision. As in many areas of the economy and society, the rule of law was not firm. The fluid and politicized nature of taxation and the pattern of industrial-state relations, for many observers, harkened back to Soviet days. For instance, Turley writes that personal connections and effective enterprise-state bargaining could alter an enterprise's tax obligations, thus carrying forward the tradition of soft budget constraints from the communist period to the postcommunist period. As in Soviet times, enterprises could obtain working capital or subsidies in the form of tax exemptions, tax breaks, and tax amnesties (Turley 2006, 24). Gustafson similarly describes Russian taxation in the 1990s as "taxation by plea bargain" and an extension of ingrained habits from the Soviet planned economic system (2000, 195). Former acting prime minister Egor Gaidar writes, "The problem of tax collection was not a problem of tax administration in the usual sense. It was more a political struggle about what constituted the essence of the emerging economic system, whether it was to be a system in which the relationship between the state and the enterprises was to be regulated by law or whether it would be business as usual, based on the political influence and personal contacts" (Gaidar 1999, quoted in Turley 2006, 23).

Taxation under the Yeltsin presidency closely reflected the distribution of power in the new federation as well as the turbulent politics of the early transition. The constant and repeated efforts to negotiate special tax deals for enterprises occurred at several levels. Lobbying was not simply directed at one official body responsible for government revenue since the tax code could be amended or reformulated in multiple ways. Legislative acts by the State Duma or by regional governments, regulatory acts and instructions by ministries and government agencies, and presidential decrees (brought to Yeltsin by members of the extended Yeltsin "family" or members of his administration) could all alter the tax obligations of individual corporate taxpayers.[3] Easter offers several examples of ad hoc tax arrangements made to favor well-connected corporate elites. One of the more striking examples Easter discusses is when

Vladimir Potanin, as acting first deputy prime minister in 1996, gave his own company, Norilsk Nickel, a tax break that saved it $100 million in taxes (2006b, 46). Likewise, Rutland describes the case of Sibneft Oil Company that saved $450 million in taxes when it began nominally basing operations in the region where its director, Roman Abramovich, served as the governor (2005, 9).

In a similar vein, regional elites lobbied for special fiscal treatment, including redefining the division of tax receipts between the state and regional levels. The large literature on Russian fiscal federalism reviews how regional and local governments negotiated special tax arrangements throughout the Yeltsin period, especially in the early transition years. Governments in politically sensitive regions, most notably in Tatarstan, Bashkortostan, Sakha, Ingushetia, and Komi, obtained enormous concessions from the federal government (Martinez-Vazquez and Boex 1999, 12). Under Yeltsin, fiscal negotiations occurred frequently, and divisions of the tax receipts changed annually according to bilaterally negotiated rates (Wallich 1994, 56, cited in Treisman 1999, 52). To highlight the extreme variation, Treisman compares the average region, which transferred 60 percent of locally collected revenues in 1992, to Tyumen, which transferred 80 percent of revenues, and to Tatarstan and Bashkortostan, which transferred almost nothing (1999, 54).[4] He argues that the system of asymmetrical federalism served to quell protest actions and appease powerful regional governments, especially those with separatist aspirations (Treisman 1999). Economic goals, like encouraging structural reform or responding to local development needs, were subordinate to political considerations (Martinez-Vazquez and Boex 1999). Those regions that lent electoral support to Yeltsin's opposition, that declared sovereignty, or that staged protest strikes received larger fiscal transfers than those regions that were politically stable and supportive of Yeltsin.[5]

Making a similar observation, Martinez-Vazquez and Boex write that ethnic republics frequently started political campaigns, known as "sovereignty parades," with the intent of achieving a special tax status and obtaining favorable bilateral treatment by the federal government (1999, 11). The early 1990s saw tremendous regional tensions, and there was a real risk that Yeltsin could not contain the separatist movements that he had encouraged in his attempt to wrest control from Mikhail Gorbachev just a few years earlier (Roeder 1991; Gorenburg 2001; Herrera 2005; Stoner-Weiss 2006). In early 1992, five regions decreased or terminated remittances to the federal government. By the end of the year, however, twenty regions failed to meet their tax-remittance obligations. By 1993 thirty regions were in violation of tax-remittance laws (Martinez-Vazquez and Boex 1999, 11, citing Wallach 1994). As pressures mounted, the Yeltsin government continually granted and enhanced special fiscal arrangements to manage the most politically sensitive regions. Between 1992 and 1994, the share of revenues allocated to regional budgets increased from 47 to 70 percent. Despite some recentralization in 1995, revenue transfers to the regions increased again in 1996, approaching 1992 levels (Grafe and Richter 2001, 151). Quite strikingly, Tatarstan and Bashkortostan, particularly resistant regions, even prohibited the federal treasury from opening local branches (Rutland 2005). Table 12 reports the formal division of revenues between state and local governments according to tax form by year.

By 1996 the high number of exemptions and formal tax concessions for firms reached 7 percent of GDP (Grafe and Richter 2001, 147). The negotiation and renegotiation of the tax regime reflected the acute weakness of the Yeltsin administration vis-à-vis regional and industrial elites (Martinez-Vazquez and Boex 1999, 6). The enfeebled state not only failed to resist lobbying pressure from governors and enterprise directors in setting and amending the tax laws, it also failed miserably to collect the taxes that remained in force. According to Gaddy and Gale, in 1996 and 1997 only 8 percent of large enterprises paid their taxes with money, 63 percent paid in kind, and 29 percent paid nothing at all (2005). When taxes were paid in kind, it allowed taxpayers to alter their obligations to federal coffers unilaterally. Gaddy and Ickes give several examples of how regions used in-kind payments to lower their obligations to the center (2002). First, a regional government might agree to accept from an enterprise a local construction project instead of cash payments, since the local project added some value to the region, and the in-kind payment could not be shared with the federal government as required by law. Second because in-kind payments were hard to measure, regions and enterprises could also alter their tax obligations unilaterally by overvaluing the in-kind goods proffered. Gaddy and Ickes give the example of Samara region that transferred goods to the Mari-El region instead of paying rubles to the federal budget. Although Samara asserted that the goods satisfied a 5 billion ruble tax obligation to a particular fund, the Federal Audit Chamber later valued the goods at no more than 800 million rubles (Gaddy and Ickes 2002, 176). According to Gaddy and Ickes, the overvaluation of in-kind tax payments and tax offsets was pervasive in the Russian fiscal system during the Yeltsin years.

According to the State Tax Service, only 17 percent of all enterprises in 1996 paid their taxes on time. Others estimate that due to underreporting, barter, and capital flight, 33 percent of firms paid no taxes at all (Grafe and

TABLE 12. Distribution of Income between Center and Regions by Year in Russia, 1991–98

| | Law on Basic Principles of Taxation, 1991 | | 1992, Q1 | | 1992, Q2–Q4 | | 1993 | | 1994, Q1 | | 1994, Q2–Q4 | | 1995 | | 1996 | | 1997 | | 1998 | |
|---|---|---|---|---|---|---|---|---|---|---|---|---|---|---|---|---|---|---|---|---|
| | Fed | Reg | Fed | Reg | Fed | Reg | Fed | Reg | Fed | Reg | Fed | Reg | Fed | Reg | Fed | Reg | Fed | Reg | Fed | Reg |
| VAT[a] | 100 | 0 | Ad hoc negotiations | | 80 | 20 | 80–50 | 20–50 | 75 | 25 | 75 | 25 | 75 | 25 | 75 | 25 | 75 | 25 | 75 | 25 |
| Profit tax | 0 | 100[b] | 47 | 53 | 41 | 59 | 31 | 69 | 37–34[c] | 63–66[c] | 37–34[c] | 63–66[c] | 34 | 66 | 34 | 66 | 34 | 66 | 34 | 66 |
| Personal income tax | 0 | 100[b] | 0 | 100 | 0 | 100 | 0 | 100 | 0 | 100 | 0 | 100 | 10 | 90 | 10 | 90 | 0 | 100 | 40 | 60 |
| Excise on alcohol | 50 | 50 | 50 | 50 | 50 | 50 | 50 | 50 | 50 | 50 | 50 | 50 | 50 | 50 | 50 | 50 | 50 | 50 | 50 | 50 |
| Energy excises | — | — | 100 | 0 | 100 | 0 | 100 | 0 | 100 | 0 | 100 | 0 | 100 | 0 | 100 | 0 | 100 | 0 | 100 | 0 |
| Excises on domestic productions | — | — | n.a. | n.a. | n.a. | n.a. | n.a. | n.a. | 0 | 100 | 0 | 100 | 0 | 100 | 0 | 100 | 0 | 100 | 0 | 100 |

*Source:* Martinez-Vazquez and Boex 1999, 115, Table 17.

[a]VAT on imports and on precious metals and stones is assigned 100 percent at the federal level.

[b]These taxes could be shared with the federal government.

[c]The federal profit tax rate is 13 percent; regional tax rates range up to 22 percent of profits (for most enterprises) and 25 percent of profits (for banks and insurance companies); the sharing percentages are calculated based on the 13/22 and 13/25 profit tax rates.

Richter 2001, 145). A special interagency commission led by Petr Karpov examined 210 of Russia's largest enterprises in order to understand why so few companies paid taxes with money. The report concluded that most enterprises were cash poor, to the point that only 20 percent of their earnings were in cash for 60 percent of the largest companies studied (Gaddy and Ickes 2002, 248). Moreover, in all but 10 percent of the enterprises studied, cash did not constitute even half of their earnings. However, according to Gaddy and Ickes, even those companies with high cash earnings took advantage of the possibility of nonmonetary tax payments whenever possible (248). An Emergency Tax Commission was created later in 1996 to try to capture tax arrears from the largest twenty corporate debtors, which collectively owed the state about 4 percent of GDP (Tanzi 2001, 62).[6] The focus on large companies seemed more fruitful since it would be harder for them to hide economic activity (Gehlbach 2008).

## Energy Taxes and Tax Arrears

The Emergency Tax Commission targeted energy companies in particular since tax arrears in this sector were especially egregious, exacerbating federal budget deficits. The oil companies' elaborate mechanisms to evade high tax levels in the 1990s were based upon complicated transfer pricing schemes (Wolosky 2000). Since tax calculations were based on trade rather than production, the oil companies could establish subsidiaries in special low tax zones in Russia or in tax havens abroad in order to reduce their official taxable income (Jones Luong and Weinthal 2004, 141). As the Yeltsin administration became more and more intent on collecting taxes from the energy sector, the oil lobby repeatedly managed to convince their sympathizers in the relevant ministries and the legislature to block tax reform. Throughout most of the 1990s, elites in the energy sector used their political connections to preempt and even overturn tax reform. Jones Luong and Weinthal highlight this point by referring to one example in which the oil lobby convinced the Duma to repeal an increase in the oil excise tax that had already been passed and in force for several months in 1997 (2004, 144).

Although the Emergency Tax Commission hoped to recover some back taxes and improve tax compliance, its job was complicated by unfavorable economic conditions and the weakness of the energy sector overall. Given how important the oil sector became for tax revenues in the 2000s, it is easy to forget that the sector was much weaker a decade earlier. First, oil production and oil profits had fallen by almost half during the transitional recession of the 1990s. By 1998, oil production had dropped to 6 million barrels per day, down from 11 million barrels in 1988 (Hill 2004, 11). A lack of investment in the industry meant that, despite the depletion of oil in older wells, drilling new wells was infeasible. Second, the recession in the Russian economy reduced domestic demand for oil by as much as 40 percent (Hill 2004). Meanwhile the decrepit state of Soviet pipelines limited the ability of the Russian oil companies to turn to world oil markets to absorb excess capacity. As a result, the federal government's receipts from export duties, excise taxes, and profit taxes from the oil sector were low.

The lobbying for energy-related tax concessions from the government did not just occur at the enterprise level. Regional governments also lobbied for a greater portion of energy revenues, thus cutting into federal tax receipts in the 1990s. Resource-rich regions like Sakha and Tyumen pressured the government successfully to grant them special tax treatment, arguing that their regions had endured the negative environmental repercussions of their resource endowments but not the material benefits (Martinez-Vazquez 2002, 15). From 1992 Yeltsin's government allocated a larger share of tax revenues from mineral resources to the region of origin for the first time in the country's history (Martinez-Vazquez 2002, 11).

The deep politicization of the tax codes, the weakness of the central administration vis-à-vis regional and corporate actors, and the underdevelopment of the energy sector limited the ability of the state to raise sufficient revenues. In addition, several observers stress that the *structure* of Russian energy taxes deserves some of the blame for the industry's weak contribution to the budget in the Yeltsin years (Jones Luong and Weinthal 2004; Easter 2006a; Gustafson 1997). First of all, the especially high tax rates discouraged the development of the sector and encouraged tax evasion (Economist Intelligence Unit 2006b, 39). Second, since both the Ministry of Fuel and Energy and the Ministry of Finance determined tax rates for the oil companies, excise taxes fluctuated irregularly and unpredictably. A third and related problem was that regional governments arbitrarily levied taxes on oil companies and required them to meet social welfare needs capriciously. In the same vein, the oil companies frequently faced tax inspections that resulted in indiscriminate fees and fines (Jones Luong and Weinthal 2004, 146). In sum, excessively high tax rates, indeterminate profit margins, and insecure property rights discouraged activity in the sector and diminished overall budgetary contributions (Gaddy and Gale 2005).

## The Inception of Russian Tax Reform

The special exemptions and politically motivated tax arrangements for regions and individual corporations led to severe budgetary shortfalls and unsustainable borrowing on the part of the government (Johnson 2000). A symptom of the ailing fiscal system was the sale of state treasury bonds at sky-high returns. Prior to the August 1998 crash of the ruble and the government's temporary default on its debt repayments, the Russian central bank was offering up to 150 percent annual return on state treasury bonds (*Moskovskie novosti,* August 18, 1998). Only once the budgetary problems approached this crisis point in 1998 did Yeltsin's government push forward the initial reforms to improve tax collection from enterprises and stabilize the division of tax revenues between the federal and regional governments (Jones Luong and Weinthal 2004).

The early stage of tax reform began under Yeltsin, spurred by the ruble crisis. It then accelerated significantly under Vladimir Putin, with the majority of tax reforms occurring between 1998 and 2002 (Jones Luong and Weinthal 2004). In the years following the 1998 crash, the government fully revamped the fiscal system by introducing a new Tax Code, the Budget Code, the *Law on Financial Foundations of Local Self-Government,* and the *Concept of Reform of Inter-Governmental Relations in the Russian Federation for 1999–2001,* among smaller tax reform measures (Martinez-Vazquez 2002, 18). The first part of the Russian tax code, which was passed by the Russian Duma on July 31, 1998, and put into force on January 1, 1999, focused on new taxes and taxpayer rights. The second part, which was passed under the Putin presidency on August 5, 2000, and entered into force in 2001 and 2002, amended the value-added tax, corporate income tax, personal income tax, excise taxes, and the mineral resource recovery tax.[7] As a result of new legislation, six primary tax reforms occurred on Putin's watch.

- A 13 percent flat tax on personal income replaced the progressive income tax system.
- A unified regressive social tax replaced separate social taxes.
- Corporate tax reform lowered the nominal rate from 35 to 24 percent, allowed for more regular business expenses, closed loopholes, and lowered the maximum supplemental regional tax rate on corporate profits.
- The value-added tax rate fell from 20 to 18 percent, and turnover taxes were eliminated.

- The government introduced a mineral extraction tax.
- The government simplified taxes on small businesses.

The revamping of the tax system occurred throughout Putin's first term and into his second term. While the flat tax came into force almost immediately in 2001, other important changes to the codes followed in subsequent years. For example, the unified social tax was reduced from 36.5 to 26 percent in 2004 for 2005. More important, the State Duma, also in 2004, adopted new legislation that closed many of the semilegal tax loopholes related to transfer pricing in the energy sector. This legislation also linked tax rates to world oil prices. Moreover, in September 2004, the government increased export duties on oil by 25 percent (*Prime-TASS News Agency,* September 15, 2004). These laws affecting the energy sector were designed to make taxes harder to shirk and thus would drastically alter the flow (and accumulation) of petrodollars from the oil companies to the state.

While the bulk of reform occurred by the end of 2004, refinements to the tax system continued. In 2006, the government eliminated inheritance taxes and lowered the tax rate on mineral extraction in East Siberia. It also introduced new allowances for education and health-care spending in 2006 in the personal income tax regime (*NTV Mir,* April 24, 2006). In 2007, the mineral extraction tax became somewhat differentiated according to the costs associated with oil extraction. In 2008 the government pushed through a bill offering tax holidays of up to fifteen years for newly developed oil fields in the Arctic Ocean and seven-year-maximum tax holidays for newly developed oil deposits in the Sea of Azov, in the Caspian Sea, on the Yamal Peninsula, and in the Timan-Pechora oil province (*ITAR-TASS,* July 11, 2008). The 2008 tax amendments also offered new deductions for low-income personal income taxpayers, as well as new corporate tax deductions for employee training and research and development. While the overhaul of the tax system is essentially complete, alterations to the tax codes continue; for example, for 2009 the government lowered the CIT rate to 20 percent and cut the tax rate on small businesses from 15 to 5 percent (*EIU Monthly Report,* April 2009, 5).

Fortunately for the Russian state, the new tax reforms occurred just in time to take advantage of the dramatic growth of the tax base. Since 1999, Russia has enjoyed a sustained period of high economic growth. With the real GDP growing an average of 6.7 percent per year from 1999 to 2005,[8] the tax base expanded significantly. For example, according to OECD figures, real wages grew more than 20 percent in 2001 and 2002, and continued to grow over 10 percent for four more years in a row (OECD, November 2006b, 25). In the case of personal income taxes, the introduction of Russia's 13 percent flat tax in 2001 was intended to widen the tax net by simplifying and improving tax compliance and lowering individual burden. Despite the lower rate, personal income tax (PIT) revenues increased 26 percent in real terms in the first year (Ivanova, Keen, and Klemm 2005, 399). Rabushka, a flat-tax enthusiast, reports a compound real ruble PIT revenue increase of 105.6 percent over the four years from 2001 through 2004 (Rabushka 2005). Further contributing to Russia's improved fiscal position, the reform of the profit tax corresponded with the industrial recovery beginning in 1999 and 2000. The 1998 ruble devaluation increased the competitiveness of Russian goods on domestic and world markets, thereby increasing tax receipts on corporate profits, especially in Russia's manufacturing sector (OECD 2006b, 23).

Finally, the tax base increased in the 2000s due to Russia's booming energy sector. While economists find it difficult to control for the energy sector when evaluating the impact of tax reforms on revenue growth, there is a clear consensus that the most important causes for the phenomenal increase in total economic activity are the increases in Russian oil and gas exports and the extraordinarily high world energy prices.[9] A 2005 World Bank report states, "Increasing hydrocarbon prices was perhaps the single most important [cause], and most persistent trigger for scaling up economic activity after the crisis" (38). While some transfer pricing makes precise estimates difficult, the oil and gas sector accounts for approximately 20 to 25 percent of Russian GDP (Economist Intelligence Unit 2006b, 35). According to 2006 OECD estimates, the energy sector (oil, gas, and coal) accounts for 62 percent of exports (OECD 2006b, 53, table 1 A1.5). Importantly, the Finance Ministry estimated the share of oil and gas revenues in the 2006 budget to be 52 percent (World Bank 2005). Figure 7 reports the structure of Russian exports.[10]

The overabundance of tax receipts and the persistently high world energy prices led the Putin administration to create the Russian Stabilization Fund. According to an amendment to the Budget Code in December 2003, the government became required to channel extraordinary revenues to the fund to hedge against a future drop in oil prices and subsequent budgetary deficits. According to the amendment, when the price of a barrel of Urals crude oil exceeds $20, the additional revenues from the crude oil export duty must be channeled to the Russian Stabilization Fund. The fund can only be tapped to offset budget deficits resulting from low oil prices, unless the fund exceeds 500

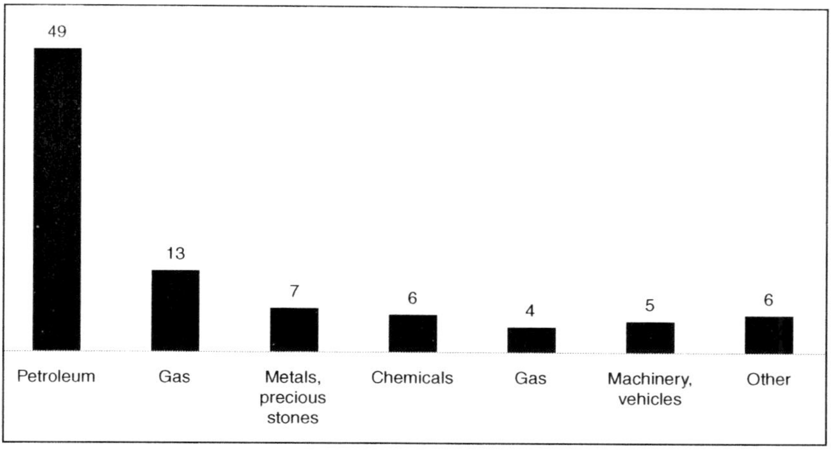


Fig. 7. Structure of Russian exports. (Data from OECD 2004b, 15.)

billion rubles. In this case, the government can agree with the Federal Assembly to draw from the fund in a formal budget law in order to repay foreign debt or to finance structural reforms (OECD 2004a, 5). Since the fund exceeded this ceiling rather quickly, the government amended the legislation such that revenues were channeled to the fund only once the price of oil exceeded $27 per barrel. Even with the revised price, the fund ballooned thanks to sustained high oil prices. The rainy-day fund grew so rapidly that in September 2006, the finance minister announced in the Duma that the government would split the fund into parts, with one part a reserve fund amounting to about 7 to 10 percent of GDP and the other part a fund for future generations. At the time of the announcement, the fund had reached 6.4 percent of GDP (*RIA Novosti,* September 22, 2006).[11] Despite these impressive efforts, the Russian government remained awash in revenues until the global financial recession hit in late 2008. According to the Ministry of Finance, the budget surplus in 2007 was 5.9 percent of GDP (*RIA Novosti,* January 17, 2008).

Given these extraordinary developments in Russian energy, it is not surprising that many credit high oil prices for Russia's fiscal recovery (Kwon 2003; Ivanova, Keen, and Klemm 2005). Certainly high oil prices and increased capacity are responsible for much of the growth of the tax base during Putin's tenure. However, it is inaccurate to attribute Russia's fiscal recovery only to oil and gas prices. Fiona Hill points out that Putin's tax reforms deserve significant credit for enabling the Russian state to capture the gains from high oil prices rather than allowing the oligarchs of the Yeltsin period to pocket the profits from the energy price surge (2004, 35). In 2000, prior to the reforms taking effect, 78 percent of the rents from improved oil and gas sales remained in the hands of the energy exporters, with the government gaining only 22 percent of the $30 billion windfall (Jones Luong and Weinthal 2004, 141). As a result of the 2004 reforms, the state linked the rate of excise taxes to world oil prices, such that if the price of oil rose above $20 per barrel (up to $25 per barrel), export duties would rise from 35 percent to 45 percent of the difference between $20 and the actual price of oil. If the price of oil surpassed $25 per barrel, the marginal duty would increase to 65 percent of the difference between $25 and the actual oil price (*Izvestiia*, October 15, 2004; *Financial Times*, March 23, 2004, 8). Given that oil prices remained above $25 per barrel after 2004, and in fact averaged $34.17 per barrel and $50.25 per barrel in 2004 and 2005 and, even more striking, $60.97 and $69.10 for 2006 and 2007, for Urals crude respectively, state coffers stayed quite flush in oil tax revenues throughout Putin's presidency.[12] Deputy finance minister Sergei Shatalov estimated in 2004 that the higher tax rates on oil would allow the government to take 96 percent of oil companies' surplus revenues. The OECD estimated in 2004 that the state would capture "about 84% of the marginal revenue from crude oil and oil products for each one dollar increase in the price of Urals crude above $25/bbl" (2006a, 5). At the time, the government explained the surge in the tax level by arguing that the oil companies would have to sacrifice in the name of social justice in order to develop Russia's other economic sectors. The higher oil taxes were also necessary to pay for the decrease in the social tax by one-third that same year (*RIA Novosti*, April 26, 2004).

These tax hikes were only possible due to the consolidation of power. By the time the legislation came to the Duma for a vote, most deputies would not oppose the government's agenda, and the tax amendments received the support of 395 out of 450 deputies. Had Putin not consolidated power and strengthened the ability of the state to reform the tax regime *and* collect the abundant revenues, the oligarchs most likely would have continued to use their personal influence and political pressure into the 2000s to capture the lion's share of oil superprofits for themselves (Appel 2008). In this sense, the depoliticization of the tax system allowed the channeling of a much larger portion of the energy superprofits to government coffers, enabling the state to afford its fiscal responsibilities.

## Depoliticizing Taxation under President Putin

Much of the depoliticization of the East European tax systems occurred because leaders were preparing for their country's entry into the European Union, which required privileging external commitments over domestic pressures. But in Russia, the impetus behind depoliticization of taxation was quite different. What accounts for the Putin administration's ability to withstand political pressures for alternative tax arrangements? How did the obligation of paying taxes become accepted by enterprise directors and regional elites?

Many factors were at play. First, the implementation of the new tax codes was facilitated by certain administrative aspects of Putin's tax reform, such as the improved training of the tax administration, the empowerment of the tax police, and the introduction of a personal tax identification number—which enabled the state to keep better tabs on taxpayers. Second, Putin revived Russia's fiscal system by strengthening the state overall.[13] He fortified the state tax apparatus and the other coercive institutions of the state, like the tax police, the regular police, and the secret service (FSB). He surrounded himself in the Kremlin with law-and-order officials whose pasts included the military, the KGB, and the police (the *siloviki*). The rise of the *siloviki* created an atmosphere of fear, which engendered greater compliance with tax laws and more modest attempts to gain special tax favors among all but a few leading companies.

Moreover, it is crucial to recognize the larger political context and the decline of democratic politics generally. The Putin administration strengthened central authority by pushing forward several initiatives to rein in the regions, such as new legislation rendering governors appointed rather than elected, allowing the president to dismiss regional governors who violated tax laws and other federal statutes, and the creation of seven superregional administrations that were led by Putin appointees. Indeed, much of Putin's first term was spent reasserting control over Russia's regions, disciplining corporate taxpayers, especially in the energy sector, and reestablishing the authority of the central government. Taxation under Putin, like under Yeltsin, was a reflection of the power of various groups in the economy—yet in the Putin case, taxation reflected the reduced power of these regional and corporate actors and the heightened power of the tax administration and the central government, with the *siloviki* populating important positions. As Richard Sakwa put it, the central goal of Putin's leadership, above all, was "state rehabilitation" (2007, 24–25).

From the perspective of the mid-1990s and the chaos of the Yeltsin years, the ability of the Putin administration to break the political stronghold of the oligarchs and assert greater central control over regional leaders is surprising. However, when Putin was elected president in the first round of the 2000 elections, he had several advantages that enabled him to consolidate power, centralize authority, and pass difficult legislation. Putin won the presidential race easily from his positions of prime minister and acting president. Quite impressively, he went from the status of an unknown bureaucrat to that of president with an 80 percent approval rating in a matter of months. This extraordinary burst of popularity came initially from his forceful response to the 1999 Chechen incursion into Dagestan and the apartment bombings throughout Russia, although Russia's favorable economic performance helped sustain his popularity in subsequent years. Putin's initial popularity not only afforded him great legitimacy and a popular mandate, it also translated into his dominance over a sympathetic and indebted legislature. After December 1999, the State Duma was dominated by Unity, the newly formed party that gained control over the lower house just three months earlier by self-identifying with the popular Putin. Thus, Putin became president with a legislature ready, if not obligated, to work with him.

Using his initial control over the legislature, the new president was able to push through institutional changes—beyond major tax reform—that cemented his dominance over the legislative branch and weakened regional actors. These changes included the ousting of governors from the upper chamber of parliament, the Federation Council, and, as noted, making governors centrally appointed instead of locally elected. Putin weakened the legislature even further by changing electoral rules that eliminated single-member district voting in favor of proportional representation. The threshold for a party to enter the legislature increased from 5 to 7 percent for subsequent elections, and no coalitions could form to overcome the threshold. The minimum turnout for elections to be valid was also eliminated. These changes strengthened large parties, which were easier for the executive branch to control than smaller parties or independent politicians.[14] Emasculating the regional governors and undercutting institutional checks by the legislative branch helped Putin's government introduce and see through an expansive set of radical energy tax reforms in 2003 to 2005—marking a decisive break from the stalled fiscal reform efforts of the previous decade.

Regional leaders at times complained about Putin's reallocation of revenues between the regions and the center in the first years of his presidency, but it was to no avail (*Nezavisimaia gazeta,* August 26, 2002; *Vedomosti,* September 17, 2003; *Gazeta,* July 14, 2003). Moreover, regional elites, watching Putin's decisive and aggressive action in the second Chechen war, must have thought twice before threatening the center with separatist intentions in order to preserve or gain tax privileges. Certainly the Chechen example helped quell any opportunistic "parades of sovereignty" for the sake of fiscal favoritism.

In a similar vein, Putin's treatment of uncooperative, noncompliant corporate elites set a discouraging example for others who might have opposed the central administration's tax agenda more aggressively. Those oligarchs who did not ascertain (quickly enough) the growing ability of the state apparatus to realize its priorities found themselves in precarious positions, as made abundantly clear by several well-known cases, like those of Boris Berezovsky and Vladimir Gusinsky. The very high profile businessmen, Gusinsky and Berezovsky, were not sufficiently deferential to the Putin agenda upon his becoming president. Rivera and Rivera describe Putin's approach then as taking "aim at the business empires and personal fortunes of several of Russia's most prominent 'oligarchs' . . . eliminat[ing] their direct or indirect influence on politics" (2006, 141). Facing criminal prosecution, Gusinsky and Berezovsky fled to Spain and Great Britain in 2000 leaving behind their media empires, NTV and ORT respectively. Their fellow oil magnate Mikhail Khodorkovsky failed to appreciate quickly enough his need to flee and abandon his plans, and thus lost his wealth and his liberty as discussed below.

## Russia's Energy Sector and Political Bargaining

In both Eastern Europe and Russia, the leadership disregarded, circumvented, or suppressed political pressures in setting tax policy. The declining status of energy sector elites and the depoliticization of taxation in Russia exemplify the government's deliberate weakening of corporate actors in the 2000s. Directors from the Russian oil companies tried to influence the government's design of the series of tax reforms, such as the tax reform linking tax rates to world prices, but with diminishing success. Some scholars describe the first wave of tax reform as a compromise between the government and the Russian oil companies. For example, based on extensive original interviews with government and energy sector insiders, Jones Luong and Weinthal characterize the new Tax Code "as a negotiated settlement" between the Russian government and the Russian oil companies in which both sides "incurred gains and losses" (2004, 140). Easter similarly describes the early period of Putin's tax reform as collaborative. He highlights the corporatist bargaining over energy tax reform in which finance minister Aleksei Kudrin met regularly with industry elites to set tax rates in 2001 and 2002 (2006a, 42).

In 2003, however, the corporatist state-business relationship fell apart over energy superprofits, at the time that the government moved to peg tax rates to world energy prices (Easter 2006a, 42). Mikhail Khodorkovsky, the chairman of the Yukos oil company, continued to pressure the government to create a more favorable energy tax regime, failing to recognize the government's will to hold its ground.[15] Easter points to the Yukos affair—namely, the arrest, prosecution, and imprisonment of the Yukos chairman and the dismemberment of the company—to demonstrate the government's new, less collaborative approach. Following Khodorkovsky's success in blocking a 2002 effort to raise oil excise taxes in the Duma, his negotiations with the China National Petroleum Corporation to build a private oil pipeline between Angarsk and Daqing, China, and his financial support of opposition parties (Easter 2006a, 45), the oil tycoon was arrested and convicted of tax evasion, privatization fraud, and illegal transfer pricing to hide oil profits (*Moskovskaia pravda,* March 28, 2005). He was sentenced to a total of nine years in a Siberian labor camp, and his company, Yukos, was required to pay back taxes and fines equaling about $33 billion (*Financial Times,* March 28, 2007; Thompson 2005). For Easter, the Yukos affair was the turning point at which the "tax system was mobilized as a coercive instrument by which the central state reasserted its dominance over the corporate elite" (2006a, 47). Boris Nemtsov and Vladimir Milov describe the Yukos affair as marking the beginning of the "tax terror" in Russia (2008, 37).

Even though Khodorkovsky was targeted substantially if not primarily for political reasons (he was funding alternative parties and civic associations), his high-profile case augmented the culture of fear and the growing deference to state authority. In this regard, the Yukos affair served as a warning to private business (Goldman 2006) and encouraged businesses to pay their tax arrears and take corporate tax obligations more seriously (Pazderka 2005; Easter 2006a, 47).

It is hard to gauge the precise effect that Khodorkovsky's imprisonment had on intimidating Putin's opponents and stifling opposition.[16] However, what is certain is that the prosecution of Russia's richest oil tycoon and the dismantling of Russia's most successful company made clear that no person or corporation was too powerful or too profitable for the state to sacrifice for the sake of consolidating power and pursuing the administration's priorities.[17] Likewise, small and midsize businesses understood that tax evasion had become much riskier. In short, despite consulting corporate actors during the revamping of the tax system from 2001 to 2002, the power dynamics between the state and business shifted, and the Putin administration became much more forceful in pursuing its agenda.

Easter writes that, beginning in 2003, "state-business bargaining over tax policy still occur[ed], but the state now dictat[ed] the terms" (2006b, 52). Richard Sakwa discussed the dismantling of Yukos and the imprisonment of Khodorkovsky in the broader context.

> The Yukos affair represented a major disciplinary act, not only ensuring the business leaders stayed out of politics, but also bringing the state back into the heart of business life. . . . The ability of political actors to act as independent agents was reduced through a not-so-subtle and at times brutal system of rewards and punishments, while the economic bases of independent political activity were systematically dismantled. (2007, 19)

Indeed, it was during the spring of 2004, with the Yukos affair developing in the background, that the government succeeded in pushing through the indexation of the oil tax system in which the oil companies' tax burden rose with the price of oil. This reform proved to be extremely important and highly favorable to the federal budget since it allowed the state to capture a much larger percentage of the rents of subsequent energy price spikes. Had the 2004 oil tax reforms failed, the state would have collected only 35 percent marginal tax on oil, rather than the 65 percent marginal tax that applied to barrels of oil selling above $25 (*Financial Times,* March 23, 2004).

In short, as Putin's authority and power grew in his first and second terms, he became much more assertive in depoliticizing and regaining control over taxation. The use of coercion not only enabled the state to collect back taxes. Putin's tougher approach, especially his treatment of the Yukos chairman, made it clear to the energy barons that countering Putin was risky and could cost them their property or their liberty. Although a handful of companies are rumored to have reached special tax arrangements through suspect means (most notably, Rosneft and Gazprom),[18] there is little doubt that most companies have been forced to accept the new tax system. Still there are some cases of regional governments negotiating special investment deals with major investors, even after eight years of Putin's presidency. However, these deals must be available to all businesses that can meet similar investment conditions, the tax savings must come out of the region's portion of the tax revenues, and ultimately these tax savings constitute a negligible portion of tax revenue when the revenues of the state are considered as a whole.[19]

Moreover, companies that seek special tax arrangements take a risk, especially if they fall out of favor with the central government. Accusations of tax fraud and tax evasion are tactics used by the Kremlin to punish disloyal businessmen, and the examples of the tax authorities using their ominous powers to harass certain businessmen or to manipulate ownership structures are legendary. The Yukos example was the most high-profile example, but there are many other prominent cases. Consider the case of Hermitage Capital, a hedge fund run by a British-American businessman, William Browder. Hermitage aggressively sought to buy shares in companies that state-owned companies sought to buy as well, which displeased the Kremlin. The Department of Tax Crime within the Interior Ministry began a formal tax fraud inquiry into Hermitage Capital, and Browder found himself unable to reenter the country (*Vedomosti,* June 26, 2007; April 28, 2007). In the case of RussNeft, its founder Mikhail Gutseriev fell out of favor with the powers that be in 2002 for trying to acquire Yukos shares, driving up the price for the state-owned Rosneft. Gutseriev too faced harassment by the federal tax authorities (*Moscow Times,* August 1, 2007, cited in Goldman 2008, 124). The years of running roughshod over the Russian leadership and public authority were over. As Putin consolidated power, the Russian state regained its autonomy from formidable actors, both regional and corporate, in setting and implementing tax policy.

The state's heightened autonomy from domestic political forces in the 2000s is only affirmed by the manner in which the additional revenues from the windfall oil profits were used. Increases in social spending and defense were easily afforded, given the large budgetary surplus.[20] Moreover, channeling the excess revenues to the Stabilization Fund, rather than using the earmarked surplus funds for social spending or tax breaks to well-connected groups or troublesome political regions, reflects the government's greater insulation from domestic politics and the weakness (and the outright suppression) of organized opposition.[21] Even when the fund doubled its 500 billion ruble minimum threshold, the government resisted the temptation to use the surplus for short-term political ends, with some minor deviation prior to the 2007 elections. For most of Putin's time in office, the government used the superprofits of the energy sector to free Russia from outside influence—paying the IMF debt in full and prepaying $15 billion of its Soviet-era Paris Club debt in 2005. In 2006, once the Stabilization Fund had nearly quadrupled the threshold amount, the Ministry of Finance decided to fund "national priority projects" and founded a $2.5 billion Investment Fund, while paying off Russia's remaining Paris Club debt in advance (Economist Intelligence Unit 2006b, 37). Although many challenged the wisdom of growing the Stabilization Fund so large, that is, before the global financial crisis of 2008, it is clear that the mighty Putin administration made this choice free from meaningful public pressure or democratic accountability. When the financial crisis hit and oil prices suddenly lost two-thirds of their value for a period in 2008, Putin's strikingly conservative fiscal approach seemed rather prescient.

## International Constraints and Tax Policy-making

Although the Russian state became more autonomous vis-à-vis domestic actors in setting tax policy, how autonomous is the Russian state from international constraints? To what extent has globalization strained Russia's tax policy-making flexibility? What international concerns does Russia share with its East European counterparts that affect the development of the tax regime? For example, how does the mobility of global finance or internationally integrated markets affect Russian tax policy-making?

On the one hand, Russia has been much freer than East European countries in designing its indirect taxes since there has been no external body promoting or requiring particular tax forms or rates.[22] Russia has not felt similar pressures and certainly has never been required to harmonize indirect taxes with existing EU members in order to pursue the foreign policy goal of EU membership. Likewise, Russia's indirect taxes are not at issue, and never have been, in negotiations with the European Union or the World Trade Organization. Although tax reform was encouraged by the IMF in the 1990s, Russia continued to receive funds even when tax reform was clearly lacking. In fact, the head of the Fiscal Affairs department at the IMF during the 1990s, Vito Tanzi, describes the lending condition of tax reform to be inconsequential for several reasons. First, tax reform was one of many conditions that had to be fulfilled for lending to continue. When tax reform was not forthcoming, the IMF simply pointed to those areas where visible progress existed, like in privatization. Second, the political pressure to continue lending, despite a lack of fiscal reform, meant that the Fiscal Affairs department had very limited leverage. Finally, Tanzi's department understood that the Russian government in the 1990s was only superficially willing and able to transform the tax system, and the IMF would simply have to accept the founding of an agency and the hanging of a plaque on the door as evidence of progress, even when the department was not convinced any reforms had occurred.[23] Even at the height of Russia's borrowing, IMF lending conditionality was essentially meaningless for Russia.

In the area of direct taxes, on the other hand, there are some commonalities between Russia and other postcommunist countries that suggest that international factors have shaped fiscal reform under Putin. Consider Russia's similar approach to personal income taxes discussed in the previous chapter. Like a dozen other countries in the region, Russia has a flat tax. But given the timing of its adoption in 2001, it is hard to argue that Russia was jumping on the bandwagon, joining international trends, or following the lead of neighboring countries. Indeed Russia was one of the earliest countries to adopt this tax form, subsequent only to the Baltic countries who had switched to a flat tax several years earlier. In other words, when it comes to the sudden succession of countries adopting a flat tax, Russia was much more of an international leader than a follower in the regional move to flatten income taxes.

The most striking similarity in tax trends between Russia and other East European countries in the area of direct taxes is the reduction of nominal corporate income tax (CIT) rates in the 2000s. Putin's government lowered the CIT rate by one-third, allowing the maximum allowable combined regional and federal rate to equal 24 percent. Moreover, as in Eastern Europe, public officials continue to stress the advantages of cutting the CIT rate further, and in 2009, a reduction of the CIT rate occurred ahead of expectations.[24]

Is Russia competing for foreign investment through its corporate tax regime, following the regional and global trend? Is the Ministry of Finance hoping a lower CIT rate will attract foreign investment? After all, the lowering of CIT is a common approach to compete for foreign investors and to encourage domestic capital to invest at home. While statements emerging from East European leaders about foreign investment are unambiguous in this regard, the formal statements by Russian government officials send mixed messages, suggesting a rather conflicted stance toward foreign investment. Contrast the statements of Czech, Polish, and Russian officials. As Agata Kudelska, an official at the Polish Agency for Information and Foreign Investment (PAIiIZ) explains, "Foreign direct investment is doubtless one of the fundamental factors of economic growth. . . . The new EU member states have been competing fiercely for such investment. If Poland wants to become a leader in this race, it has to have an attractive package of investment incentives" (*Rzeczpospolita,* December 18–19, 2004, B5). Former Czech finance minister Bohuslav Sobotka explained, "We have to take changes in the neighboring countries into account. This is why I am glad that we managed to push through the decrease of the corporate income tax despite the opposition's pressure. Investors perceive that we have a certain plan to cut down this tax. The curve is clear and it will certainly help more foreign investments to flow into the Czech Republic" (*Právo*, December 4, 2003). In contrast, the current Russian president, Dmitry Medvedev, explained at the 2007 World Economy Forum in Davos, Switzerland, that there would be no "tax concessions that would distort the rational distribution of resources in the economy. . . . Taxes should be as low as it is possible at the moment . . . and this should be the case for everyone" (*Interfax*, January 27, 2007).[25]

Formal statements notwithstanding, the slashing of the corporate tax rate suggests that Russia wants to compete for mobile foreign capital. On the other hand, the corporate tax regime exists within a larger business environment, which, in many respects, is inhospitable to foreign investment. The government has contemporaneously weakened the stability of property rights through the coercive dismantling of Yukos, through the Natural Resource Ministry's treatment of the Shell-led Sakhalin-2 oil and gas project, Russia's largest single foreign investment, and through the harassment of foreign investors. High-profile examples include the British-American director of Hermitage Capital, William Browder, and the British Petroleum CEO for the joint venture with TNK, Robert Dudley, who, along with most of his British Petroleum staff, confronted problems with the renewal of Russian work visas (*Vedomosti*, October 27, 2008; *Moscow Times*, July 18, 2008; *Financial Times*, October 10, 2006).[26] In a similar vein, the government has made clear that foreign control is not welcome in certain sectors. For example, the government has limited the exploration of new oil fields to companies that are majority-owned by Russian citizens (and who are loyal to the government—as the case of Russneft's sale demonstrates). Moreover, the Putin administration has discouraged foreign participation in industries beyond those that exploit natural resources. In May 2008, the Duma passed a new law that identified forty-two sectors in which private foreign investors could not hold a majority stake and in which state-owned foreign companies could not acquire more than a 25 percent stake without the permission of a special government commission, chaired by Putin himself. The sectors include aviation, telecoms, media, space, nuclear energy, and natural monopolies (*Moscow Times*, June 3, 2008).

Indeed, there is frequent speculation that Khodorkovsky's discussions with foreign oil companies, Chevron-Texaco and Exxon Mobile, over a potential merger with Yukos contributed to, if they did not hasten, the government's prosecution of the tycoon (*Financial Times*, October 31, 2003; August 4, 2003; *FT Investor*, December 1, 2003). Moreover, Khodorkovsky's pipeline negotiations with a Chinese public company countered the government's preference to maintain a Russian state monopoly over the energy export channels (Rutland 2005). Overall, the government has seemed intent on bolstering its control over industries it considers vital for Russia's international power and status, thereby limiting foreign involvement. In this regard, the Russian government seems to prefer state ownership over foreign or even domestic private ownership.

Recent acquisitions exemplify the state's aim of acquiring control over the commanding heights of the economy, especially in natural resources.[27] Just consider the slew of purchases by state-owned companies during Putin's second term in office: The government solidified state control of Russia's natural gas monopoly, Gazprom, through the purchase of a 10.7 percent share in July 2005 by state-owned Rosneftegaz. As a result of the purchase, the state decisively augmented its direct stake in Gazprom to 50 percent. Furthermore, Gazprom itself has repeatedly served as the vehicle to acquire shares in companies that the government considers to be in the state's strategic interest. Since 2005, Gazprom and its affiliates have purchased important stakes in OMZ (machine building); Sibneftegaz, Novatek, and Sibneft (energy); Atomstroieksport (nuclear construction); Mosenergo, Northgas, and RAO UES (power); and Izvestiia and Chas pik (media).[28] Hence, given the larger context, it is not clear that the corporate tax cuts can be interpreted as part of a broad strategy to attract foreign investment. Russia does not appear to embrace an overall strategy of opening its markets and competing for investment in a global economy as its strategy for growth, like smaller economies in Eastern Europe do. On the contrary, Putin's administration in the 2000s pursued an alternative path to economic development, more akin to France's dirigisme or Japan's industrial policy in the postwar period. In short, Russia's approach is markedly different from that of midlevel developing countries that use tax policy and other investment incentives to compete fiercely for foreign investment in order to boost domestic production.

## Russian International Autonomy

The aggressive pursuit of an economic development strategy that would increase Russia's international status and that would bolster Russian sovereignty constituted the core of Putin's agenda. As others have argued, the achievement of greater autonomy in Russia was not accidental; it was deliberate (Goldman 2008). Putin's priorities included recapturing the rents from the oil windfall to decrease public debt and to hedge against future fluctuations in world oil prices—both of which serve to maintain and augment Russia's autonomy from the global economy. This achievement is often overlooked given the enrichment of Putin insiders and the growing concentration of wealth in Russia. However, significant portions of the oil wealth were directed toward ridding Russia of foreign debt. On this point, Putin stated in 2004 that diminishing Russia's "humiliating dependency on international financial organisations" has been one of his greatest achievements (*Financial Times*, March 17, 2004).

The Putin strategy contrasts with the foreign policies and development strategies of other postcommunist European governments, who instead have displayed a dramatic willingness to relinquish control over policy-making—in tax policy and in many other areas—to foreign bodies and actors. As in many places in the world, East European leaders see foreign direct investment and increasing domestic capital as the central means to economic development. However, the structure of Russia's economy, the potential size of the domestic market, and its comparative advantage in natural resources enables the Russian state to relate to the global economy quite differently. With the world's third largest foreign exchange reserves and an external public debt that fell from 38.8 percent of GDP in 2001 to 10.8 percent in 2005, Russia's position became quite enviable. Russia's foreign exchange reserves and low foreign debt have improved private firms' access to capital in international capital markets in a way that is quite different from the access of East European firms.[29]

Is Russia thus free from many or most of the constraints and pressures of the international economy in setting tax policy and other economic policies? In short, Russia is freer than the other countries studied in this book, but certainly far from immune. The Russian economy depends heavily on world energy prices. It is this dependence that motivates the government to safeguard its newfound autonomy over policy-making, as seen with Putin's cautious and conservative use of the Stabilization Fund. The Russian government's need to create a fund to hedge against future dips in energy prices only serves to underscore how tied Russia is to global markets. Most important, the government knows it must diversify the economy to increase autonomy from world markets, and, for this reason, business-friendly taxes in the manufacturing and service sectors make sense. The Russian government's white paper, the Strategy for Social and Economic Development, specifies the government's goal to diversify the economy in the medium run in order to make growth less reliant on world energy prices. A 2005 World Bank report notes that Russia's economy is excessively dependent on exporting natural resources to the point that only

1 percent of the workforce is responsible for one-fifth of Russia's GDP (11, 18). Most likely, lowering corporate taxes ultimately stems from the need to strengthen nonenergy sectors of the economy.

Putin's success in achieving significant autonomy for the state in tax policy-making, both domestically and internationally, appears to be a function of the structure of the Russian economy, favorable international terms of trade, and, most important, the deliberate efforts of Putin to pursue greater autonomy for Russia. Putin's desire to minimize policy constraints—whether coming from within Russia or from without—informed his priorities, like regaining control over Russia's fiscal health and ridding the country of its high foreign debt. Certainly, Putin was strongly abetted by the abundance of corporate, excise, and mineral extraction taxes flowing into state coffers due to high world energy prices—but the intent to pay back the loans was very much a consequence of Putin's vision. Even within his small entourage of advisers, the majority opinion was not in favor of repaying the Western debt.[30] But policy autonomy was part of his plan to strengthen Russia.

In sum, the Putin administration revamped the tax system and increased state autonomy in policy-making vis-à-vis international and domestic forces. His administration saw through the transformation of a tax regime that, under the Yeltsin administration, could not satisfy the revenue needs of the state. A malignant fiscal system, helped substantially by oil prices, became a robust, prolific revenue-producer under Putin. Russia is more autonomous—indeed quite autonomous—from the international pressures transforming the tax regimes in the rest of postcommunist Europe (Millar 2007). So even if the government does not court investment in several sectors, it wants to create an environment in which foreigners want to invest in Russia as minority shareholders, or even majority shareholders in manufacturing sectors, which are strategically less important to the government. In sum, although Russia is not the example that demonstrates the survival of domestic politics in determining tax policy, the reasons relate primarily to eight years of Putin's governing style and national priorities, and the inability or unwillingness of his successor, President Medvedev, to reverse this antidemocratic trend. The lesson from the Russian case is that high oil prices or some other aspect of an economy, like a large domestic market, can give an individual country more autonomy; and this international autonomy may allow a state to respond closely to societal pressures or national leaders' preferences in policy-making.

## CHAPTER 7

# Globalization, Electoral Politics, and European Taxation

The myriad external constraints that discourage East European governments from responding to domestic constituents when setting certain tax policies seem much less binding for Russia's governments. An important lesson learned from the comparison of the tax experiences in Eastern Europe and Russia is that any broad statements about the impact of international economic integration on policy-making—fiscal or otherwise—need to reflect directly the varying positions of countries in the global economy. Thus, even if the trends in postcommunist Europe strongly suggest the depoliticization of key areas of taxation resulting from international economic integration, it is not at all clear whether these regional trends represent an anomaly or whether tax politics is in decline elsewhere. What country conditions or characteristics allow domestic politics more influence on taxation? Variation within the postcommunist region suggests some possible avenues to explore. For example, does domestic politics have a greater impact on taxation in large economies relative to small economies? How significant for tax policy-making is the extent of a country's reliance on foreign direct investment or its degree of openness? Likewise, how important is a country's wealth or the size of its internal market? Within the European Union, does electoral politics have a stronger impact on tax policy in West European countries than in East European ones? This chapter examines possible variables that influence a country's ability to resist some of the pressures on tax policy-making that stem from globalization, giving special consideration to the possible differences between Western EU members and the newer postcommunist members.

## Globalization, Domestic Politics, and Taxation

In order to make certain arguments about the evolution of taxation under growing regional and global integration, this book has thus far relied upon a quantitative analysis of tax trends across postcommunist Europe and qualitative case studies of individual countries. This analysis has led to two sets of observations that can be summarized as follows.

First, domestic politics has mattered little in indirect tax policy for post-communist Europe. Indirect taxes have been determined by the imperatives of international integration (especially European integration) and not by the distribution of power among political actors.

Second, corporate taxes, which are part of direct taxation, have not followed traditional party lines. Both the Left and the Right have been active in depressing corporate tax rates largely due to the global competition for mobile investment. In personal income taxes, traditional partisan politics remains important for tax outcomes, and parties have sought to advance the interests of their traditional constituents when in power. Accordingly, parties on the left have favored more progressive taxation. Parties on the right have favored less progressive taxation, and right-wing parties have been the driving force behind the spread of the flat tax in the region. This concluding chapter now examines whether these observations are supported by regression analysis conducted on a panel of East and West European countries.

## Data Description

In order to examine statistically the role of domestic politics on tax policy, an ideology index was created using the expert survey data of Benoit and Laver (2006). In the survey, Benoit and Laver construct several indices of political ideology. The index that is most relevant for tax policies is the "Spending versus Taxes" policy dimension, which considers whether a party promotes raising taxes to increase public services or instead promotes cutting public services to decrease taxes. In Benoit and Laver (2006) the index score ranges from 1 to 20 for each political party (from left to right). Thus, a party with a score of 1 takes a very left-wing position on tax matters and favors higher taxes and greater public services. A party with a score of 20 takes a very right-wing position on tax matters and prefers lower taxes and fewer services. To construct the index for each country in each year from 1995 to 2007 in my analysis, the vote share for each party in the legislature is multiplied by the Benoit and Laver party score. Because the Benoit and Laver scores are available for only one survey year, I assume that the ideological position of the same party does not change over the time period studied (1995–2007). In this way I can construct the ideological position of a country's legislature, say in 1995, using the expert survey results conducted on the positions of parties in the year 2003 and adjusting the government score according to the share of the vote each party received in the prior election.

In several instances, new parties formed and others dissolved. In these cases I had to rely upon alternative imputations. Consider first the imputation for parties that were no longer present at the time of the survey. If these parties merged into a new party, then I assign the score of the new party to each of its merging members. If the party split into new parties, then I assign the average weighted score of the new parties. Now consider the imputation for new parties formed after the survey date. For those parties resulting from the split of an existing party, I assign the score of the existing party. For the parties resulting from the merger of existing parties, I assign a score based on the weighted average of the predecessors. In very few instances, there were newly formed parties that could not be traced back to any predecessor party. In these cases I use qualitative information and assign a score equal to the party that can be considered closest to it from an ideological point of view (on fiscal matters specifically). Once I have the ideology score for all parties, countries, and years, the ideology index is constructed as the average of the party scores weighted by their voting share in the previous, most recent election. The vote share for each of the eighteen countries used in the regression analyses is assembled from multiple sources.[1]

Six types of taxes are considered: Value-Added Taxes, Capital Income Taxes, Personal Income Taxes, Social Taxes, Indirect Taxes, and Direct Taxes. For each tax, two measures were initially considered: the tax as a percentage of GDP and as a percentage of total taxation. Sixteen countries are included in the quantitative analysis, nine in Eastern Europe (Bulgaria, Czech Republic, Estonia, Hungary, Lithuania, Poland, Romania, Slovakia, and Slovenia)[2] and seven in Western Europe (Belgium, Germany, France, United Kingdom, Ireland, Italy, and Sweden). The choice is dictated by data availability. The analysis is also conducted for the adoption of Flat Income Taxes. In this case the sample includes Russia and Ukraine. Since no West European countries have adopted a flat tax, the analysis of the flat tax is limited to the eleven postcommunist countries. The data on taxation are from Eurostat 2009.

The results reported below are based on 1995–2007 data and for taxes as a percentage of total taxation. Similar findings apply when the period is limited to the 2000s (2000–2007) and when taxes are measured as a percentage of GDP. This is especially the case for the most relevant variable: ideology. The choice to report and discuss the results for taxes as a percentage of total taxation is based on the broader interest in the variation of the tax mix as a reflection of the distribution of the tax burden across different groupings. This political consideration is better captured by examining the allocation of tax revenues across different sources than by looking at its level relative to the size of the economy. Moreover, the trends in corporate taxes as a percentage of GDP have attracted some concern by economists who see inconsistencies (or a lag) in the impact of nominal corporate tax cuts (Piotrowska and Vanborren 2008). Of course, there are important limitations in using both measures of taxes, whether in terms of GDP or total taxation. Indeed a better index of the tax burden on different revenue sources would be based on implicit tax rates. Unfortunately, data on implicit tax rates are limited to fewer years and many fewer countries in Western and Eastern Europe. Ultimately, even if not ideal, these other measures (percentage of GDP and total taxation) provide some insight into the relevance of partisan politics on tax policy-making and are complete enough to submit to a simple probabilistic statistical analysis.

In addition to examining the relationship between electoral outcomes (the ideology index) and tax policy, the analysis considers various economic indicators as well. These indicators shed light upon the importance of the size of an economy, the level of development, and the trade and capital account openness of a country (which together can serve as a proxy for the degree of international economic integration). In the statistical model, the economic indicators are capital account openness, trade, foreign direct investment (inflows and outflows), the size of the economy (GDP), and the stage of development (per capita GDP). The index of capital account openness is from Chinn and Ito (2005).[3] The index is based on binary dummy variables that codify the restrictions on cross-border financial transactions reported in the IMF's *Annual Report on Exchange Arrangements and Exchange Restrictions* (AREAER). The dummy variables reflect the four major categories of restrictions: multiple exchange rates, restrictions on current account transactions, restrictions on capital account transactions, and requirements for the surrender of export proceeds. Higher numbers denote more openness to cross-border capital transactions. The other economic variables are from the World Bank "World Development Indicators."

## The Statistical Model

The model posits the following statistical relation:

$$T_{it} = c_i + \alpha I_{it} + \beta I_{it} D_{WE} + \gamma T_{-it} + \lambda X_{it} + \varepsilon_{it}$$

where $T_{it}$ is the tax variable, $c_i$ is the country fixed effect, $I_{it}$ is the logarithm of the ideology index, $D_{WE}$ is a dummy variable that takes the value of 1 for the West European countries and zero otherwise, $T_{-it}$ is the average of the tax measure in the other countries included in the sample, $X_{it}$ includes a set of economic variables (current account openness, trade/GDP, foreign direct investment as a share of GDP [inflows and outflows], the logarithm of total GDP, and the logarithm of per capita GDP). The coefficient $\alpha$ captures the association between ideology and the particular tax measure used in the left-hand side of the equation. The coefficient $\beta$ is for the interaction term between ideology and the dummy variable for Western Europe. This coefficient, if statistically significant, captures the different role that ideology plays in Eastern and Western Europe. If it is not statistically significant then there are no differences between the two regional blocs. The coefficient $\gamma$, which multiplies the average of the tax measure in the other countries included in the sample, captures the imitation effect, that is, whether countries try to mimic the tax policies of other countries.

Before presenting the results, it should be noted that the estimation simply tries to establish conditional correlations, not necessarily causation. Establishing causation is a much more difficult task that requires addressing the endogeneity of the dependent variables. Nevertheless, establishing the statistical significance of conditional correlations provides useful information about potential associations among key variables of interest, complementing the more in-depth analysis of tax policy-making conducted in earlier chapters.

## Results

Table 13 reports the summary statistics for the variables of interest. The results from the country fixed effect regression are reported in table 14. The standard error is reported in parentheses under the coefficient estimate.

### INDIRECT TAXES

For indirect taxes, the ideology variable is not statistically significant. Instead the openness index is statistically significant at the 5 percent level (.029) and is positively correlated with the level of indirect taxes as a share of total taxation. Thus, the more open a country is, the higher the level of indirect taxes as a share of total tax revenue. The variables for foreign direct investment inflows and outflows are also statistically significant at the 5 percent level (.035 and .048). The more foreign direct investment flowing into the country, the higher the level of indirect taxes is. The more foreign direct investment flowing out of a country, the lower the level of indirect taxes is.

More narrowly, if only the VAT is considered, other variables become relevant. Once again, the ideology index is not statistically correlated with the VAT as a share of total taxation. The openness of the capital account is the only variable significantly correlated with the level of VAT (at a 1 percent level, .000). Hence, the more open a country is, the greater the contribution of the VAT to total taxation. This is true for East and West European countries, which is not surprising given that they engaged in VAT harmonization quite early.

To summarize, the above findings reaffirm that domestic politics has mattered little in affecting indirect tax policies. Instead, variables related to regional and global economic integration seem to have a greater significance. As discussed below, the results in direct taxes are quite different.

### DIRECT TAXES

For direct taxes, the ideology index is statistically significant at the 1 percent level (.007). The more right-wing politicians elected to parliament, the greater is the contribution of direct taxes as a share of total taxation. If I disaggregate direct taxes by personal income taxes and corporate income taxes, the ideology variable remains statistically significant in both cases.

For corporate income taxes, the ideology index is statistically significant at the 1 percent level (.004) and is negatively correlated with the share of corporate taxes within total tax revenues. Hence, lower corporate taxes are associated with left-wing governments. This result is compatible with the observation in chapter 4 that the declines in corporate tax levels that occurred when the Right was in power were not undone when the Left took power, and, in fact, the Left

**TABLE 13. Summary Statistics**

| Variable | Number of Observations | Mean | Standard Deviation | Minimum | Maximum |
|---|---|---|---|---|---|
| Indirect taxes | 201 | 0.3797 | 0.0532 | 0.290 | 0.584 |
| VAT | 201 | 0.2024 | 0.0545 | 0 | 0.374 |
| Direct taxes | 201 | 0.2974 | 0.0803 | 0.169 | 0.466 |
| PIT | 201 | 0.2040 | 0.0716 | 0.081 | 0.343 |
| CIT | 201 | 0.7165 | 0.0287 | 0.013 | 0.150 |
| Social | 201 | 0.3252 | 0.0803 | 0.13 | 0.443 |
| Flat tax | 143 | 0.2517 | 0.4355 | 0 | 1 |

maintained or further reduced corporate tax obligations. That said, the relevance of the ideology index is region specific. If I run the regression with only the nine postcommunist countries in the sample, then the ideology index becomes significant only at the 10 percent level, and the significant variables become GDP and per-capita GDP. The bigger economies in Eastern Europe rely more on corporate taxes, but richer economies rely less on corporate taxes. If only the seven West European countries are included in the regression from 1995 to 2007, the only variable significant at the 10 percent level is the openness index. The less open a country is, the more it relies on corporate taxes.

For personal income taxes, the ideology index is significant at the 5 percent level (.019). Accordingly, the better the right-wing parties performed in the previous election, the higher is the contribution of personal income taxes to total taxation. The other variable that is statistically significant (at the 1 percent level, .005) is the average personal income tax rate of other countries in the sample of eighteen European countries. This is hard to interpret since it is negatively correlated.[4]

**TABLE 14. Indirect and Direct Taxes**

| Variable | Indirect Taxes | VAT | Direct Taxes | Personal Income | Corporate Income | Social Taxes | Flat Tax |
|---|---|---|---|---|---|---|---|
| Ideology | –.0075 | .0120 | .0806*** | .0519** | .486*** | –.0626** | .8169*** |
| | (.0244) | (.0257) | (.0297) | (.0220) | (.0165) | (.0247) | (.3080) |
| Imitation | –.0399 | –.0810 | .0419 | –.5322*** | –.1733 | .4016* | 1.3133*** |
| | (.2622) | (.1591) | (.2144) | (.1848) | (.2098) | (.2232) | (.2904) |
| Openness | .0053** | .0150*** | –.0015 | .0015 | –.0029* | –.0042* | .0690* |
| | (.0024) | (.0025) | (.0030) | (.0022) | (.0016) | (.0024) | (.0398) |
| Trade | –.000001 | .0002 | .0002 | 2.25e-06 | .0002 | –.0002 | –.0033 |
| | (.0002) | (.0002) | (.0002) | (.0002) | (.0001) | (.0002) | (.0027) |
| FDI inflow | .0613** | .0449 | –.0263 | –.0208 | –.0144 | –.0426 | .0432 |
| | (.0288) | (.0300) | (.0345) | (.0258) | (.0192) | (.0285) | (.9034) |
| FDI outflow | –.0601** | –.0452 | .0472 | .0382 | .0212 | .0210 | .3050 |
| | (.0301) | (.0313) | (.0362) | (.0270) | (.0201) | (.0298) | (.7331) |
| GDP | –.1097 | .1180 | –.1077 | –.1363* | .0325 | .0032 | –.2485 |
| | (.0913) | (.0595) | (.1028) | (.0808) | (.0554) | (.0813) | (2.8963) |
| GDP/capita | .1396 | –.0832 | .1431 | .0210 | .0095 | .0081 | .0769 |
| | (.0939) | (.0986) | (.1095) | (.0836) | (.0596) | (.0882) | (2.7008) |
| EU ideology | .0082 | –.0300 | –.0884 | –.0590 | –.0370 | .0717 | (dropped) |
| | (.0487) | (.0505) | (.0583) | (.0436) | (.0326) | (.0482) | |
| Constant | .9352** | –.3971 | –.3444 | .9311** | –.1593 | .2628 | –.4986 |
| | (.4164) | (.4579) | (.5255) | (.4141) | (.2715) | (.4078) | (13.6401) |

*Note:* Standard errors are in parentheses underneath the coefficient estimates.
***significant at 1 percent; **significant at 5 percent; *significant at 10 percent.

## FLAT INCOME TAXES

In order to examine the importance of the ideology variable for the adoption of the flat tax, only postcommunist countries are included in the sample. Russia and Ukraine are added to the sample since data on flat taxes are also available for these two additional countries. In this regression, the ideology index is significant at the 1 percent level (.009). According to the data from 1995 to 2007, the more votes the right-wing parties won in the previous election, the more likely the flat tax is adopted. This is consistent with the qualitative analysis in chapter 5 and is consistent with the regression analysis of Baturo and Gray (2009) discussed in the same chapter. The other variable that is statistically significant at the 1 percent level (.000) is the number of other countries employing the flat tax. In other words, the more countries that have adopted the flat tax, the more likely it is that a country adopts the flat tax. No other variables are statistically significant except the openness of the economy, but only at the 10 percent level (.08).

To summarize, the second finding from the fixed-effect regression partially confirms the hypothesis about direct taxation. In personal income taxes, traditional partisan politics remains significant for tax outcomes. In corporate taxes, partisan politics proves significant, but not in the way one might have expected. Before running the regressions, a natural hypothesis based on the case studies was that the ideology index would not prove statistically significant. Instead, the variable is statistically significant, but it comes out negative. Hence politics matters, just not traditional partisan politics. The most natural interpretation of the results is that the Left embraced—and then more aggressively advanced—the traditional right-wing approach to taxation (which sees high corporate taxes as depressing economic activity).

Given the availability of the data, it was also possible to examine a third major category of revenue: taxes or fees for social programs.

## SOCIAL TAXES

Although this was not analyzed in other areas of the book, it is interesting to consider which variables correlate with the percentage contribution of social taxes to total tax revenues. The ideology index is significant at the 5 percent level (.012). The more votes the left-wing parties receive, the higher the level of social taxes as a share of total revenues. The level of social taxes in other countries is also significant at the 10 percent level (.074), as is a country's degree of openness (.079). Hence, countries are weakly following the trends in other countries, and more-open countries have lower levels of social taxes.

One way to interpret the negative association between openness and lower social taxes is that countries may try to reduce the cost of labor in order to attract foreign capital. In fact, from an economic point of view, many of the most common social taxes are effectively taxes on labor income. Irrespective of whether they are paid by employers or employees, they ultimately increase the effective cost of labor. One strategy to attract foreign capital is to reduce the cost of labor, and some governments may consider this strategy more effective than reducing the corporate tax burden. Moreover, since many investment incentives and corporate tax holidays are forbidden by the European Union (as discussed in chapter 4), lowering social taxes to reduce the tax wedge remains a possible strategy for attracting investment after joining the EU.

### EASTERN VERSUS WESTERN EUROPE

Each regression discussed above also considers the interaction between the ideology variable and the dummy for Western Europe. The dummy variable captures whether the ideology index mattered differently for East European countries and West European countries. According to the regression results, ideology does not seem to matter more in the seven West European countries than it does in the nine postcommunist European countries. Only in the separate regressions run for corporate taxes is the ideology index for Western Europe statistically different from Eastern Europe (dropping out for the former but remaining significant for the latter—albeit at the 10 percent level). In the regressions run separately for each region in the other tax areas, the ideology index does not change meaningfully. That is, if it is significant for one region, it remains significant for the other. In sum, there does not seem to be a significant difference in the way ideology shapes tax policy in Eastern and Western Europe, with the exception of corporate taxes. Although not reported here, I also estimated the equation presented above using implicit taxes on corporate incomes. As noted above, this is clearly a better indicator of the tax burden of corporations overall. However, too much of the data was missing, and the findings were inconclusive.

## The Politics of East European Taxation

It is surprising that postcommunist Europe does not differ more from Western Europe according to the results of the analysis. The most likely reason for the similarity of the tax mix (and the similar influence of electoral politics on taxation) is that the postcommunist countries looked to Western Europe when designing many areas of taxation long before the accession process began, as discussed in chapters 2 and 3. Some scholars of the region have noted a related reason, namely, that many of the consultants who advised in the early years of setting up new tax systems in Eastern Europe came from the United States and Europe (via the multilateral financial institutions). These foreign consultants in conjunction with local politicians succeeded in presenting taxation as a technical matter that should be sheltered from politics (Bonker 2007; Easter 2009). As chapter 2 notes, the IMF, the OECD, and the European Community cofunded and coordinated many groups of foreign tax consultants based on a common agreement on the main principles of tax systems (Easter 2009). These consultants drew from past models and agreed-upon "best practices"—which they could not necessarily do in other areas of economic reform like privatization, since there was no template for large-scale, economy-wide privatization (Bonker 2007).

Why did postcommunist leaders so fully yield to foreign consultants and EU treaties? Indeed, their willingness to import large tracts of fiscal legislation, and essentially relinquish control over many economic areas, is surprising and difficult to explain. The same question might be posed to older EU members whose citizens have long accepted the authority of external regional organs in setting indirect and some direct tax policy. Yet the West Europeans helped develop the common fiscal approaches at the supranational level, whereas the East Europeans simply absorbed them. Why would newly elected East European leaders be so willing to disregard the concerns of their traditional domestic constituents and adopt particular tax structures in response to external imperatives?

The most straightforward explanation would rely on the leaders' perception of the electorate's hierarchy of values and preferences and the leaders' understanding of the sacrifices required to advance these preferences. Because the majority of postcommunist European citizens wanted to join the European Union, most politicians did not want to assume responsibility for postponing or thwarting membership. Ultimately, politicians were willing to make many sacrifices and surrender policy-making control in order to achieve this goal. Popular support for EU membership remained high, and democratically accountable politicians recognized the cost of failing to achieve full membership.

From a larger perspective, the move to join Europe extends far beyond the political calculations of leaders hoping to be reelected. East Europeans were determined to join the European Union for multiple overlapping reasons. For some, the appeal of membership was economic. They expected that the material benefits of joining the EU exceeded the expected costs and sacrifices to policy autonomy. On a material level, the possibility for individuals to travel and work abroad and the opportunities for businesses to trade and invest more freely were broadly attractive. Furthermore, workers in depressed regions or struggling industries anticipated structural funds, and national governments looked forward to cash infusions into their budgets and hoped for new investments on their territory. Granted, the high expectations of significant economic transfers were not always met, and many complained that the EU had been more generous in previous rounds of enlargement. For example, there was widespread disappointment that the Common Agricultural Policy offered less beneficial terms to new members than to existing members. Nonetheless, new resources flowed in that would otherwise have been unavailable. EU membership was materially advantageous, and for many it justified the necessary compromise of policy sovereignty.

For others, the appeal of EU membership (and the willingness to make the necessary sacrifices to achieve this goal) related to the desire to reorient the country away from the Russian sphere toward Europe and the West. This reorientation mattered first on the level of national security, as Czech president Václav Havel made clear (*ČTK Newswire*, June 12, 2003). The East European experience within the Soviet bloc in the postwar period, especially in those countries that experienced violent conflict during the Cold War, like Hungary in 1956, Czechoslovakia in 1968, and Poland in 1953, expected to find greater security by joining Western bodies, like NATO and the EU. The security advantages in the case of NATO membership were straightforward since membership required that all members defend each other in case of attack. Yet even the EU offered some security dividend in that greater economic integration and economic interdependence would alter the security calculations of East European adversaries.

Finally, the loss of policy sovereignty required for EU membership may have been made more acceptable by prevailing ideas on national identity. For some East Europeans, reorienting the country toward the West and becoming members of Europe were akin to returning to one's rightful place in the heart of Europe. Joining the European Union was part and parcel of cementing a postcommunist, European identity (Holy 1996, 202; Appel 2004). The Czech case demonstrates this especially clearly. This desire to join Europe and break with its past was made explicit in the slogan "Return to Europe," which was the leading slogan of all of Civic Forum in the June 1990 elections. A pro-European stance was a popular position to take among numerous politicians, and many politicians incorporated "Europeanizing" elements in their policy proposals.

The widely held belief that the Czechs—or the Poles or the Hungarians, for that matter—constituted a European nation that had been artificially separated from this region for over four decades mattered for the evolution of the fiscal system by precluding proposals that would erect tax structures incompatible with West European neighboring countries. A prevailing European identity led policy elites to sacrifice policy autonomy and adopt structures compatible with, or identical to, European structures as a means of asserting one's identity and enabling one's membership in the community of European states.

In short, the desire to join the European Union and the willingness to adopt vast EU tax codes resulted from an overlap of economic benefits, security advantages, and a prevailing national identity. Outside Europe there may very well be no parallel examples where so many countries voluntarily adopted such large bodies of legislation wholesale. EU enlargement emerged within a remarkable convergence of economic, security, and historical supporting factors. It is questionable whether such conditions could once again emerge in another region of the world that would lead to such a great sacrifice of economic sovereignty and so many concessions in policy-making.

All of these factors causing East European leaders and citizens to privilege external considerations over domestic political preferences in tax policy explain only those areas covered by EU treaties, most notably indirect taxation. Direct taxation is only partly constrained by EU treaties. In areas outside the EU competence, the West and East face similar global constraints and imperatives that help to explain similarities in taxation as seen in the regression analysis above. Global pressures affect how governments tax labor, capital, and corporate profits. As noted, newer and older EU members alike are concerned with attracting investment and want to perform well in the interregional and intraregional competition for capital. Especially for smaller states, global pressures can be quite significant and contribute importantly to growing similarities in economic policy.

Furthermore, policy officials do not design economic policy in isolation. As chapter 5 argues, politicians pay attention to the policy experiments of their counterparts abroad. They seek out new ideas and strategies to solve common problems or to cope with similar constraints. The result in the regression analysis that countries are more likely to adopt a flat tax when more countries already have a flat tax (the imitation variable) lends support to theories of the transnational diffusion of policy ideas and policy bandwagoning (Ikenberry 1990; Eichengreen 2001; Weyland 2005; Orenstein 2008). While the findings in corporate income tax did not prove statistically significant in this study, the case studies in chapter 4 suggest a similar logic at work in the downward movement of corporate taxes. On the level of political rhetoric, certainly, politicians in Eastern Europe have repeatedly referred to the tax regimes of other countries in justifying lower corporate income taxes at home. The relevance of policy bandwagoning theories in the international decline of corporate income taxes should be explored further, perhaps even on a global scale, in future research.

The analysis of the impact of domestic politics on taxation deserves repeating in other regions where countries participate in alternative regional arrangements. The similarities found between Eastern and Western Europe may very well be replicated in comparative studies of Latin America and Asia, depending on how individual countries participate in the global economy and the structure of their domestic economies. As noted in chapter 6, countries participate in the global economy in multifaceted ways. Thus, leaders in some countries will maintain greater fiscal policy autonomy despite the powerful constraints of globalization given their special positions in the international economy and given the prevailing terms of trade, as the Russian case shows. It is likely that other oil-rich countries will maintain greater autonomy in tax policy such that corporate taxes or labor taxes are less reflective of the competition for foreign direct investment. Perhaps for this reason the tax systems in major OPEC countries do not resemble the tax systems of other wealthy countries. In Saudi Arabia, for instance, the most common tax forms are not levied; there is no sales tax, income tax, property tax, inheritance tax, or municipal tax for Saudi citizens and nationals. Instead, Saudis pay a religion-based wealth tax (a *zakat* of 2.5 percent of assets) and some limited corporate taxes, excise taxes, and import duties (like an excise tax on tobacco). Most significant, Saudi oil accounts for 75 percent of tax revenues (Cheminigui and Lofgren 2004, 2). The tax systems in the largest economies, like the United States, Japan, and China, also suggest that some countries are rule makers rather than rule takers in the international economy. Further investigation of the conditions and characteristics of a wide range of countries in the global economy will help scholars understand the role of domestic politics in fiscal policy-making in the twenty-first century and the continuing possibility for democratic politics to remain meaningful under conditions of deepening international integration.

# Notes

## Chapter 1

1. The value-added tax is a form of sales tax based on the value a producer adds to a product over the course of its production. Excise duties are taxes paid on a narrow set of goods typically on a per-unit basis (rather than proportionate to the value of the good). Excise duties typically intend to discourage the consumption of a good or pay for the externalities associated with the consumption of a good. Common examples include the taxes on alcohol, tobacco, and gasoline.

2. Interview with Pavel Mertlík, Prague, May 29, 2002.

3. The three common acronyms found in this book are PIT, CIT, and VAT. PIT is short for personal income tax, which is the tax paid by individuals on their income, like their salaries. CIT refers to corporate income tax, which is a tax on corporate profits. Finally, VAT stands for value-added tax. A value-added tax is a type of sales tax that is based on the value a producer adds to a product over the course of its production. For consumers, it is a kind of sales tax that they indirectly pay on goods and services. Separate chapters are devoted to each of these tax areas.

4. Campbell is an exception, who avoids data limitations by developing small case studies on fiscal deficits to shed light upon the issues. He asks whether global pressures or domestic political institutions and attitudes toward deficits in particular better explain neoliberal fiscal reforms after communism. He argues that politics and political institutions refract global pressures and account for a variation in deficit spending in Poland, Hungary, and the Czech Republic over the 1990s (2001a).

## Chapter 2

1. All calculations are based on data from European Bank for Reconstruction and Development for years 1990, 1991, and 1992 (EBRD 2000, 4).

2. According to a World Bank publication, the level of arrears reached 27.7 percent of Russia's total public-sector wages in March 1997 (World Bank 1998, 6).

3. For a breakdown of unemployment benefits by country over the 1990s, see Vodopivec, Wörgötter, and Raju 2005, table 2.

4. This figure is based on author's calculations from World Bank data. For data on Bulgarian privatization receipts, see http://www.worldbank.org/ecspf/PSD-Yearbook/bulgaria.html (accessed June 1, 2009).

5. Interview with Vito Tanzi, Washington, DC, June 4, 2008.

6. On civil service reform in Poland and Russia, see Berenson 2006, chapter 3; Berenson 2010.

7. Interview with Stoyan Aleksandrov, Sofia, August 14, 2007.

8. Interview with Stoyan Aleksandrov, Sofia, August 14, 2007.

9. Interview with Vito Tanzi, Washington, DC, June 4, 2008.

10. Interview with Vito Tanzi, Washington, DC, June 4, 2008.

11. Interview with Vito Tanzi, Washington, DC, June 4, 2008.

12. In his memoirs on his time working in postcommunist fiscal reform, Tanzi acknowledges the hurdles to reform created by conflicting interpretations of the most basic tax concepts, like income. Vito Tanzi, Unpublished memoirs, 2008.

13. The theoretical literature on tax illusions is extensive, developed and popularized by James Buchanan (1967), Anthony Downs (1957), and Richard Wagner (1976), and more recently by John Cullis and Philip Jones (1992).

14. This added value is measured by the price at which a producer sells his output minus the price he paid for his inputs.

15. For example, in one study on the distributional impact of the VAT rates on the Czech and Slovak poor, Heady and Smith concluded that increasing the lower rate would burden poorer citizens more in proportion to their income, even though richer citizens would face the greatest absolute increases. The micro household data showed that the burden was especially acute for pensioners and single parents (1995, 33).

## Chapter 3

1. As seen in table 5, indirect taxes can be on par with, and sometimes smaller than, social security payments. That said, some experts do not formally categorize all social payments as taxes, since the level of benefits received can depend on the amount an individual has contributed, as in pension programs.

2. This added value is measured by the price at which a producer sells his output minus the price he paid for his inputs. France was the first country in Europe to introduce a VAT in 1954.

3. These special tariff regimes for certain North African and Middle Eastern countries are negotiated for twelve-year periods, must be ratified by the EU member states, and are compatible with WTO stipulations. See European Commission, Euro-Med Association Agreements Implementation Guide, Relex F, Brussels, July 30, 2004. http://ec.europa.eu/external_relations/euromed/docs/asso_agree_guide_en.pdf (accessed April 20, 2010).

4. The European Neighbourhood Policy, a program initiated in 2004, applies to many countries in the Euro-Mediterranean Association Agreements but also extends to several postcommunist countries like Armenia, Azerbaijan, Belarus Moldova, and Ukraine (but not Russia). Special trade and political regimes are negotiated bilaterally between the European Commission and the neighboring country.

5. Interview with Oleksiy Balabushko, Kiev, July 24, 2009.

6. See European documents at http://ec.europa.eu/enlargement/archives/enlarge

ment_process/future_prospects/negotiations/eu10_bulgaria_romania/chapters/chap_10_en.htm (accessed February 25, 2008).

7. For the text of the directive, see http://eur-lex.europa.eu/LexUriServ/LexUriServ.do?uri =OJ:L:2006:347:0001:0118:EN:PDF (accessed February 25, 2008).

8. For further details see European Commission, Taxation and Customs Union. "How VAT Works." http://ec.europa.eu/taxation_customs/taxation/vat/how_vat_works/index_en.htm.

9. European Commission, Taxation and Customs Union. "How VAT Works." http://ec.europa.eu/taxation_customs/taxation/vat/how_vat_works/index_en.htm.

10. In table 7, as the final column with data from 2004 demonstrates, Russia is less reliant on VAT for overall revenues for several reasons. As discussed extensively in chapter 6, the Russian tax structure relies heavily on energy-related taxes, especially export duties and the mineral extraction tax. Second, post-Soviet Russia has continued to rely heavily on taxing large enterprises (Gehlbach 2008). Finally, and most important for this chapter, Russia's indirect tax regime has evolved without consideration of EU directives.

11. Interview with László Kékesi, deputy state secretary at the Hungarian Ministry of Finance, Budapest, June 13, 2002.

12. Kopstein and Reilly write that it is not membership per se that accounts for the adoption of "institutions similar to the EU" but the anticipation of membership (2001, 25).

13. Interview with Václav Klaus, Claremont, California, January 17, 2001.

14. Interview with Pavel Telika (chief negotiator for the Czech Republic), Claremont, California, April 18, 2005.

15. As one negotiator explained, "With this 57 percent rule, it is almost double [the] price and it is quite sensitive for the politicians to say [to their constituents] now you will have cigarettes double [the] price." Interview with Tomáš Kuirek (Mission of the Czech Republic to the EU), Brussels, June 28, 2002.

16. See the report by Jan Truszczynski, Poland's chief negotiator during EU accession (2002, 9).

17. For a summary of the reports, see the archives for the Czech Republic at the official EU Web site: http://europa.eu/legislation_summaries/taxation/e10107_en.htm (accessed October 8, 2008).

18. Interview with Alain Bothorel (counselor, Delegation of the European Commission to Hungary), Budapest, June 14, 2002.

19. Interview with Pavel Mertlík, former Czech finance minister, Prague, May 29, 2002.

20. Interview with Václav Klaus, Claremont, California, January 17, 2001.

21. Magyar Nemzet, quoted in Kopstein and Reilly 2000, note 44, 27.

## Chapter 4

1. That is, an increasing tax burden may be hidden by a decreasing tax base.

2. Justifying the availability of effective tax-rate data for only 19 OECD countries, the 2007 report explains, "The definition involves a vast range of legislation covering everything from allowances for capital expenditures, to the deductibility of contributions to pension reserves, the valuation of assets and inventories and the extent to which different expenses can be deducted" (OECD 2007a, 24).

3. OECD 2000, 127.

4. An OECD report characterizes the exemptions associated with Poland's corporate income taxes as "generous." Poland has "more than 40 investment allowances, 63 depreciation schedules, and investors enjoy 5–10 years of tax holidays in 17 Special Economic Zones." OECD 2000, 127.

5. European Commission, DG XXI, *Final Report: Structures of the Tax Systems in Estonia, Poland, Hungary, the Czech Republic, and Slovenia* (Reference Contract XXI/99/801, 2000).

6. OECD 2000, 123, figure 33.

7. Cited in and translated by Paczynska (2009).

8. European Commission 2000, DG XXI, *Final Report.*

9. OECD 2007b Statistics.

10. It should be noted that shareholders did not pay an additional tax on these dividends since 20 percent of the profits were withheld by the company, primarily as a way to improve compliance.

11. Interview with Gabor Kiss, Hungarian Central Bank, Budapest, June 13, 2002. One Hungarian tax specialist in the Ministry of the Economy went so far as to describe Hungary as a tax haven for corporations. Interview with Tamás Révész, Ministry of Economy, Budapest, June 17, 2002.

12. Hungary offers more nonstandard deductions to taxpayers than in neighboring states, however. Whereas Poland and the Czech Republic provide tax allowances for mortgage interest payments, charitable donations, and home improvement, in Hungary, additional nonstandard deductions and credits include employee contributions to mutual pension or health insurance, life insurance, certain income from intellectual activities, charitable contributions, investments in certain qualifying securities, mortgage interest payments, and savings for home mortgages, among others (Martinez-Serrano and Patterson 2003, 42–43).

13. OECD 2000, 123, figure 33. For comparative purposes, in the UK, 75 percent of taxpayers fall in the middle bracket (22 percent) with the remaining taxpayers divided nearly evenly between the lowest (10 percent) and highest (40 percent) brackets (Heimann 2001, 56).

14. KPMG, "Tax Rates: EU Accession Countries" (2003), www.kpmg.com.

15. As a share of total taxation, consumption taxes equaled 40.3 percent in 1995, 39 percent in 2000, 40 percent in 2004, and 38.9 percent in 2005 (OECD 2007).

16. European Commission 2000, DG XXI, *Final Report,* and OECD 2007b.

17. European Commission 2000, DG XXI, *Final Report,* and OECD 2007b.

18. The drop in CIT rates resulting from the 2007 reform package would coincide

with the introduction of a flat personal income tax. It is unclear the effect this has had since a shift in income classification may occur due to tax optimization efforts.

19. Fico stated that his government would consider the lower rate for textbooks and the Internet in the future (*ČTK Business Newswire,* April 23, 2007).

20. Interview with Alain Bothorel, EU Delegation in Hungary, Budapest, June 14, 2002.

21. More details are found in "EU Dreams Force Polish Evolution," *International Tax Review* 10, no. 10 (November 1999), 13–14.

22. For a full description of tax incentives, see chapter 3 on investment incentives of PriceWaterhouseCoopers Report entitled "Doing Business in Hungary," http://www.pwcglobal.com/hu/eng/ins-sol/business/main/ins_chp3.html (accessed June 4, 2002).

23. The EU appeared willing to increase the tax incentives allowed in order to close the chapter with Poland. For instance, one compromise under discussion was to increase the allowable tax break to equal 75 rather than 50 percent of the value of the investment. For more detail, see Piotr Apanowicz, "Polska-UE Problem specjalnych stref ekonomicznych coraz bliżej rozwiązania" Warsaw ["Problem of special economic zone closer solution more"], *Rzeczpospolita,* June 17 2002; "Porozumienie w polowie drogi" ["Meeting halfway"], *Rzeczpospolita,* April 12, 2002; Rząd i firmy chcą porozumienia" ["The Government wants to reach an agreement"], *Rzeczpospolita,* May 15, 2002. Interview with Warsaw University professor and adviser to the deputy minister of finance, Hanna Litwinczuk, June 28, 2002.

24. Squire, Sanders, & Dempsey L.L.P., "EU State Aid (Slovak Republic)," October 2003. http://www.ssd.com/files/tbl_s29Publications/FileUpload5689/8559/EUStateAid01.pdf (accessed July 8, 2009).

25. *International Tax Review,* "EU Dreams Force Polish Evolution," *International Tax Review* 10 (November 1999): 19–20.

26. Interview with Pavel Mertlík, Prague, May 29, 2002.

27. In Poland the state sought to keep inflation low by imposing limits on wage growth (relative to the inflation rate). Until 1992, the Solidarity-led government taxed companies that allowed wages to grow beyond the state-controlled level.

28. European Commission 2000, DG XXI, *Final Report.*

29. The report continues, "A growing body of evidence now points to a strong negative effect of high labour taxes on the level of employment and growth in Europe" (Commission of the European Communities 1997, 3).

30. Structures of the Taxation Systems in the European Union: Data 1995–2002, European Communities, 2004.

31. For example, Garrett and Mitchell (2001) seek to counter the position expressed by globalization critics, like Rodrik (1997), who portend the end of the welfare state, at least in its current form, as governments find themselves increasingly unable to afford past welfare commitments. Winner (2005) does find evidence to support the "race to the bottom" thesis: namely, that globalization drives down corporate income tax rates. Winner (2005) finds that capital mobility has depressed capital tax rates and increased the effective tax rate on labor income.

32. Personal interviews with the two finance ministers most directly involved in tax reform and accession in Poland and the Czech Republic left me with the impression that they wholly supported the direction that the EU was taking them in fiscal reform. Interview with Leszek Balcerowicz, Warsaw, June 27, 2002; interview with Pavel Mertlík, Prague, May 29, 2002.

## Chapter 5

1. Serbia's flat tax applies a single tax rate on labor income. That said, Serbia's PIT is not strictly flat in that the tax codes apply an additional tax on the sum of income from all sources above a threshold, although the threshold is very high (Keen, Kim, and Varsano 2006, 5).

2. The Czech 15 percent flat tax rate is less straightforward than that of other countries since the rate quite exceptionally includes social security benefits in the calculation of the base.

3. Jamaica and Bolivia have had a flat tax since 1986, and Hong Kong since 1947. On non-Soviet cases, see Alm and Wallace 2004; Keen, Klemm, and Ivanova 2005; Keen, Kim, and Varsano 2006; Mitchell 2007.

4. Rabushka maintains a blog on flat taxes. See http://flattaxes.blogspot.com.

5. A *Laffer effect* here refers to a boost in revenues that follows from a lower tax rate. This effect is based on insights from the work of Arthur Laffer, who theorized that as tax rates rise beyond an optimal point, revenues will fall since the disincentive to work becomes very strong.

6. Dissenters include Gaddy and Gale (2005, 988).

7. For country-specific data, see figure 1, Keen, Kim, and Varsano 2006, 6, 13. The authors of this study note that in the cases of Latvia and Lithuania, the flat tax rate was set at the highest marginal tax rate prior to reform.

8. Speech by Mart Laar, CEPOS Copenhagen Flat-tax Conference, online video stream: http://www.cepos.dk/cms/index.php?id=138 (accessed July 11, 2007). For the ideological and partisan orientations of parties in Ukraine, see Kuzio 2005; Krauchuk 2005; Anieri 2005.

9. Interview with Ardo Hansson in "Talking Taxes: A City Paper Interview with Ardo Hansson," *City Paper*, http://www.balticsww.com/news/features/talking_taxes.htm (accessed July 11, 2007).

10. Eurostat: 1995–2004 and Ministry of Finance of Estonia (http://www.fin.ee/?id=621, accessed June 15, 2009).

11. Laar writes, "After the introduction of the flat tax, revenues of the state budget in Estonia started to increase very quickly. The Estonian state-budget moved rapidly to a surplus of more than 10 percent and it became necessary to pass two supplementary budgets during one year." Mart Laar, *The Small Country That Could*, http://www.idee.org/cubalaar.html (accessed July 10, 2007). Also see Laar 2002.

12. The exception was that some areas became untaxed, like dividends, inheritance,

gifts, and real estate transfers, with the stated goal of ending double taxation. Otherwise the 19 percent rate applied. Also, excise taxes followed EU codes and were not part of the reform program.

13. These goals were specified in the Program Declaration of the Slovak Government, 2002. Also see Mikloš, Jakoby, and Morvay 2005.

14. Interview with Martin Bruncko, Bratislava, May 17, 2007.

15. This assessment should be taken with a grain of salt certainly—since it was also repeated that strong leftist economists are a contradiction in terms.

16. On Slovak unions, see Malová and Rybář 2005.

17. On the role of experts from particularly influential NGOs (MESA 10, INEKO, F. A. Hayek Foundation, and IVO), see Fisher, Gould, and Haughton 2007; Mathernová and Renčko 2006; Fisher 2006.

18. Interview with Ivan Mikloš, Bratislava, May 18, 2007.

19. Foreign companies already avoided taxes on dividends according to EU laws by establishing parent companies in the Netherlands (*ČTK*, April 28, 2006).

20. Interview with Martin Barto (National Bank of Slovakia), Bratislava, May 17, 2007.

21. There are challenges in the Baltic countries to the flat tax that ultimately fail.

22. In the March 2003 Budget Committee, there were 17 members from United Ukraine, 12 members from Our Ukraine, 2 members from the Communist Party, 2 members from the Social Democrats, 1 from Yulia Tymoshenko's bloc, and 3 nonaffiliated members of parliament

23. I would like to thank Edward Rakhimkulov of the Ukrainian Parliamentary Development Project for providing insight into the Ukrainian story. Interview with Edward Rakhimkulov, Kyiv, Ukraine, July 23, 2009.

24. The former finance minister of the NMS2 (the right-wing, ex-King Simeon's party) stated, "The adoption of a flat tax on income has to happen gradually, starting with 9 and 19% and eventually reaching its final version." *Pari,* May 19, 2005. Also see *Pari,* May 11, 2005; May 18, 2006.

25. Interview with Svetla Kostadinov, Sofia, August 13, 2007, and with Gyorgy Angelov, Sofia, August 13, 2007.

26. Interview with Kristina Karagyozova (National Bank of Bulgaria), Sofia, August 15, 2007.

27. Although official figures from Eurostat calculate a surplus of 1 percent of GDP, the minister of finance calculated the budget surplus to be over three times that figure for 2006 and 2007 (*US Fed News,* June 5, 2008).

28. Interview with Stoyan Aleksandrov, Sofia, August 14, 2007.

29. Interview with Gyorgy Ganev, Sofia, August 13, 2007.

30. Interview with Gyorgy Ganev, Sofia, August 13, 2007.

31. Gray and Baturo (2009) use data from Benoit and Laver for the 2000s and Huber and Inglehart for the 1990s in order to place parties along a left-right spectrum.

32. Interview with Ivan Mikloš, Bratislava, May 18, 2007.

33. David Ellerman from the World Bank writes, "The Western advisers were marketing themselves as the intellectual saviors of the benighted East by putting the scientific prestige of neoclassical economics behind one of the most cockamamie social engineering schemes (voucher privatization) of the twentieth century." Ellerman contends, "Only the mixture of American triumphalism and the academic arrogance of neoclassical economics could produce such a lethal dose of gall" (Ellerman 2001, 32).

34. Interview with past EU representative in the Czech Republic, Santa Monica, CA.

35. The IMF has published recommendations for the design of tax systems for developing and transition countries in which it suggests a moderate to low CIT rate aligned with the top PIT rate, low import taxes, and a heavy reliance on sales taxes (VAT), among other suggestions (Shome 1995).

36. Interview with Ludovit Odor (National Bank of Slovakia), Bratislava, May 16, 2007.

37. Interview with Vito Tanzi, Washington, DC, June 4, 2008.

38. Ivan Mikloš explains, "A few people went to Estonia, people on the technical level. Of course we knew about this concept. We knew about the Hall and Rabushka book. We knew about the reform in Estonia in 1994, and Russia and Ukraine [in 2001 and 2004]."

39. Curiously, Czech economists also served as consultants for Slovak parties. For example, Czech economist Petr Mach wrote a flat tax proposal for Slovakia's ANO party.

40. Interview with Ludovit Odor (National Bank of Slovakia), Bratislava, May 16, 2007.

41. Interview with Petr Mach, Prague, May 18, 2007.

42. Interview with Petr Mach, Prague, May 18, 2007.

43. Interview with Gyorgy Angelov, August 13, 2007.

44. See Mart Laar's ode to Milton Friedman at http://blog.irl.ee/Mart/2007/01/28/milton-friedman-day/ and Václav Klaus's memorial address at the University of Chicago, http://www.hrad.cz/cms/en/prezident_cr/klaus_projevy/4259.shtml. Both accessed on July 10, 2007.

45. Daniel Mitchell is the chief expert on tax policy for the Heritage Foundation and visits the region frequently since the flat tax experiments began.

46. Interview with Martin Bruncko, Bratislava, May 17, 2007.

47. Quote of a Polish tax lawyer, Tomasz Michalik, in *International Tax Review* (April 2005).

## Chapter 6

1. For a discussion of the appropriate comparative referent for Russia, see Shleifer and Treisman 2004, 20.

2. Barter remained a problem for Russian tax collection into part of the Putin era. Gaddy cites 2004 estimates of nonmonetary exchange for the Russian enterprise sector as a whole to be 14.5 percent. In the machine-building sector, however, 50 percent of payments were nonmonetary settlements (Gaddy 2004).

3. Easter writes, "By 1997, the tax code consisted of nearly two hundred different taxes augmented by twelve hundred presidential decrees and government orders; three thousand legislative acts; and four thousand regulatory acts and instructions from ministries and agencies. In addition, regional governments added more than one hundred of their own additional taxes to the system" (2006a, 32).

4. Although Tyumen is an oil-producing region and was an important contributor to the central budget, other oil-producing regions like the Komi republic, Tatarstan, and Bashkortostan were granted tremendous tax retention deals from Moscow (Treisman 1999, 55).

5. Although Treisman breaks from other authors in that he did not find that formal lobbying and access to parliamentarians in the early 1990s account for the variation in revenue sharing, he does concede that more informal contacts may account for some of the regional variation (1999, 74).

6. Tanzi reports that the level of total tax arrears reached 5 percent of GDP by October 1996 (2001).

7. The full text of parts one and two of the Russian Tax Code can be found at www.garweb.ru/project/mns/en/law/garweb_law/10800200/10800200-001.htm.

8. For growth rates by year, see OECD 2006a, 23, table 1.1.

9. The IMF estimates four-fifths of the increase in total revenue between 1999 and 2001 resulted from gains in the oil sector (Kwon 2003, 7, cited in Hill 2004).

10. OECD 2004b, 15.

11. The fund exceeded $100 billion in 2007 (*Financial Times*, February 8, 2007).

12. Official Energy Statistics from the U.S. Government, http://tonto.eia.doe.gov/dnav/pet/hist/wepcuralsw.htm (accessed September 24, 2008). Urals blend crude peaked at $139 a barrel on July 11, 2008.

13. The tax police were eliminated by Presidential Decree no. 306, since they were considered to be agents of harassment and extortion. That said, tax-related harassment in Russia certainly did not end with the 2003 decree (Aslund 2007, 217).

14. These changes, enfeebling the legislature, followed the Beslan school crisis in 2004.

15. The Russian economics minister, German Gref, described Khodorkovsky's political pressure in an interview, quoting him threatening Gref, "Either you withdraw that law or I will make sure you are sacked" (Pazderka 2005).

16. On the Council of Europe's assessment of the Khodorkovsky affair, and its effect on weakening political opponents and intimidating Russia's business elites, see Council of Europe 2004, cited in McFaul and Tatic 2005.

17. Although many of the oligarchs can be characterized as businessmen who wanted to maximize profit and minimize tax obligations, Khodorkovsky stands out as an oligarch who also wanted to transform the Russian business environment. Yukos was relatively transparent, highly profitable, and the largest single contributor to the Russian budget before its breakup. Interview with Andrei Illarionov, April 2, 2008. He also had supporters and patrons in many of Russia's smaller alternative political parties (*Izvestiia*, May 17, 2005).

18. One adviser to the Ministry of Finance estimated that the effective tax rate on Gazprom is between 30 and 35 percent. For the oil companies, the effective rate ranges from 60 to 65 percent, according to his estimates, however. Interview with Evsey Gurvich, Moscow, July 25, 2008.

19. Interview with Nikolai Petrov, Moscow, July 24, 2008.

20. For example, the 2005 budget included a 38 percent increase in police and defense spending and a 35 percent increase in social spending.

21. Only 1 billion out of 49 billion dollars in excess revenue in 2005 was allocated to fund the deficit in the pension fund. The remaining 48 billion remained in the fund or went to early debt repayment (OECD 2006a, 3).

22. On EU pressures and constraints see Vachudova 2005; Grzymala Busse and Innes 2003.

23. Interview with Vito Tanzi, Washington, DC, June 4, 2008.

24. According to the Ministry of Finance, the government was considering lowering the profit tax from 24 to 20 percent for 2010. See 2007 remarks by Deputy Finance Minister Sergei Shatalov in "MinFin to Consider Lowering Profit Tax to 20% in 2008–2010—Shatalov," *Interfax*, March 1, 2007 (World News Connection).

25. "Russia Vows to Create Comfortable Environment for Private Capital," *Interfax*, January 27, 2007 (World News Connection).

26. In fact 148 of British Petroleum's employees working for the joint venture TNK-BP found difficulties in renewing their visas in March 2008 (*Moscow Times*, July 23, 2008).

27. Goldman 2008 elaborates this point.

28. For a list of more than two dozen major state acquisitions between 2004 and 2006 by Gazprom and other state proxies, see OECD 2005, 3, table 1.5.

29. Between 2000 and 2003, private borrowing from abroad increased by 20 billion dollars (OECD 2004b, 14, table 1.8).

30. Interview with Andrei Illarionov, Los Angeles, April 2, 2008.

## Chapter 7

1. The following sources are used to determine the vote share: Beck et al. 2009; Carr 2009; Center on Democratic Performance 2009; Inter-Parliamentary Union (IPU) 2009; Muller and Overstreet 2008, 1061.

2. Other countries like Latvia and Serbia could not be included due to limitations of comparable tax data.

3. For further explanation of the calculation of the Chinn and Ito index, see Chinn and Ito 2005 at http://www.ssc.wisc.edu/~mchinn/Readme_kaopen163.pdf.

4. The negative correlation could mean that countries do not imitate the personal income tax approach in neighboring countries and explicitly depart from patterns in nearby countries.

# Bibliography

Alfandari, Gilles, and Mark E. Schaffer. 1996. "On 'Arrears' in the Russian Enterprise Sector." In *Enterprise Restructuring and Economic Policy in Russia,* edited by Simon Commander, Qimiao Fan, and Mark E. Schaffer. Washington, DC: World Bank.

Alm, James, and Benno Torgler. 2003. "Culture Differences and Tax Morale in the United States and in Europe." CREMA Working Paper No. 2004-14. Center for Research in Economics, Management and the Arts, July.

Alm, James, and Sally Wallace. 2004. *The Jamaican Individual Income Tax.* Atlanta: Andrew Young School of Policy Studies, Georgia State University.

Appel, Hilary. 2004. *A New Capitalist Order: Privatization and Ideology in Russia and Eastern Europe.* Pittsburgh: University of Pittsburgh Press.

Appel, Hilary. 2006. "International Imperatives and Tax Reform: Lessons from Post-communist Europe." *Comparative Politics* 39 (October): 43–62.

Appel, Hilary. 2008. "Is It Putin or Is It Oil? Explaining Russia's Fiscal Recovery." *Post-Soviet Affairs* 24 (October–December): 301–23.

Aslund, Anders. 2007. *How Capitalism Was Built: The Transformation of Central and Eastern Europe, Russia, and Central Asia.* Cambridge: Cambridge University Press.

Avi-Yonah, Reuven. 2000. "Globalization, Tax Competition, and the Fiscal Crisis of the Welfare State." *Harvard Law Review* 113, no. 1573: 1575–1676.

Balcerowicz, Leszek. 1995. "Understanding Post-communist Transitions." *Journal of Democracy* 5, no. 4: 75–89.

Barnes, Andrew. 2006. "Giving Oil Its Due, but No More: How Petroleum Revenues Do and Do Not Affect the Russian Political Economy." Paper presented at the American Association for the Advancement of Slavic Studies, New Orleans, November 15–18.

Bates, Robert H. 2001. *Prosperity and Violence: The Political Economy of Development.* New York: W. W. Norton.

Baturo, Alexander, and Julia Gray. 2009. "Flatliners: Ideology and Rational Learning in the Adoption of the Flat Tax." *European Journal of Political Research* 48, no. 1 (January): 130–59.

Beck, Thorsten, George Clarke, Alberto Groff, Philip E. Keefer, and Patrich Walsh. 2009. "Database of Political Institutions." The World Bank. Available at http://econ.worldbank.org/WBSITE/EXTERNAL/EXTDEC/EXTRESEARCH/0,,contentMDK:20649465~pagePK: 64214825~piPK:64214943~theSitePK:469382,00 .html. Accessed July 30, 2009.

Belien, Paul. 2005. "Walking on Water: How to Do It." *Brussels Journal,* August 27.

Benoit, Kenneth, and Michael Laver. 2006. *Party Policy in Modern Democracies.* London: Routledge.

Berenson, Marc. 2006. "Recreating the State: Governance and Power in Poland and Russia." PhD dissertation, Princeton University.

Berenson, Marc. 2007. "Becoming Citizens: Attitudes towards Tax Compliance in Poland, Russia, and Ukraine." Annual Bank Conference on Development Economics (ABCDE), Bled, Slovenia, May 17.

Boix, Carles. 2001. "Democracy and Development and the Public Sector." *American Journal of Political Science* 45, no. 1: 1–17.

Bonker, Frank. 2007. *The Political Economy of Fiscal Reform in Central-Eastern Europe: Hungary, Poland, and the Czech Republic from 1989 to EU Accession.* Cheltenham, UK: Edward Elgar.

Boyarchuk, Dmytro, Lilia Maliar, and Serguei Maliar. 2005. "The Consumption and Welfare Implications of Wage Arrears in Transition Economies." *Journal of Comparative Economics* 33, no. 3 (September): 540–64.

Brady, David, Martin Seeleib-Kaiser, and Jason Beckfield. 2005. "Economic Globalization and the Welfare State in Affluent Democracies, 1975–2001." *American Sociological Review* 70, no. 6 (December): 921–48.

Braithwaite, John. 2005. "A Good Century for Tax? Globalisation, Redistribution, and Tax Avoidance." *Public Policy Research* (June–August): 85–92.

Bräutigam, Deborah. 2008. "Introduction: Taxation and State-Building in Developing Countries." In *Taxation and State-Building in Developing Countries: Capacity and Consent,* ed. Deborah Bräutigam, Odd-Helge Fjeldstad, and Mick Moore. Cambridge: Cambridge University Press.

Brewer, John. 1989. *The Sinews of Power: War, Money, and the English State, 1688–1783.* New York: Alfred A. Knopf.

Bronchi, Carla, and Andrew Burns. 2000. "The Tax System in the Czech Republic." Working Paper. Paris: OECD Economics Department.

Brooks, Clem, and Jeff Manza. 2006. "Why Do Welfare States Persist?" *Journal of Politics* 68, no. 4 (November): 816–27.

Brooks, Sarah. 2007. "When Does Diffusion Matter? Explaining the Spread of Structural Pension Reforms across Nations." *Journal of Politics* 69:701–15.

Buchanan, James. 1967. *Public Finance in Democratic Process: Fiscal Institutions and Individual Choice.* Chapel Hill: University of North Carolina Press.

Burgoon, Brian. 2001. "Globalization and Welfare Compensation: Disentangling the Ties that Bind." *International Organization* 3 (Summer).

Bútorová, Zora, Olga Gyárfášová, and Marián Velšic. 2005. "Public Opinion." In *Slovakia 2004: A Global Report on the State of Society,* ed. Grigorij Mesežnikov and Miroslav Kollár. Bratislava: IVO.

Cameron, David. 2003. "The Challenges of Accession." *East European Politics and Societies* 17, no. 1 (Winter): 24–41.

Campbell, John L. 1995. "State Building and Post-communist Budget Deficits." *American Behavioral Scientist* 38 (March–April): 761–88.

Campbell, John L. 2001a. "Convergence or Divergence? Globalization, Neoliberalism, and Fiscal Policy in Post-communist Europe." In *Globalization and the European Political Economy*, ed. Steven Weber, 107–39. New York: Columbia University Press.

Campbell, John L. 2001b. "Convergence or Divergence? Globalization, Neoliberalism, and Fiscal Policy in Postcommunist Europe." In *Successful Transitions: Political Factors of Socio-economic Progress in Postsocialist Countries*, ed. Jurgen Beyer, Jan Wielgohs, and Helmust Wiesenthal, 95–119. Baden Baden: Nomos.

Carlin, Wendy, Steven Fries, Mark Schaffer, and Paul Seabright. 2000. "Barter and Non-Monetary Transactions in Transition Countries: Evidence from a Cross-Country Survey." Centre for Economic Reform and Transformation Discussion Paper, 2000/04.

Carothers, Thomas. 1999. *Aiding Democracy Abroad: The Learning Curve*. Washington, DC: Carnegie Endowment for International Peace.

Carr, Adam. 2009. "Psephos: Adam Carr's Election Archive." http://psephos.adam-carr.net/.

Center on Democratic Performance. 2009. "Election Results Archive." University of Binghamton. Available at http://cdp.binghamton.edu/era/index.html. Accessed July 30, 2009.

Cerami, Alfio. 2006. *Social Policy in Central and Eastern Europe: The Emergence of a New European Welfare Regime*. Berlin: LIT Verlag.

Cheibub, Jose. 1998. "Political Regimes and the Extractive Capacity of Governments: Taxation in Democracies and Dictatorships." *World Politics* 50, no. 3: 349–76.

Cheminigui, Mohamed Abdelbasset, and Hans Lofgren. 2004. "Tax Policy and Reform in Saudi Arabia: A General Equilibrium Analysis." Mimeo.

Chinn, Menzie, and Hiro Ito. 2005. "Notes on the Calculation of the Chinn-Ito Financial Openness Variable." Mimeo, July 20. Available at http://www.ssc.wisc.edu/~mchinn/Readme_kaopen163.pdf. Accessed October 29, 2009.

Commander, Simon, Irina Dolinskaya, and Christian Mumssen. 2000. "Determinants of Barter in Russia: An Empirical Analysis." IMF Working Paper, WP/00/155.

Commission of the European Communities. 1997. *Communication from the Commission to the Council: A Package to Tackle Harmful Tax Competition in the European Union*. COM (97) 564 final.

Council of Europe. 2004. "The Circumstances Surrounding the Arrest and Prosecution of Leading Yukos Executives." Strasbourg: Council of Europe Parliamentary Assembly, Committee on Legal Affairs and Human Rights, Doc. 100368, November 29.

Csontos, László, János Kornai, and István Gyorgy Tóth. 1998. "Tax Awareness and Reform of the Welfare State: Hungarian Survey Results." *Economics of Transition* 6.

Cullis, John, and Philip Jones. 1992. *Public Finance and Public Choice*. New York: McGraw-Hill.

D'Anieri, Paul. 2003. "Leonid Kuchma and the Personalization of the Ukrainian Presidency." *Problems of Post-Communism* 50, no. 5: 58–65.

Darden, Keith, and Anna Grzymala-Busse. 2006. "The Great Divide: Pre-communist Schooling and Post-communist Trajectories." *World Politics* 59, no. 1: 83–115.

Darendorf, Ralf. 1990. *Reflections on the Revolution in Europe.* New York: Random House.

Davis, Jeffrey, Rolando Ossowski, Thomas Richardson, and Steven Barnett. 2000. "Fiscal and Macroeconomic Impact of Privatization." International Monetary Fund, Occasional Paper No. 194.

Deegan-Krause, Kevin. 2003. "Slovakia's Second Transition." *Journal of Democracy* 14 (April): 65–79.

Dehejia,Vivek, and Philipp Genschel. 1999. "Tax Competition and the European Union." *Politics and Society* 27 (September).

Downs, Anthony. 1957. *An Economic Theory of Democracy.* New York: Harper.

Dyba, Karel, and Jan Svejnar. 1994. "Stabilization and Transition in Czechoslovakia." In *The Transition in Eastern Europe,* vol. 1, ed. Olivier Blanchard, Kenneth Froot, and Jeffrey Sachs. Chicago: University of Chicago Press.

Easson, Alex. 1998. "Tax Competition Heats Up in Central Europe." *Bulletin for International Fiscal Documentation* 52.

Easter, Gerald. 2006a. "Building Fiscal Capacity." In *The State After Communism,* ed. Timothy Colton and Stephen Holmes. Lanham, MD: Rowman and Littlefield.

Easter, Gerald. 2006b. "Comparative Politics of Tax Reform in Eastern Europe." Paper presented to the Post-communist Workshop, December.

Easter, Gerald. 2008. "Capacity, Consent, and Tax Collection in Post-communist States." In *Taxation and State-Building in Developing Countries: Capacity and Consent,* ed. Deborah Bräutigam, Odd-Helge Fjeldstad, and Mick Moore, 64–89. New York: Cambridge University Press.

Easter, Gerald. 2009. "International Leverage versus Institutional Mimicry: Explaining Tax Reform in Eastern Europe." Paper presented at the American Political Science Association Annual Meeting, September.

Ebrill, Liam, and Oleh Havrylyshyn. 1999. "Tax Reform in the Baltics, Russia, and Other Countries of the Former Soviet Union." IMF Occasional Paper no. 182.

Economist Intelligence Unit. 2006a. *Country Profile: Hungary.*

Economist Intelligence Unit. 2006b. *Country Profile: Russian Federation.*

Eichengreen, Barry. 2001. "Capital Account Liberalization: What Do Cross-Country Studies Tell Us?" *World Bank Economic Review* 15, no. 3: 341–65.

Ellerman, David. 2001. "Lessons from Eastern Europe's Voucher Privatization." *Challenge* 44, no. 4: 14–37.

Erickson, Christopher, and Sarah Kuruvilla. 1994. "Labor Costs and the Social Dumping Debate in the European Union." *Industrial and Labor Relations Review* 48 (October): 28–48.

European Bank for Reconstruction and Development. 2000. *Transition Report Update: May 2000.* London: EBRD Publications.

European Bank for Reconstruction and Development. 2001. *Transition Report: Energy in Transition.* London: EBRD Publications.

European Commission. 2000. DG XXI, *Final Report: Structures of the Tax Systems in Estonia, Poland, Hungary, the Czech Republic, and Slovenia.* Reference Contract XXI/99/801.

European Commission. 2003. *Report on the Results of the Negotiations on the Accession of Cyprus, Malta, Hungary, Poland, the Slovak Republic, Latvia, Estonia, Lithuania, the Czech Republic, and Slovenia to the European Union.* Brussels, 2003, 1–64. Available at http://europa.eu.int/comm/enlargement/negotiations/pdf/negotitions_report_to_ep.pdf. Accessed June 11, 2004.

European Commission and Organisation for Economic Co-operation and Development. 1998. "Value Added Taxes in Central and Eastern European Countries: A Comparative Survey and Evaluation." Paris.

Eurostat. 2004. *Structures of the Taxation Systems in the European Union.* Luxembourg: European Communities, 2004.

Feige, Edgar, and Ivica Urban. 2008. "Measuring Underground (Unobserved, Non-observed, Unrecorded) Economies in Transition Countries: Can We Trust GDP?" *Journal of Comparative Economics* 36:287–306.

Fish, M. Steven. 1998. "The Determinants of Economic Reform in the Post-communist World." *East European Politics and Societies* 12, no. 1: 31–78.

Fish, M. Steven. 2005. *Democracy Derailed in Russia: The Failure of Open Politics.* Cambridge: Cambridge University Press.

Fisher, Sharon. 2006. *Political Change in Post-communist Slovakia and Croatia: From Nationalist to Europeanist.* New York: Palgrave.

Fisher, Sharon, John Gould, and Tim Haughton. 2007. "Slovakia's Neoliberal Turn." *Europe-Asia Studies* 59, no. 6 (September): 977–98.

Fjeldstad, Odd-Helge, and Mick Moore. 2008. "Tax Reform and State-Building in a Globalized World." In *Taxation and State-Building in Developing Countries: Capacity and Consent,* ed. Deborah Bräutigam, Odd-Helge Fjeldstad, and Mick Moore. Cambridge: Cambridge University Press.

Fukuyama, Francis. 2004. *State-Building: Governance and World Order in the 21st Century.* Ithaca: Cornell University Press.

Gaddy, Clifford. 2004. "Four More Years of Putin?" March 15. Available at http://www.aei.org/events/filter.all,eventID.760/transcript.asp. Accessed March 1, 2007.

Gaddy, Clifford, and W. Gale. 2005. "Demythologizing the Russian Flat Tax." *Tax Notes International* 14 (March): 983–88.

Gaddy, Clifford, and Barry Ickes. 2002. *Russia's Virtual Economy.* Washington, DC: Brookings Institution Press.

Gaidar, Egor. 1999. "Lessons of the Russian Crisis for Transition Economies." *Finance and Development* 36, no. 2 (June): 6–8.

Ganev, Venelin. 2007. "The Annulled Tax State: An Essay on the Fiscal Sociology of the Early Postcommunism." Paper presented at the AAASS Annual Conference, New Orleans, November.

Gardawski, Juliusz. 2002. "Unemployment Benefits Examined." Eironline, October 29. Available at http://www.eurofound.europa.eu/eiro/2002/10/feature/pl0210107f.htm. Accessed June 16, 2009.

Garrett, Geoffrey. 1998. *Partisan Politics in the Global Economy.* New York: Cambridge University Press.

Garrett, Geoffrey, and Peter Lange. 1996. "Internationalization, Institutions, and Political Change." In *Internationalization and Domestic Politics,* ed. Robert Keohane and Helen Milner. Cambridge, MA: Cambridge University Press.

Garrett, Geoffrey, and Deborah Mitchell. 2001. "Globalization, Government Spending, and Taxation in the OECD." *European Journal of Political Research* 39:145–77.

Gehlbach, Scott. 2008. *Representation Through Taxation: Revenue, Politics, and Development in Postcommunist States.* Cambridge: Cambridge University Press.

Genschel, Phillip. 2002. "Globalization, Tax Competition, and the Welfare State." *Politics and Society* 30 (June): 245–75.

Genschel, Phillip. 2004. "Globalization and the Welfare State: A Retrospective." *Journal of European Public Policy* 11, no. 4 (August): 613–36.

Gitter, Robert, and Markus Scheuer. 1998. "Low Unemployment in the Czech Republic: 'Miracle' or 'Mirage'?" *Monthly Labor Review* 121 (August ): 31–37.

Gizelis, Theodora. 2005. "Globalization, Integration, and the European Welfare State." *International Interactions* 31:139–62.

Goldman, Marshall. 2006. "Putin and the Oligarchs." *Foreign Affairs* 83, no. 6 (January–February): 33–44.

Goldman, Marshall. 2008. *Petrostate: Putin, Power, and the New Russia.* Oxford: Oxford University Press.

Goliaš, Peter, and Robert Kičina. 2005. "Slovak Tax Reform: One Year After." Mimeo (April): 10–11.

Gorenburg, Dmitry. 2001. "Nationalism for the Masses: Popular Support for Nationalism in Russia's Ethnic Republics." *Europe-Asia Studies* 53, no. 1: 73–104.

Gorodnichenko, Yuriy, Jorge Martinez-Vazquez, and Klara Sabirianova Peter. 2009. "Myth and Reality of Flat Tax Reform: Micro Estimates of Tax Evasion Response and Welfare Effects in Russia." *Journal of Political Economy* 117, no. 3: 504–54.

Grabbe, Heather. 1999. "A Partnership for Accession? The Implications of EU Conditionality for the Central and East European Applicants." EUI Working Paper 99/12, European University Institute.

Grabbe, Heather. 2002. "European Union Conditionality and the Acquis Communautaire." *International Political Science Review* 23, no. 3: 249–68.

Grafe, Clemens, and Kaspar Richter. 2001. "Taxation and Public Expenditure." In *Russia's Post-communist Economy,* ed. Brigitte Granville and Peter Oppenheimer. Oxford: Oxford University Press.

Gray, Julia, and Alexander Baturo. 2007. "Flatliners: Ideology and Rational Learning in the Diffusion of the Flat Tax." IIIS Discussion Paper no. 210, March.

Grennes, Thomas. 1997. "The Economic Transition in the Baltic Countries." *Journal of Baltic Studies* 28, no. 1 (Spring): 9–24.

Grzymala-Busse, Anna, and Abby Innes. 2003. "Great Expectations: The EU and Domestic Political Competition in East Central Europe." *East European Politics and Societies* 17 (Winter): 64–73.

Grzymala-Busse, Anna, and Pauline Jones Luong. 2002. "Re-conceptualizing the State: Lessons from Post-Communism." *Politics and Society* 30, no. 4: 529–54.

Gustafson, Thane. 2000. *Capitalism Russian-Style.* Cambridge: Cambridge University Press.

Haggard, Stephen, and Robert Kaufman. 2001. "Introduction." In *Reforming the State: Fiscal and Welfare Reforms in Post-Socialist Countries,* ed. Kanos Kornai, Stephan Haggard, and Robert Kaufman. New York: Cambridge University Press.

Hall, Robert, and Alvin Rabushka. 1995. *The Flat Tax.* Stanford: Hoover Institution Press.

Haughton, Timothy. 2003. "We'll Finish What We've Started: The 2002 Slovak Elections." *Journal of Communist Studies and Transition Politics* 19, no. 4: 65–90.

Haughton, Timothy. 2004. "Explaining the Limited Success of the Communist-Successor Left in Slovakia: The Case of the Party of the Democratic Left (SDL)." *Party Politics* 10, no. 2: 177–91.

Heady, Christopher, and Stephen Smith. 1995. "Tax and Benefit Reform in the Czech and Slovak Republics." In *Tax and Benefit Reform in Central and Eastern Europe,* ed. David Newberry. London: Centre for Economic Policy Research.

Heimann, Beata. 2001. "Recent Trends in Personal Income Taxation in Poland and in the UK." *Berichte aus dem Weltwirtschalflichen Colloquium der Universitat Bremen* 76 (November).

Hellman, Joel. 1998. "Winners Take All: The Politics of Partial Reform in Post-communist Transitions." *World Politics* 50, no. 2: 203–34.

Herrera, Yoshiko. 2005. *Imagined Economies: The Sources of Russian Regionalism.* Cambridge: Cambridge University Press.

Hill, Fiona. 2004. *Energy Empire: Oil, Gas, and Russia's Revival.* London: Foreign Policy Center.

Holmes, Stephen. 1997. "What Russia Teaches Us Now: How Weak States Threaten Freedom." *American Prospect* 33:30–39.

Holmes, Stephen. 2003. "A European Doppelstaat?" *East European Politics and Societies* 17 (Winter): 107–18.

Holy, Ladislav. 1996. *The Little Czech and the Great Czech Nation.* Cambridge: Cambridge University Press.

Hunter, Richard, and Robert Shapiro. 2000. "Reform of the Polish Tax System: Triumph of Politics over Policy?" *International Tax Journal* 26 (Fall).

Ikenberry, G. John. 1990. "The International Spread of Privatization Policies: Inducements, Learning, and 'Policy Bandwagoning.'" In *The Political Economy of Public Sector Reform and Privatization,* ed. Ezra Suleiman and John Waterbury, 88–110. Boulder: Westview Press.

International Tax Review. 1999. "EU Dreams Force Polish Evolution." *International Tax Review* 10 (November).

International Tax Review. 1999–2000. "Poland Steers Tax Reforms through Crisis." *International Tax Review* 11 (December–January).

International Tax Review. 2005. "Polish Government Proposes Flat-Rate Tax System." *International Tax Review* (April).

Inter Parliamentary Union (IPU). 2009. "PARLINE Database on National Parliaments." Available at http://www.ipu.org/parline/. Accessed July 30, 2009.

Ivanova, Anna, Michael Keen, and Alexander Klemm. 2005. "The Russian 'Flat Tax' Reform." *Economic Policy* 20, no. 43 (July): 397–444.

Jacoby, Wade. 2000. *Imitation and Politics: Redesigning Modern Germany.* Ithaca: Cornell University Press.

Jacoby, Wade. 2006. *The Enlargement of the EU and NATO: Ordering from the Menu in Central Europe.* New York: Cambridge University Press.

Johnson, Juliet. 2000. *A Fist Full of Rubles: The Rise and Fall of the Russian Banking System.* Ithaca: Cornell University Press.

Johnson, Simon, and Daniel Kaufmann. 2001. "Institutions and the Underground Economy." In *A Decade of Transition: Achievements and Challenges,* ed. Oleh Havrylyshyn and Saleh M. Nsouli, 212–28. Washington, DC: IMF Institute.

Jones Luong, Pauline, and Erika Weinthal. 2004. "Contra Coercion: Russian Tax Reform, Exogenous Shocks, and Negotiated Institutional Change." *American Political Science Review* 98, no. 1: 139–52.

Joshi, Anuradha, and Joseph Ayee. 2008. "Associational Taxation: A Pathway into the Informal Sector?" In *Taxation and State-Building in Developing Countries: Capacity and Consent,* ed. Deborah Bräutigam, Odd-Helge Fjeldstad, and Mick Moore, 183–211. Cambridge: Cambridge University Press.

Kandell, Jonathan. 2004. "The Year of Accession: Slovakian Overdrive." *Institutional Investor,* February.

Kaufman, Robert, and Alex Segura-Ubiergo. 2001. "Globalization, Domestic Politics, and Social Spending in Latin America: A Time-Series Cross-Section Analysis, 1973–97." *World Politics* 53, no. 4 (July): 553–87.

Keen, Michael, Stephen Smith, Richard Baldwin, and Vidar Christiansen. 1996. "The Future of Value Added Tax in the European Union." *Economic Policy* 11, no. 23 (October).

Kelley, Judith. 2004. *Ethnic Politics in Europe: The Power of Norms and Incentives.* Princeton: Princeton University Press.

Kemme, David, and Ryszard Rapacki. 2000. "Fiscal Reform, Policy, and Constraints during Transition in Poland." *Post-Soviet Geography and Economics* 41:1–28.

Kiss, Gabor, and Gyorgy Szapáry. 2000. "Fiscal Adjustment in the Transition Process: Hungary, 1990–1999." *Post-Soviet Geography and Economics* 41: 1–28.

Kitschelt, Herbert. 2003. "Accounting for Postcommunist Regime Diversity: What Counts as a Good Cause?" In *Capitalism and Democracy in Central and Eastern Eu-*

*rope: Assessing the Legacy of Communist Rule,* ed. G. Ekiert and S. Hanson. Cambridge: Cambridge University Press.

Kitschelt, Herbert, Peter Lange, Gary Marks, and John Stephens, eds. 1999. *Continuity and Change in Contemporary Capitalism.* New York: Cambridge University Press.

Klugman, Jeni, and Alexandre Kolev. 2001. "The Welfare Repercussions of Single-Parenthood in Russia in Transition." In *Parents and Child Welfare in the New Russia,* ed. Jeni Klugman and Albert Motivans. New York: Palgrave.

Kolev, Alexandre. 1998. "Labour Supply in the Informal Economy in Russia during Transition." CEPR Discussion Paper no. 2024 (November), 1–35.

Kopstein, Jeffrey, and David Reilly. 2000. "Geographic Diffusion and the Transformation of the Post-communist World." *World Politics* 53 (October): 1–37.

Kornai, Janos. 1986. "The Soft Budget Constraint." *Kyklos* 39:3–30.

Kornai, Janos. 1990. *The Road to a Free Economy: Shifting from a Socialist System; The Example of Hungary.* New York: W. W. Norton.

Kornai, Janos. 1997. *Struggle and Hope: Essays on Stablization and Reform in a Post-Socialist Economy.* Northampton, MA: Edward Elgar.

Kramer, Mark. 1995. "Polish Workers and the Post-communist Transition, 1989–1993." *Europe-Asia Studies* 47 (June): 669–712.

Kramer, Mark. 1997. "Social Protection Policies and Safety Nets in East-Central Europe: Dilemmas of the Post-communist Transformation." In *Sustaining the Transition: The Social Safety Net in Post-communist Europe,* ed. Ethan B. Kapstein and Michael Mandelbaum, 46–123. New York: Council on Foreign Relations.

Krauchuk, Robert S. 2005. "Kuchma as Economic Reformer." *Problems of Post-Communism* 52, no. 5: 48–58.

Kupa, M. 1991. "Implementation of Tax Reform in Hungary." In *The Role of Tax Reform in Central and Eastern European Economies.* Paris: OECD.

Kuzio, Taras. 2005. "From Kuchma to Yushchenko: Ukraine's 2004 Presidential Election and the Orange Revolution." *Problems of Post-Communism* 52, no. 2: 29–44.

Kwon, Gohoon. 2003. "Post-crisis Fiscal Revenue Developments in Russia: From an Oil Perspective." *Public Finance and Management* 3, no. 4: 503–30.

Laar, Mart. 2002. *The Little Country That Could.* London: CRCE.

Laar, Mart. 2005. "The Small Country That Could." IDEE. Available at http://www.idee.org/cubalaar.html. Accessed July 10, 2007.

Laar, Mart. 2007. CEPOS Copenhagen Flat-Tax Conference. Online video stream available at http://www.cepos.dk/cms/index.php?id=138. Accessed July 11, 2007.

Lehmann, Hartmut, Jonathan Wadsworth, and Alessandro Acquisti. 1999. "Grime and Punishment: Job Insecurity and Wage Arrears in the Russian Federation." *Journal of Comparative Economics* 27, no. 4: 595–617.

Levi, Margaret. 1998. *Of Rule and Revenue.* Berkeley: University of California Press.

Levitsky, Steven, and Lucan Way. 1998. "Between a Shock and a Hard Place: The Dynamics of Labor-Backed Adjustments in Poland and Argentina." *Comparative Politics* 30 (January).

Lieberman, Evan. 2003. *Race and Regionalism in the Politics of Taxation in Brazil and South Africa*. Cambridge: Cambridge University Press.

Mahon, James. 2004. "Causes of Tax Reform in Latin America, 1977–96." *Latin American Research Review* 39, no. 1: 3–30.

Mahon, James. 2005. "Liberal States and Fiscal Contracts: Aspects of the Political Economy of Public Finance." Paper prepared for the American Political Science Association, Washington, DC, September 1–4.

Malová, Darina, and Marek Rybář. 2005. "Organized Interests." In *Slovakia 2004: A Global Report on the State of Society*, ed. Grigorij Mesežnikov and Miroslav Kollár. Bratislava: IVO.

Martinez-Mongay, Carlos. 2000. "ECFIN's Effective Tax Rates: Properties and Comparisons with Other Tax Indicators." *Economics Papers of the European Commission ECFIN* 146 (October).

Martinez-Serrano, Alicia, and Ben Patterson. 2003. "Taxation in Europe: Recent Developments." European Parliament Working Paper ECON 131 EN 01-2003. Luxembourg: European Commission.

Martinez-Vazquez, Jorge. 2002. "Asymmetric Federalism in Russia: Cure or Poison." Georgia State University ISP Working Paper 03-04, December.

Martinez-Vazquez, Jorge, and L. F. Jameson Boex. 1999. "Fiscal Decentralization in the Russian Federation during the Transition." Georgia State University ISP Working Paper 99-03, July.

Martinez-Vazquez, Jorge, and Robert McNab. 2000. "The Tax Reform Experiment in Transitional Countries." Georgia State University ISP Working Paper 00-01.

Mathernová, Katarína, and Juraj Renčko. 2006. "'Reformology': The Case of Slovakia." *Orbis* (Fall).

McFaul, Michael, and Sanja Tatic. 2005. "Countries at the Crossroads 2005: Russia." Freedom House, Washington, DC, June. Available on-line at http://www.freedomhouse.org.

Menn, Svetlana. 2005. "Tax Developments in the European Union since 2004 Enlargement." *Tax Planning International Review* (November).

Mertens, Jo Beth, and Jean E. Tesche. 2002. "VAT Revenues in the Russian Federation: The Role of Tax Administration in Their Decline." *Public Budgeting and Finance* 22:87–113.

Michonski, Arkadiusz. 2002. "The Accession Negotiations and the Shape of Polish Membership of the European Union." In *Negotiations on Poland's Accession to the European Union: Selected Issues*, ed. Jan Barcz and Arkadiusz Michonski. Warsaw: Ministry of Foreign Affairs.

Micklewright, John, and Gyula Nagy. 1994. "How Does the Hungarian Unemployment Insurance System Really Work?" *Economies in Transition* 2, no. 2: 209–32.

Micklewright, John, and Gyula Nagy. 1995. "Unemployment Insurance and Incentives in Hungary. " CEPR Discussion Paper no. 1118, January.

Mikloš, Ivan. 2008. "Slovakia: A Story of Reforms." In *Growth versus Security: Old and*

*New EU Members' Quest for a New Economic and Social Model*, ed. Wojciech Bienkowski, Josef Brada, and Mariusz-Jan Radlo. New York: Palgrave Macmillan.

Mikloš, Ivan, Marek Jakoby, and Karol Morvay. 2005. "Tax Reform in the Slovak Republic." CESifo DICE Report 3.

Milanovi, Branko. 1998. *Income, Inequality, and Poverty during the Transition from Planned to Market Economy.* Washington, DC: World Bank.

Millar, Janems. 2007. "Putin and the Economy." In *Putin's Russia: Past Imperfect, Future Uncertain*, ed. Dale Herspring. Lanham, MD: Rowman and Littlefield.

Milner, Helen, and Robert Keohane, eds. 1996. *Internationalization and Domestic Politics.* New York: Cambridge University Press.

Mishra, Ramesh. 1998. "Beyond the Nation State: Social Policy in an Age of Globalization." *Social Policy and Administration* 32, no. 5 (December): 481–500.

Mitchell, Daniel. 2003. "Russia's Flat Tax Miracle." *Capitalist Magazine*, April 20. Available at http://www.capmag.com/article.asp?ID=2612. Accessed July 9, 2007.

Mitchell, Sydney Knox. 1951. *Taxation in Medieval England.* New Haven: Yale University Press.

Mitra, Pradeep, and Nicholas Stern. 2002. "Tax Systems in Transition." World Bank Working Paper, October.

Moravcsik, Andrew, and Milada Anna Vachudova. 2003. "National Interests, State Power, and EU Enlargement." *East European Politics and Societies* 17 (Winter): 42–57.

Mosley, Layna. 2000. "Room to Move: International Financial Markets and National Welfare States." *International Organization* 54 (Autumn): 737–73.

Muller, Thomas, and William Overstreet. 2008. *Political Handbook of the World 2008.* Washington, DC: CQ Press.

Nemtsov, Boris, and Vladimir Milov. 2008. *Putin. Itogi: Nezavisimyi Ekspertnyi Doklad.* Moscow: Novaya Gazeta. Available at http://www.nemtsov.ru/docs/putin-itogi.pdf. Accessed April 28, 3008.

Newberry, David, ed. 1995. *Tax and Benefit Reform in Central and Eastern Europe.* London: Centre for Economic Policy Research.

North, Douglass. 1981. *Structure and Change in Economic History.* New York: W. W. Norton.

North, Douglass, and Barry Weingast. 1989. "Constitutions and Commitment: The Evolution of Institutions Governing Public Choice in Seventeenth-Century England." *Journal of Economic History* 49, no. 4: 803–32.

Orenstein, Mitchell A. 2008. *Privatizing Pensions: The Transnational Campaign for Social Security Reform.* Princeton: Princeton University Press.

Organization for Economic Cooperation and Development. 1991. *The Role of Tax Reform in Central and Eastern European Economies.* Paris: OECD.

Organization for Economic Cooperation and Development. 2000. *OECD Economic Surveys: Poland 1999–2000.* Paris: OECD.

Organization for Economic Cooperation and Development. 2004a. *Economic Survey of the Russian Federation 2004: The Challenge of Sustaining Growth.* Paris: OECD.

Organization for Economic Cooperation and Development. 2004b. *Economic Survey of the Russian Federation 2004: The Sources of Russian Economic Growth.* Paris: OECD.

Organization for Economic Cooperation and Development. 2005. *Economic Surveys: Russian Federation.* Paris: OECD.

Organization for Economic Cooperation and Development. 2006a. *Economic Survey of the Russian Federation 2006: Fiscal Policy: The Principal Tool for Macroeconomic Management,* Chapter 2, November 17. Paris: OECD.

Organization for Economic Cooperation and Development. 2006b. *Survey of the Russian Federation.* 2006/17, November 2006. Paris: OECD.

Organization for Economic Cooperation and Development. 2007a. *OECD Economic Outlook* 1, no. 81 (June).

Organization for Economic Cooperation and Development. 2007b. *Revenue Statistics 1965–2006.* Paris: OECD.

Ostaszewska, Aleksandra. 2001. "Poland: Corporate Income Tax Law Amendments." *European Taxation* 41 (February).

Paczynska, Agnieszka. 2009. *State, Labor, and the Transition to a Market Economy.* University Park: Penn State Press.

Palata, Lubos. 2006. "Elections: Almost Like Old Times." *Transitions On-Line,* June 1.

Pazderka, Josef. 2005. "Russia: End of a Messy Affair." *Transitions On-Line,* June 1.

Piotrowska, Joanna, and Werner Vanborren. 2008. "Taxation Papers: The Corporate Income Tax Rate-Revenue Paradox: Evidence in the EU." Working Paper no. 12-2007, February.

Political Transformation and the Electoral Process in Post-communist Europe. 2009. Election Results. University of Essex. Available at http://www.essex.ac.uk/elections/. Accessed August 30, 2009.

Pommerehne, Werner, and Bruno Frey. 1992. "The Effects of Tax Administration on Tax Morale." Unpublished manuscript, University of Zurich.

Przeworski, Adam. 1991. *Democracy and the Market.* Cambridge: Cambridge University Press.

Rabushka, Alvin. 2005. "The Flat Tax at Work in Russia: Year Four, 2004." Hoover Institution Comments, Essays, and Speeches, January 26. Available at http://www.hoover.org/research/russianecon/essays/5146322.html. Accessed March 15, 2007.

Rivera, Sharon Werning, and David S. Rivera. 2006. "The Russian Elite under Putin: Militocratic or Bourgeois?" *Post-Soviet Affairs* 22 (April–June): 124–44.

Rodrik, Dani. 1997. *Has Globalization Gone Too Far?* Washington, DC: Institute for International Economics.

Roeder, Philip. 1991. "Soviet Federalism and Ethnic Mobilization." *World Politics* 43 (January): 196–232.

Rose, Richard. 1993. *Lesson-Drawing in Public Policy.* Chatham, MA: Chatham House.

Ross, Michael. 2004. "Does Taxation Lead to Representation?" *British Journal of Political Science* 34, no. 2: 229–49.

Rutland, Peter. 2005. "Putin's Economic Record." In *Developments in Russian Politics VI,* ed. Stephen White, Zvi Gitelman, and Richard Sakwa. Durham: Duke University Press.

Sakwa, Richard. 2007. "Putin's Leadership." In *Putin's Russia: Past Imperfect, Future Uncertain*, 3rd ed., ed. Dale R. Herspring. Lanham, MD: Rowman and Littlefield.

Schimmelfennig, Frank. 2003. *The EU, NATO, and the Integration of Europe: Rules and Rhetoric*. Cambridge: Cambridge University Press.

Schwartz, Andrew. 1997. "The Czech Approach to Residual Share Management." In *Between State and Market: Mass Privatization in Transition Economies*, ed. Ira Lieberman, Stilpon Nestor, and Raj Desai. Washington, DC: World Bank.

Shields, Janice. 1995. "'Social Dumping' in Mexico under NAFTA." *Multinational Monitor* 16 (April).

Shleifer, Andrei, and Daniel Treisman. 2004. "A Normal Country." *Foreign Affairs* 83, no. 2 (March–April): 151–74.

Shome, Parthasarathi. 1995. *Tax Policy Handbook*. Washington, DC: International Monetary Fund.

Simmons, Beth, and Zachary Elkins. 2004. "The Globalization of Liberalization: Policy Diffusion in the International Political Economy." *American Political Science Review* 98, no. 1: 171–90.

Stepanyan, Vahram. 2003. "Reforming Tax Systems: Experience of the Baltics, Russia, and Other Countries of the Former Soviet Union." IMF Working Paper 03/173, September.

Stiglitz, Joseph. 2002. *Globalization and Its Discontents*. New York: W. W. Norton.

Stoner-Weiss, Kathryn. 2006. *Resisting the State: Reform and Retrenchment in Post-Soviet Russia*. Cambridge: Cambridge University Press.

Swank, Duane. 2006. "Tax Policy in an Era of Internationalization: Explaining the Spread of Neoliberalism." *International Organization* 60, no. 4: 847–82.

Swank, Duane, and Sven Steinmo. 2002. "The New Political Economy of Taxation in Advanced Capitalist Democracies." *American Journal of Political Science* 46 (July): 642–55.

Tait, A., ed. 1992. *Fiscal Issues in Economies in Transition*. Washington, DC: International Monetary Fund.

"Talking Taxes: A City Paper Interview with Ardo Hansson." 2007. *City Paper*. http://www.balticsww.com/news/features/talking_taxes.htm. Accessed July 11, 2007.

Tang, Helena, Edda Zoli, and Irina Klytchnikova. 2000. "Banking Crises in Transition Economies: Fiscal Costs and Related Issues." World Bank Policy Research Working Paper 2484, November.

Tanzi, Vito. 1991. "Tax Reform and the Move to a Market Economy: Overview of the Issues." In *The Role of Tax Reform in Central and Eastern European Economies*. Paris: OECD.

Tanzi, Vito. 1992. *Fiscal Policies in Economies in Transition*. Washington, DC: International Monetary Fund.

Tanzi, Vito. 2001. "Creating Effective Tax Administrations: The Experience of Russia and Georgia." In *Reforming the State: Fiscal and Welfare Reform in Post-Socialist Countries,* ed. Janos Kornai, Stephan Haggard, and Robert Kaufman. Cambridge: Cambridge University Press.

Tanzi, Vito, and George Tsibouris. 2000. "Fiscal Reform over Ten Years of Transition." IMF Working Paper no. 113. Washington, DC: IMF Publications.

Thompson, William. 2005. "Putting Yukos in Perspective." *Post-Soviet Affairs* 21, no. 2: 159–81.

Tilly, Charles. 1985. "Warmaking and State Making as Organized Crime." In *Bringing the State Back In,* ed. Peter Evans, Dietrich Rueschemeyer, and Theda Skocpol, 161–91. Cambridge: Cambridge University Press.

Torgler, Benno. 2003. "Tax Morale in Transition Countries." *Post-Communist Economies* 15, no. 3 (September): 357–81.

Treisman, Daniel. 1999. *After the Deluge: Regional Crises and Political Consolidation in Russia.* Ann Arbor: University of Michigan Press.

Trezziová, Dana. 2001. "Czech Republic: Income Tax and VAT Amendments." *European Taxation* 41 (February).

Truszczynski, Jan. 2002. "Status and Prospects of Poland's Accession Negotiations with the European Union." In *Negotiations on Poland's Accession to the European Union: Selected Issues,* ed. Jan Barcz and Arkadiusz Michonski. Warsaw: Ministry of Foreign Affairs.

Turley, Gerard. 2006. *Transition, Taxation, and the State.* Aldershot, UK: Ashgate.

Vachudova, Milada Anna. 2005. *Europe Undivided: Democracy, Leverage, and Integration after Communism.* New York: Oxford University Press.

Vámosi-Nagy, Szabolcs, Imre Kocsis, and Luis Alvaro Sanchez. 1998. "Tax-Policy Reforms in Hungary." In *Public Finance Reform during Transition: The Experience of Hungary,* ed. Lajos Bokros and Jean Jacques Dethier. Washington, DC: World Bank Publisher.

Vasilieva, A., E. Gurvich, and V. Subbotin. 2003. "Analyzing the Tax Reform from an Economic Perspective." *Voprosy Economiki,* no. 6.

Vazquez-Caro, Jaime, Carlos Cavalcanti, Kim Allen Bak, and Sijbren Cnossen. 2001. *Tax Reforms in Light of EU Accession: The Case of Poland.* Washington, DC: World Bank Country Study.

Véghelyi, Mária. 1997. "An Overview of Trends in Tax Reforms in Selected Central European Countries." *Bulletin for International Fiscal Documentation* 51 (February).

Vodopivec, Milan, Andreas Wörgötter, and Dhushyanth Raju. 2005. "Unemployment Benefit Systems in Central and Eastern Europe: A Review of the 1990s." *Comparative Economic Studies* 47, no. 4: 615–51.

Wagner, Richard. 1976. "Revenue Structure: Fiscal Illusion and Budgetary Choice." *Public Choice* 25, no. 1: 127–30.

Wallich, Christine, ed. 1994. *Russia and the Challenge of Fiscal Federalism.* Washington, DC: World Bank.

Waterbury, John. 1997. "Fortuitous By-Products." *Comparative Politics* 29, no. 3: 383–412.

Way, Lucan. 2002. "The Dilemmas of Reform in Weak States: The Case of Post-Soviet Fiscal Decentralization." *Politics and Society* 30, no. 4: 579–98.

Weber, Steven, ed. 2001. *Globalization and the European Political Economy.* New York: Columbia University Press.

Weyland, Kurt. 2005. "Theories of Policy Diffusion: Lessons from Latin American Pension Reform." *World Politics* 57 (2005): 262–95.

Weyland, Kurt. 2007. *Bounded Rationality and Policy Diffusion: Social Sector Reform in Latin America.* Princeton: Princeton University Press.

Winner, Hannes. 2005. "Has Tax Competition Emerged in OECD Countries?" *International Tax and Public Finance* 12:667–87.

Wolff, Joachim. 2001. "The Hungarian Unemployment Benefit System and Incentives to Return to Work." Sonderforschungbereich 386 Discussion Paper 253.

Wolosky, Lee. 2000. "Putin's Plutocrat Problem." *Foreign Affairs* 79, no. 2 (March–April): 18–31.

Woodruff, David. 1999. *Money Unmade: Barter and the Fate of Russian Capitalism.* Ithaca: Cornell University Press.

World Bank. 1998. "Will Wage Arrears Continue in Russia?" *Beyond Transition,* March–April. Available at http://www.worldbank.org/html/prddr/trans/marapr98/pgs6-8.htm.

World Bank. 2005. *From Transition to Development.* Moscow: World Bank Group.

# Index

*Note:* Italic page numbers signify tables or figures.